Masculinity and Dress in Roman Antiquity

In *Masculinity and Dress in Roman Antiquity,* Olson argues that clothing functioned as part of the process of communication by which elite male influence, masculinity, and sexuality were made known and acknowledged, and furthermore that these concepts interconnected in socially significant ways. This volume also sets out the details of masculine dress from literary and artistic evidence and the connection of clothing to rank, status, and ritual. This is the first monograph in English to draw together the myriad evidence for male dress in the Roman world, and examine it as evidence for men's self-presentation, status, and social convention.

Kelly Olson is Associate Professor of Classics at the University of Western Ontario, Canada. Her other works include *Dress and the Roman Woman* (Routledge, 2008).

Routledge Monographs in Classical Studies

Titles include:

Athens Transformed, 404-262 BC: From Popular Sovereignty to the Dominion of the Elite
Phillip Harding

Translating Classical Plays: The Collected Papers
J. Michael Walton

Athens: The City as University
Niall Livingstone

Resemblance and Reality in Greek Thought
Edited by Arum Park

An Ancient Theory of Religion: Euhemerism from Antiquity to the Present
Nickolas P. Roubekas

Attic Oratory and Performance
Andreas Serafim

Forthcoming:

TransAntiquity: Cross-Dressing and Transgender Dynamics in the Ancient World
Edited by Domitilla Campanile, Filippo Carlà-Uhink, and Margherita Facella

Aeschylus and War: Comparative Perspectives on 'Seven Against Thebes'
Edited by Isabelle Torrance

The Etruscans and the History of Dentistry: The Golden Smile through the Ages
Marshall J. Becker and Jean MacIntosh Turfa

Masculinity and Dress in Roman Antiquity

Kelly Olson

LONDON AND NEW YORK

First published 2017
by Routledge

2 Park Square, Milton Park, Abingdon, Oxfordshire OX14 4RN
52 Vanderbilt Avenue, New York, NY 10017

Routledge is an imprint of the Taylor & Francis Group, an informa business

First issued in paperback 2020

Copyright © 2017 Kelly Olson

The right of Kelly Olson to be identified as author of this work has been asserted by her in accordance with sections 77 and 78 of the Copyright, Designs and Patents Act 1988.

All rights reserved. No part of this book may be reprinted or reproduced or utilised in any form or by any electronic, mechanical, or other means, now known or hereafter invented, including photocopying and recording, or in any information storage or retrieval system, without permission in writing from the publishers.

Notice:
Product or corporate names may be trademarks or registered trademarks, and are used only for identification and explanation without intent to infringe.

British Library Cataloguing in Publication Data
A catalogue record for this book is available from the British Library

Library of Congress Cataloging in Publication Data
Names: Olson, K. (Kelly), author.
Title: Masculinity and dress in Roman antiquity / Kelly Olson.
Description: Abingdon, Oxon ; New York : Routledge, [2017] | Series: Routledge monographs in classical studies | Includes bibliographical references and index.
Identifiers: LCCN 2016033106 | ISBN 9781138932937 (hardback : alk. paper) | ISBN 9781315678887 (ebook)
Subjects: LCSH: Clothing and dress--Social aspects--Rome. | Clothing and dress--Symbolic aspects--Rome. | Men's clothing--Rome. | Masculinity--Rome.
Classification: LCC GT555 .O46 2017 | DDC 391/.10945632--dc23
LC record available at https://lccn.loc.gov/2016033106

ISBN: 978-1-138-93293-7 (hbk)
ISBN: 978-0-367-59517-3 (pbk)

Typeset in Times New Roman
by Taylor & Francis Books

Norma Mae Olson
Optimae matri

To see is only a language

(S.T. Coleridge, *Hexameters*)

Even if utterance is muted... my very clothing speaks.
etsi eloquium quiescat,... ipse habitus sonat

(Tert. *Pall.* 6.1.1)

Contents

List of illustrations viii
Acknowledgments x
Abbreviations xii

Introduction: Roman clothing 1
1 Tunic and toga: clothing and rank 13
2 Other aspects of costume 62
3 Poverty, mourning, and *sordes* 91
4 Clothing and status 105
5 Class and sexuality 135
Conclusion 167

Bibliography 171
Index 197

Illustrations

1.1	Tunic drawing (rendered by K. Olson-Lamari). After Croom 2002, 21 fig. 3	14
1.2	Sign from the shop of Verecundus the *vestiarius*. Pompeii (IX,7,5). First century CE	15
1.3	South-west panel of the Ara Pacis Augustae, Aeneas or Numa. Rome. 13–9 BCE	17
1.4	Banquet scene from Pompeii. Museo Archeologico Nazionale, Naples. First century CE	21
1.5	Painted wooden funerary portrait of a man in encaustic, from Thebes, Greco-Roman period. Fourth century CE	22
1.6	The Arringatore (Aulus Metellus). Museo Archeologico, Florence. Not before 100 BCE	24
1.7	North frieze, Ara Pacis Augustae, Rome. 13–9 BCE	25
1.8	Relief from the Ara dei Vicomagistri. Museo Gregoriano Profano, Vatican Museums, Rome. 20–40 CE	26
1.9	Commercial scene of knife-sellers. Vatican Museums, Galleria Lapidaria 147, Rome	27
1.10	Tombstone erected by Publicia Glypte to two young boys (rendered by K. Olson-Lamari). Museo di Villa Albani, Rome. Early second century CE	28
1.11	Roman funerary relief from the Via Statilia. Centrale Montremartini, Rome. 80–50 BCE	30
1.12	Statue of Augustus from the Via Labicana. Museo Nazionale Romano (Palazzo Massimo alle Terme), Rome. First century CE	32
1.13	Relief, arch of Titus. Rome. 70 CE	33
1.14	Statue of Vespasian. Museo Pio Clementino, Vatican Museums, Rome. 69–79 CE	34
1.15	*Extispicium* relief with Trajan. Forum of Trajan, Rome. 120/130 CE	35
1.16	Statue of Hadrian; Musei Capitolini, Rome. 120–8 CE	36
1.17	Great Antonine altar, dynastic scene, from Ephesus. Vienna, Kunsthistorisches Museum. After 169 CE	37

1.18	Panel relief of M. Aurelius. Musei Capitolini, Rome. 176–80 CE	38
1.19	Panel from the Arch of Marcus Aurelius (now on the Arch of Constantine). Rome. 176–80 CE	39
1.20	Decorative element from the base of the stage, Roman theatre at Sabratha, Libya. Early third century CE	40
1.21	*Toga contabulata.* Palazzo Doria-Pamphili. Rome. 260s CE	41
1.22	Acilia Sarcophagus, from Acilia. Museo Nazionale Romano (Palazzo Massimo alle Terme), Rome. 238 CE	42
1.23	The Arringatore (Aulus Metellus). Museo Archeologico, Florence. Not before 100 BCE	46
1.24	Painting from a *lararium.* House of the Vettii, Pompeii (VI, 15,1). First century CE	47
1.25	Mosaic rondel, Basilica of Santa Maria Assunta. Aquileia. Fifth century CE	47
1.26	Fresco from the François Tomb, Vulci. Museo di Villa Albani, Rome. Fourth century BCE	50
1.27	Coin of Augustus. Roman denarius. Cordoba. Muenzkabinett, Staatliche Museen, Berlin, Germany. ca. 18 BCE	51
2.1	Gold *bulla* from the Casa del Menandro, Pompeii. Museo Archeologico Nazionale, Naples. First century CE	63
2.2	Statue of a togate boy wearing the bulla. The head is of Nero as a young child. Rome. 41–54 CE	64
2.3	Sarcophagus, man in hood. Centrale Montremartini, Rome. Late third–early fourth century CE	70
2.4	Bronze statue of boy in a *pallium.* Late first century BCE–early first century CE. Rome	75
2.5	Bronze statue of Hadrian in a *himation.* Archaeological Museum, Istanbul. Second century CE	76
2.6	Patrician, 'equestrian,' and senatorial *calcei* (rendered by D. Fletcher). After Goette 1988, 459.	83
2.7	Fresco: distribution of bread in a bakery at Pompeii. Museo Archeologico Nazionale, Naples. Late first century CE	83
2.8	Detail, statue of Augustus from the Via Labicana. Museo Nazionale Romano (Palazzo Massimo alle Terme), Rome. First century CE	84
4.1	Detail of toga, Roman funerary relief from the Via Statilia. Centrale Montremartini, Rome. 80–50 BCE	120
5.1	Detail, south frieze, Ara Pacis Augustae, Rome. 13–9 BCE	143

Acknowledgments

Many people have provided comments on this manuscript, from its first draft to the finished project. I owe Keith Bradley an enormous debt of gratitude for his tremendous support over the years, both personal and scholarly. I presented portions of the manuscript as conference papers around North America and Europe, and I thank audience and panel members for their suggestions and comments, especially Mary Harlow, Lloyd Llewellyn-Jones, and Ursula Rothe. Gratitude too is due to the anonymous readers at Routledge: they provided enormously helpful ideas for several of the chapters and I have incorporated their suggestions liberally. Of course, I absolve all those acknowledged here from any complicity in the mistakes which inevitably remain.

Assistance with administrative and research concerns at the Univ. of Western Ontario was generously provided by Judy La Forme and Kathleen Beharrell. Funding for the project and research trips to Rome was made available by the Social Sciences and Humanities Research Council of Canada, and the Faculty of Arts and Humanities at the University of Western Ontario. Photos were supplied by Art Resource, New York and the Deutsches Archäologisches Institut, and funding for their reproduction provided by the J. B. Smallman Fund, University of Western Ontario. Line drawings were rendered by Darian Fletcher and the fearless Katie Olson-Lamari. Translations throughout are from the Loeb Classical Library, with minor adjustments. Translations of Tertullian are taken from Hunink 2005. Translations of Isidore are from Barney *et al.* 2010. Translations of the *Digest* are by Watson 1985. All translations of Nonius, Festus, and Servius are my own.

I wish especially to thank my warm colleagues A. Kim Clark, Michael Dewar, Kyle Gervais, Elizabeth M. Greene, Amanda Grzyb, Mark McDayter, Alexander Meyer, †Ilse Mueller, Randy Pogorzelski, Kendall and Hope Sharp, and Tim Wright. My daughters Katharine and Isabella have proven gracious in the face of their mother's peculiar obsession with Roman antiquity, and I love and thank them for that. This book is dedicated to my own mother, Norma Mae Olson, without a doubt the strongest, most loving, and hardest-working woman I have ever met. My scholarly successes, such as they are, could never have been achieved without her support and encouragement. Thanks, Mom.

K. Olson
London, Ontario, Canada 2016

Abbreviations

Abbreviations of journal titles are taken from L'Année Philologique. Abbreviations of ancient authors and their works are taken from the Oxford Latin Dictionary.

BMC	1923–65. Coins of the Roman Empire in the British Museum, edited by Harrold Mattingly. 6 vols.
BNP	2002–11. Brill's New Pauly: Encyclopedia of the Ancient World, edited by H. Cancik, H. Schneider, C. Salazar, and D. Orton. Leiden: Brill.
CIL	1863– . Corpus Inscriptionum Latinarum. Berlin: G. Reiner.
Digest	1985. The Digest of Justinian. Latin text edited by Th. Mommsen with the aid of P. Kreuger. Translated by A. Watson. Philadelphia: University of Pennsylvania Press.
Edict	1940. "The Edict of Diocletian on Maximum Prices," edited by E. Graser. In Frank 1940.
FGrH	1950–8. Fragmente der griechischen Historiker. Leiden: Brill.
ILS	1892–1916. Inscriptiones Latinae Selectae, edited by H. Dessau. 3 vols. Berlin: Weidemann.
ORF	1955. Oratorum Romanorum Fragmenta Liberae Rei Publicae, edited by H. Malcovati. 2nd ed. Turin: Paravia.
OLD	1968–82. The Oxford Latin Dictionary. Oxford.
Paul. Sent	1968–9. Fontes Iuris Romani Antejustiniani, ii. 319–417, edited by S. Riccobono. Florence: G. Barbèra.
PIR	1952–66. Prosopographia Imperii Romani, edited by A. Stein and L. Peterson. Berlin and Leipzig: Walter de Gruyter & Co.
P Oxy.	1898– . The Oxyrhynchus Papyri, edited by B. P. Grenfell and A. S. Hunt. London: Egypt Exploration Society.
RE	1894–1978. Real-Encyclopädie der classichen Altertumswissenschaft, edited by A. Pauly, C. Walz, and W. S. Teuffel. Stuttgart: J. B. Metzler.
RIC	1923–2007. Roman Imperial Coinage, edited by H. Mattingly. London: Spink.

ILLRP	1963, 1965. Inscriptiones Latinae Liberae Reipublicae, edited by A. Degrassi. Florence: La Nuova Italia.
TLL	1900– . Thesaurus Linguae Latinae. Leipzig: B.G. Teubner.

Introduction
Roman clothing

One may say that the body is articulated socially through clothing and ornament, and that these are what make the human body culturally visible.[1] Valerie Steele has noted that "the history of fashion is as complex as any other branch of history" (1985, 96). It is even more complex for historians of ancient fashion, who "do not, for the most part, have the luxury of artefact-based research… we rely heavily on visual representations in a range of media, and literary texts from a range of genres" (Harlow 2005, 143). In addition, Llewellyn-Jones reminds us that many clothing terms have unexplainable meanings. "We have probably lost many nuanced and colloquial terms for items of clothing which varied according to time and place. The ancient Greeks themselves were very relaxed about naming their items of dress" (2003, 25). Thus, the historian of ancient costume is "coping with an incomplete vocabulary of changing technical and colloquial terms" (ibid).

Writing on ancient Roman costume in English has traditionally lagged sadly behind fashion studies in other fields.[2] Lillian Wilson published *The Roman Toga* and *The Clothing of the Ancient Romans* in 1924 and 1938 respectively. Meyer Reinhold published two seminal studies on clothing, one on the history of purple (1970) and the other on the usurpation of status symbols (1971). Bonfante-Warren began her invaluable work on the clothing of the Etruscans in 1973 (and her *Etruscan Dress* has recently been re-issued in an updated edition [Bonfante 2003]). Even so, for many years studies of ancient clothing, when they appeared at all, seemed to deal only with matters of interest to the antiquarian: the precise shape and size of the toga, for instance, or speculations on shades of clothing dyes.[3] It is really only in the last twenty years or so that interest in the area of appearance has burgeoned. Sebesta and Bonfante published *The World of Roman Costume* in 1994, a book which consists of short articles on many aspects of Roman costume in literature and art, including men's and women's clothing, jewelry, and shoes. This work, along with Croom's book of 2002 (*Roman Clothing and Fashion*), must now be regarded as the starting place for all English-speaking historians of Roman costume, although more recent collections have also appeared (Edmondson and Keith 2008; Harlow 2012a). Volumes on ancient textiles are also numerous: (recently, Gillis and Nosch 2007; Harlow and Nosch 2014).

2 *Introduction*

German work too has been substantial, with monographs appearing on the toga (Goette 1990), the *stola* (Scholz 1992), the tunic (Pausch 2008) as well as a host of articles on Roman cloaks, shoes, and other ornaments (Gabelmann 1977; Goette 1986 and 1990; Wrede 1988; and the chapters in Tellenbach *et al.* 2013). In French, Chausson and Inglebert 2003 will be of interest; Florence Gherchanoc's work has been most influential (see the collections Gherchanoc *et al.* 2011; Gherchanoc and Huet 2012) and recently three articles have appeared in *Revue Historique* entitled *S'habiller et se déshabiller en Grèce et à Rome* (I and III are listed in the bibliography as Baroin and Valette-Cagnac 2007 and Gherchanoc and Huet 2007). A special issue of *Mètis* (2008, no. 6) is on various aspects of ancient costume;[4] a special issue of *Dialogues d'histoire ancienne* is a series of articles on the state of the field of scholarship on ancient clothing and the body (Gherchanoc 2015).

Because of the traditional focus in classical studies on men and male culture, there has been more published on the clothing of men in Roman Italy than on female clothing.[5] And because the sources are more concerned with men generally, there is more primary evidence for male clothing: descriptions of what it looked like, accounts of how it was worn, indications of certain infractions of normal dress. Much excellent work has been done on the toga and symbols in male clothing,[6] and notions of effeminacy and self-presentation of the male body.[7] Other areas of dress have received scholarly attention as well: Roman military historians have also achieved much in the area of the soldiers' and officers' garments,[8] and there is now a wealth of publications on dress in the late antique Roman empire, and on Christian attitudes to clothing.[9] Unfortunately, space here precludes me from considering these fascinating areas in detail in this book, each of which would require their own sizeable volume. Instead, I concentrate on male 'civilian' clothing and its social and sexual resonances.

Method

To elucidate the manifold ways dress could communicate social status and identity in Roman antiquity, I maintain that we need first to understand (as best as our sources allow us to reconstruct) the sartorial vocabulary of ancient Romans, their clothing technology, and the details of the garments which were worn. In order to reconstruct these minutiae, we need to look at a variety of sources (literary and artistic), across geographic and historical periods.

The chronological range covered in this volumes spans the years 200 BCE to ca. 235 CE (the 'central period'), although where I feel it is warranted I have not hesitated to make use of sources outside this era. In addition to the usual written sources – histories, biographies, and the like – I also utilize in a limited way more imaginative literature, such as Artemidorus' *Oneirocritica*, and the historically dubious *Historia Augusta*.[10] Although not perhaps strictly veridical, these types of sources offer a "plausible glimpse into Roman mentalities" (Brennan 2008, 262). In some ways, Rome was a different world in

235 CE than it had been in 200 BCE – certainly culturally and politically – and where possible I make note of chronological developments in male dress. This is however enormously difficult to trace: truthfully, one of the fascinating things about Roman society is in fact the *lack* of change over time – in *mentalité*, in dress, in social ideology – despite deep historical and political transformations. (There is always the possibility that there was sartorial change and that we cannot discern it from the relatively few surviving comments on clothing that we possess). My geographical range tends to be fairly narrow; I try to concentrate on Rome and Roman Italy, but again, sometimes I make use of subject matter outside this region.

Roman cultural studies is a broad and fascinating area, and one in which much work remains to be done; yet classical scholars have not yet come to any real consensus concerning the proper selection and use of sources. It is a field not strictly philologically based; the scholar needs to consider different genres of literary sources together; and s/he needs especially to combine artistic, literary, and epigraphical sources to achieve a desirable 'thick description.'[11] In addition, it is also useful to draw on comparative evidence, to formulate new hypotheses or shed a new and interesting light on antiquity. This means that the discipline of *mentalité* or cultural studies (and its often somewhat impressionistic conclusions) is frequently viewed with suspicion. Susan Treggiari helpfully cautions on pressing the evidence too far: "we must not claim to have proved what we have merely shown to be plausible" (Treggiari 2002, 39). In this study, I have done my best to label speculation.

There are caveats of course concerning all types of evidence. I would argue, for instance, that there is always a danger that mention of the function and use of clothing in the literary sources can be idealistic/prescriptive rather than descriptive – what may be termed the rhetoric of clothing,[12] and in many ways this kind of symbolism is easier to trace than the materiality of ancient clothing. Unfortunately there is simply no way to know if an item of clothing is mentioned in the sources because a) it reflects real-life practice (description); b) is used metonymically (i.e., an item of clothing worn in the distant past and worn no longer, but rife with symbolism); or c) represents an idealized world-view on the part of the author (prescription). Despite these problems, no historian of clothing can afford to ignore written sources. I try to flag this difficulty by inserting phrases such as "the literary evidence states that..." to indicate the source and probable limitations of this kind of information.

In this study, I also make use of art.[13] Scholars today are rightly concerned with how to securely utilize iconography as evidence for ancient dress in the face of written sources, which often contradict it. It is difficult to engage with this debate without implying that art is 'truer' or must in some way be privileged over literature, or vice versa.[14] Some scholars feel that literary evidence presents a more accurate picture of sartorial life in Greco-Roman antiquity (Clark 1993, 105; Dixon 2001c, 125; Kampen 1981, 101; Llewellyn-Jones 2003, 10; Stone 1994, 21; Vout 1996, 206); others that art is on the whole more reliable than written sources (George 2001, 188, n. 8; Kockel 1993, 53;

4   Introduction

Olson 2008, 3–4). This is an argument that may never be resolved among scholars. While art is not a slice of life, and embellishes and omits for its own purposes, the disjunction between literary and artistic sources for ancient clothing remains fascinating, if difficult, to explain. I hope this book provides a balanced view of the merits and drawbacks of studying clothing from both written and visual evidence.

I also draw on archaeological evidence to a certain extent. Finds of remnants of cloth and clothing as well as discoveries of dyeing, fulling, textile production equipment, and implements mean that "a more elaborate picture of the Roman clothing and textile industry is developing" (Mannering 2000b, 10). Much valuable work has been done at Mons Claudianus and Didymoi in Egypt;[15] sites in pre-Roman Italy;[16] Vindolanda and Northern Europe;[17] the Cave of Letters on the Dead Sea;[18] Roman Spain;[19] and Pompeii.[20] Archaeological finds are naturally valuable for what they can tell us of the origins, production, workmanship, and physical materials of clothing, but can also contain helpful information about clothing and social status, styles of provincial clothing, and reuse of garments.

Terminology

Harlow (2004, 46) defines *costume* as 'traditional dress:' a garment or set of garments that has existed over a long period of time and has undergone little change, the signs and nuances of which could be easily understood by contemporaries. *Fashion* comprises non-traditional dress elements which are short-lived, often as a result of restless search *after* change; this is often harder to track for antiquity. Fashion elements can eventually become part of traditional dress (e.g., barbarian trousers in antiquity); and vice versa, but generally, costume is 'anti-fashion.'[21] Although I use the phrase "male sartorial code" throughout this book to mean "the accepted male *habitus* which establishes and reaffirms masculinity and inclusion in the masculine hegemony," this is not what I define as "fashion," but rather as "costume." (The dress of dandies is different in this regard: see below, Chapter 5). A series of prevailing styles in male clothing and deportment which rapidly succeeded one another ("fashion") does not seem to have existed in Roman antiquity.

'Dress' to the Romans meant more than solely garments: it also encompassed the grooming of the body (haircut and beard if any, the presence of body hair; perfume), the wearing of jewelry. The two terms used most often for dress/appearance are *habitus* and *cultus*.[22] '*Habitus*' in the *Oxford Latin Dictionary* is defined as "style of dress, toilet, etc., 'get-up' (esp. proper to a particular class or occasion);" whether of the military (Virg. *A*. 3.596, 8.723), *equites* (Hor. *S*. 2.7.54), persons in mourning (Ov. *Fast*. 2.817), or an orator (Quint. *Inst*. 8 pr. 20). The *OLD* gives as the first definition of the word "state of being, condition a. (of the body)" which matches the Roman conviction that clothing (with a few exceptions) displayed one's inner character.

The *OLD* defines *cultus* (2, p. 467) as "4. Personal care and maintenance... also, the state of being well-groomed. 5. a. The adorning (of anything); esp. the decking or attiring (of a person, his body, etc.). b. a style of dress or ornament, 'get-up;' also *cultus corporis*. 6. Adornments, esp. personal adornments, clothes, finery, etc." As Maria Wyke has noted, *cultus* is that which civilizes, or that which softens ("not only the Roman citizen and the body politic but also the written word").[23] But it can also mean comfort (Livy 26.49.11), elegance (Suet. *Nero* 31.1), urbane sophistication (Caes. *Gal*. 1.1.3), or over-refinement or luxury (Sall. *Cat*. 13.3; Plin. *Nat*. 34.163; Tac. *Ann*. 11.16). A lack of *cultus* marked out slaves and the lower classes: dirty clothing and an unwashed body.

One final word we should consider is *lautus*. It primarily means 'washed, clean' (Ter. *Ph*. 339, Cic. *Flac*. 70) but has secondary meanings of 'being well-turned out, having an air of respectability, substance' (Cic. *Att*. 8.1.3, 13.52.2, *Phil*. 3.18, *Verr*. 2.1.17), and finally 'sumptuous, luxurious, wealthy' (Mart. 4.54.8, 11.31.20, Sen. *Epp*. 94.70. Petr. 26.9, Tac. *Dial*. 22.4). In other words, 'clean' comes to mean by extension 'luxurious,' because being clean is the province of those with enough money and leisure to do so.[24]

Masculinity studies

Studies of men and masculinity to date have been most abundant in the social sciences, and usually concentrate on contemporary Western society; "disciplines concerned with past societies have to date rarely focused on men as men" (Foxhall 1998, 2). This is changing as masculinity becomes an important and stimulating field of inquiry for scholars working in ancient Roman cultural and gender studies.[25]

In most societies, there is "some fundamental, generally agreed concept of maleness" (Foxhall 1998, 4), often described by scholars as 'hegemonic masculinity,' that is, a dominant masculinity exercised by an economic, social and political elite[26] (Gleason 1990, 392; McDonnell 2006, 165), invariably masquerading as unitary (Cornwall and Lindisfarne 1994, 20). "An immediate consequence of this is that the culturally exalted form of masculinity... may only correspond to the actual characters of a small number of men. Yet very large numbers of men are complicit in sustaining the hegemonic model" (Carrigan *et al*. 1985, 592). Masculinity is thus presented in many societies, including Roman antiquity, as an essence or commodity which can be measured, possessed, or lost (Cornwall and Lindisfarne 1994, 12); as precarious, elusive, and exclusionary (McDonnell 2006, 10; Wray 2001, 62). Masculinity is also in the main a social demonstration or performance, a finding which originated in comparative scholarship (Butler 1990) but which has also been noted for Roman antiquity (Gleason 1995; Edwards 1993, 63–97) in which a man's appearance and behavior was subject to "ideological evaluation" (Wray 2001, 60).

Hegemonic discourse tends to produce subordinate and subversive variants (Cornwall and Lindisfarne 1994, 18), and recent work in the social sciences has concluded that in any society there is not one, but a variety of masculinities, some deemed by the dominant group as inadequate or inferior in one way or another (Connell 1995; Foxhall 1998, 4; Gilmore 1990; Herzfeld 1985; McDonnell 2006, 165). Masculinities invariably reflect power relationships, as gendered identities are "necessarily constructed with reference to others who are represented as different and/or dominated" (Cornwall and Lindisfarne 1994, 43), and this was certainly true for Roman antiquity (Edwards 1993; Gleason 1995; McDonnell 2006, 166 n. 13;). In addition, in other disciplines, the monolithic, polarized divisions of 'man' and 'woman' are beginning to be broken down in favor of a more complex spectrum of categories.[27] "It is plain for any broadly historical discipline that historical moment, life stage, age, class, status, wealth, race/ethnicity and so on profoundly shape what can be understood as the masculinity or femininity of any individual" (Foxhall 1998, 3).

I try to argue in the chapters that follow that there were many ways of performing masculinity in ancient Rome; that men operated according to many different notions of masculinity; and that there was a wide repertoire from which masculine identities could be assembled (after Cornwall and Lindisfarne 1994, 12, 16). Male clothing and ornament played a large part in how gender roles and behaviors overlapped, or were blurred, transcended or even obliterated: there were many ways in Roman antiquity of being a man.[28]

Rank and status

Ideally, "the form, fabric, and color of a garment announced a person's condition, quality, and estate. It did so juridically, clearly, unabashedly, and without justifications" (Perrot 1994, 15). 'Status' I define as one's informal prestige among peers or one's financial standing, 'rank' as one's actual juridical category (senator, equestrian, etc.). Obviously, rank and status were intertwined in crucial and complicated ways, sartorially and otherwise (slavery, both a juridical and a status category, is just one example), and that fact is highlighted in many of the chapters which follow. While there was no established *legal* hierarchy of clothing at Rome, there was an idealized system of sartorial signs which was unofficial, understood, and acknowledged.

Clothing was so important to visualizing social strata that the Romans conceptualized juridical category in part as the right to wear certain articles of clothing. Thus, the right to stand for office was termed the right of the *latus clavus* (the wide stripe on a magistrate's toga; see Suet. *Aug.* 38.2), incorporation into the rank of *eques* the *ius anuli aurei* (the 'right of the gold ring;' see Reinhold 1971, 279, with references). The phrase *calceos mutare*, 'to change into shoeboots' meant 'to become a senator' (Cic. *Phil.* 13.28). Cicero uses the phrase *usque a toga pura* ("all the way from the un-bordered toga") to mean 'from the day he came of age' (*Att.* 7.8.5). Such details were important because the visual was fundamental to the way in which Romans constructed social meaning: "Romans were accustomed to and highly attuned to visual modes of communication so that visual literacy reigned supreme over verbal literacy; pictures and visual clues often took priority over words" (Petersen 2009, 182; Elsner 1998, 11). Often rank was inseparable from the clothing people wore.

But stating juridical position was not clothing's sole function in antiquity. Aspects of appearance also conceptualized status, which often (although not always) had to do with wealth and power, another concern of the present study. A man may not have been legally entitled to wear the broad-striped tunic, for instance – but he could certainly demonstrate financial status by the use of Tyrian purple elsewhere on his clothing and gems on his fingers. Such indicators helped in the recognition of one's peers and superiors, as well as those of lower social station. Clothing thus had a strong legal and social dimension: it was an important way in which symbol-conscious Romans demonstrated rank and status.

As is well-known to scholars of Roman antiquity, social standing was made apparent by visual symbols, and that the hierarchy of status (and often rank as well) had a material form which in turn generated conflict. Social symbols were not the exclusive property of the dominant class, nor could they be regulated as such: because many status symbols were an effect of wealth, any rich man could appropriate them. The reason the Romans tried so hard to control the symbols of rank and status informally was precisely because the social hierarchy was fluid, status symbols easily manipulated: it was often difficult to discern rank by appearance alone. Clothing could lie, and dress could produce confusion, rather than clarification, of social and juridical boundaries: "for the eyes do not seem to bring accurate results, but the judgment is often deceived by it," Vitruvius wrote.[29] Usurpation of equestrian symbols of rank seems to have been widespread in the Imperial period, and ancient sources tell of men illegally wearing the *angustus clavus* and the gold ring (see below, Chapter 2). Slaves, for instance, conventionally appeared in shabby garments, but some were dressed in expensive clothing and ornamented, a practice which called attention to the fact that their master or mistress was wealthy. In addition, we may detect in the literary sources the often surprising omission of sartorial symbols of rank such as the toga.

The Romans also wore imported dress items, from Greece and Europe (e.g. Gaul), such as the *synthesis* (dinner-costume) and *bardocucullus* (the hooded cloak), and the significance of such items is not always easy to discern. If our literary sources are to be believed, Greek dress in particular was fraught with complications for a Roman wearer. The nobleman who assumed the *pallium* and Greek sandals in public could perhaps expect a range of reactions from those around him (admiration, disgust, indifference). A comparative situation might be the adoption of Persian garments by Greek men in fifth-century Athens: Achaemenid items were prestige-laden, and for a time they functioned as fashionable exotic luxuries (Miller 1997, 187). Greek items of clothing were likewise prestigious for the Romans, as it perhaps allowed one to visualize education, erudition, and taste, a discussion I take up below (Chapter 2). The *cucullus* and *bardocucullus* probably came to Roman attention through military conquest, and were perhaps adopted by the Romans as eminently practical items.

Cloth as economic staple

The noted art historian Anne Hollander asserted in 1978 that cloth "did not become an economic staple... a manufactured commodity of prime importance" until the Middle Ages. Only then did cloth "have something of the status of wrought gold or glass, representing a triumph of man's impulses towards artificial luxury" (Hollander 1978, 15). This assertion will come as something of a surprise to the Roman historian; cloth definitely counted as an "artificial luxury" in antiquity.

In addition, at Rome cloth was very much an economic staple. Clothing was so valuable that it was often the target of thieves (Mart. 8.48, 8.59; Petr. *Satyr.* 12, 30; Cat. 25), or could be pawned or sold outright for ready cash:[30] at Petr. *Satyr.* 44.15 a poor man has to sell his rags (*pannos*) to eat. This is because cloth and clothing were expensive in antiquity in a way unknown today: J. P. Wild (1994, 30–1) calculates that the cost of materials and labour for a late-antique tunic totaled 2,296 denarii.[31] Wild supposes that it would have been much cheaper to make one's clothes at home – provided one had a loom and skilled labour (and could gather the right materials; 1994, 31). But Liu states that "recent estimations of the (low) work rates in textile production (especially spinning and weaving) in ancient Greece and Rome have made it quite difficult to believe that household self-sufficiency in textile could be achieved."[32] Thus the household would likely be forced to purchase ready-made clothing and soft furnishings from the Roman markets. Cloth as well as clothing was used in the service of status display and conspicuous consumption, not only in clothing, but in forms like brilliantly colored sails and awnings.[33] "Such 'backdrops' can be considered analogous to clothing in presenting a public persona ... color and fabric in the Empire were covert social weapons" (Sebesta 1994b, 70).

Where could the elite buy cloth and clothing and other items of personal adornment in Roman antiquity? In Holleran's detailed study of the retail trade in ancient Rome, she notes that there were several areas in the city where one could go for luxury goods. There was a Vicus Unguentarius (street of the perfume sellers) in the forum; the Via Sacra was dominated by goldsmiths (*aurifices; CIL* 6.9207, 9212), pearl dealers (*margaritarii, CIL* 6.9545–49, 33872, 10.6492), and jewelers (*gemmarii; CIL* 6.9434–9435), who proudly recorded the fashionable and prestigious location of their workshops on funerary monuments.[34] The remains of *tabernae* along the Via Sacra perhaps at one time housed such workshops.[35] The Vicus Tuscus, a street linking the Forum Romanum to the Forum Boarium and the Circus Maximus, "was also connected with the sale of luxury items" including silks, purple dye, perfumes, ointments.[36] At Mart. 2.57 a man pawns a ring at the table of one Cladus in the Saepta to buy his dinner, suggesting "not only that it was possible to pawn goods in the Saepta, but also that traders were buying, as well as selling, luxury items."[37] Tradesmen may have called on the wealthy in their homes as well (Pl. *Aul.* 505–20).

Clothing and items of ornament were sold elsewhere in Rome too. The Subura sold linen goods and shoes (*lintearius, CIL* 6.9526; *crepidarius, CIL* 6.9284); the Horrea Agrippiana were home to sellers of cloth and clothing. One *purpurarius* had his shop in the Trastevere area.[38] The paintings from the *praedia* of Julia Felix show vendors in the Pompeiian forum selling cloth and shoes.[39] Clothes were also sold by street sellers, *institores*.[40] There was also a thriving trade in secondhand clothing dealers: "many in Rome wore ragged, patched, and secondhand clothes."[41] A fourth-century regionary catalogue records an Area Pannaria (secondhand clothing dealers) near the Porta Capena. Slave clothes were often bought from secondhand patchers or clothing dealers, the *centonarii* (Cato *R.* 135.1; Petr. *Satyr.* 45).[42] *Scrutarii* dealt in secondhand goods such as shoes.[43] Papyri provide much evidence of the secondhand clothing trade.[44] At Mart. 7.10 one Olus still owes money on his *togula*, his little toga (thus clothing could be had on credit).

Outline

In this book I try to discard the conventional discrete categories (boy, senator, *eques*, etc.) often used by modern authors to organize the description and elucidation of clothing items. I feel this is misleading inasmuch as such categories imply there were isolated kinds of appearance. Sartorial categories in fact bled into one another in antiquity, as is shown in part by the fact that many items of clothing and ornament crossed economic, social, even ideological boundaries. The *lacerna* or cloak was a garment for all economic statuses; a violet silk tunic denoted both wealth and effeminacy; the toga could appear on citizen males of every rank. Appearance was fluid, unstable, and adaptable.

This study is in large part a detailed and descriptive account of Roman male dress using literary and artistic sources. This may seem to some to border on the antiquarian, but I would argue that such details of dress need to be provided (along with an up-to-date bibliography). Such particulars provide us with the terminology of clothing and many incidental details of Roman sartorial practices and technology. In addition, ways in which dress served as a means for social and cultural definition need to be thoroughly grounded in an understanding of the physical articles of dress themselves.

I begin with a chapter entitled 'Tunic and toga: clothing and rank.' The tunic (*tunica*) was the simple sleeved garment worn by men of all ages and ranks. Here I summarize and illustrate the differences between the Republican and Imperial tunics, examine the *tunica recta*, sleeves and cincture, and striped tunics, among other topics. The toga was of course the Roman garment *par excellence*, although the form may have been Etruscan (Bonfante 2003, 45), and I look at the basic form of the toga from the Republican *toga exigua* to those togas sporting the *balteus* in the third century CE; different toga drapes for different occasions; the proper cut and draping of an orator's toga; and the *toga pura*. I also examine in detail the high symbolic content of the toga, the *toga virilis* ceremony, and the toga as the mark of the male citizen. Finally, for all its importance as a symbol of rank and sophistication, there are several examples of the omission of the toga, which I collect and explicate in this chapter.

In Chapter 2 ('Other aspects of costume') I examine the evidence for capes and cloaks worn by men (*lacerna, cucullus, paenula*), the different kinds of garments that could be worn by men under their tunics (*subligar, subligaculum, campestre*, etc.), and how shoes ideally reflected Roman ideas of rank. Also included here are items of jewelry which denoted rank such as the *bulla* and men's rings, and hats. I also survey the tradition of the *sumere saga* and rituals involving the *paludamentum*.

The second half of the book is slightly more analytical. In Chapter 3 ('Poverty, mourning, and *sordes*') I examine the clothing of the poor, mourning clothing, and *vestes sordidae*, and the connections amongst these. Chapter 4 is entitled "Clothing and status," which examines aspects of male appearance which indicated status (as opposed to rank). I look here at status reflected in expensive or excess fabrics used for the toga (silk, for example), luxury dyes (purple and scarlet), and male jewelry. Here I also examine the *toga candida*, the *toga purpurea, toga picta, tunica palmata*, and the *trabea*. More generally, in this chapter I try to determine why the normative code at Rome dictated that the appearance of the Roman man was sober and dull – an association of flamboyant clothing with *luxuria*, the *nouveaux riches*, or effeminacy, or a combination of all three.

A strong interest in personal appearance was thought by some Romans to smack of effeminacy – but not to groom at all was thought to be rustic and unsophisticated (Mart. 6.55). A Roman therefore may have walked a fine line between what was expected grooming practice and what was considered sexually suspicious. In Chapter five ("Effeminacy and the dandy: class and sexuality) I argue for the existence of the dandy in Roman antiquity, as opposed to the *cinaedus*, and draw together the available evidence for the dress of both. I also argue there confusion existed between signs of 'masculinity' (male wealth, power, influence, privilege) and signs of 'effeminacy.'

The book ends with a chapter drawing together some conclusions about appearance, sexuality, and masculinity in Roman antiquity. With certain exceptions, far from holding a notion that the 'true' self lay hidden within the shell of clothing and the body, the self for the Romans was literally a projection of exterior signs (Kellum 1999, 288). Dress performances and clothing had the ability to negotiate, resist, and challenge well-established (even legally constrained) sartorial rules, as well as norms of masculinity.

Notes

1 Silverman 1986, 145.
2 For Greek clothing, see most recently Cohen 2001; Gheranchoc and Huet 2007, 10–13; Lee 2005 and her excellent monograph of 2015; Llewellyn-Jones 2002b and 2003; van Wees 2005.

3 For an excellent summary of the move within the field from costume history to modern dress studies, see Gherchanoc and Huet 2007, 5–10; Edmondson and Keith 2008; Lee 2015, 10–32.
4 A forthcoming volume, F. Gherchanoc, J.-B. Bonnard and V. Huet is entitled *Corps, gestes et vêtements: les manifestations du politique dan l'Antiquité* (Kentron).
5 Although this is changing: see for instance Blanck 1997; Dixon 2014; Fantham 2008; Gallia 2014; Harlow 2012b and 2013; Holtheide 1980; Lovén 2013; Olson 2008; Sebesta 1994 and 1997; Scholz 1992.
6 Christ 1997; Davies 2005; Deniaux 2003; Dolansky 2008; Edmondson 2008; George 2008; Goette 2013; Palmer 1998; Sebesta 2005; Stone 1994; and Vout 1996.
7 Connolly 1998 (in part); Dyck 2001; Gleason 1990 and 1995 (in part); McDonnell 2006 (in part); and Williams 2010 (again only in part). Nudity in the Roman world is an intriguing topic (again, space precludes a discussion in this study): see Benoist 2012; Hallett 2005, 61–101.
8 On military dress, see most recently Nosch and Koefoed 2012; Southern 2006; Speidel 2012, 1994, and 1997; Sumner 2002 and 2009.
9 See for instance Daniel-Hughes 2011, 45–51; Delmaire 2004; Dewar 2008; Doerfler 2014; Harlow 2004; Métraux 2008; Parani 2008; Upson-Saia 2011; and those essays collected in Upson-Saia *et al.* 2014.
10 On the role of clothing in the *HA*, see Callu 2004; Harlow 2005; Martorelli 2004; Moliner-Arbo 2003.
11 Geertz 1973, 3–30. Barton (1993, 5–6) terms this the "mosaicist approach."
12 See Olson 2008, 35, 39–40, 50, 113–14. See McGinn 2014, 91–7 for a pointed critique of this.
13 On visual sources and ancient history, see Hölscher [1987] 2004. Smith 2002 is an excellent overview of the subject.
14 For the problems which arise when pictorial representations of clothing are used as empirical evidence, see Emberley 1997, 127–31.
15 At Mons Claudianus in Egypt's Eastern desert, "one of the richest archaeological textile assemblages of the twentieth century has been unearthed." Excavations carried out brought to light an estimated 50,000 textiles, well preserved in rubbish dumps (Mannering 2000b: 10; see also Bender-Jørgensen 2004). Most of the finds date from 104–155 CE. On the textile finds in the rubbish heaps at Didymoi, occupied 76/77–240 CE, see Cardon et al. 2011.
16 See Gleba 2000, 2004, and 2008b, with references.
17 See G. W. Taylor 1983; Wild 1977, 1979, 1992b, 1993, 2011.
18 Yadin 1963; Granger-Taylor 2006, with references.
19 Alfaro Giner 2001 and 2005.
20 On the fulleries at Pompeii, see Flohr 2003 and 2013b; Wilson 2003. On those at Ostia, see De Ruyt 2001. On textile production at Pompeii and Herculaneum, see Borgard and Puybaret 2004; Flohr 2013a; Moeller 1976; Monteix 2010.
21 For the links between 'costume' and 'fashion,' and the ways in which the two terms have been used by dress historians, see Paulicelli 2014, 4–12.
22 For the term *ornatus* see Olson 2008, 8–9.
23 Wyke 1994, 143, 145–6. Quotation: 145.
24 See now Blonski 2014, 241–8.
25 See Corbeill 1996; Foxhall and Salmon 1998a and 1998b; Gleason 1995; Harlow 2004; Kuefler 2001; McDonnell 2006; Williams 2010.
26 By 'elite,' I mean those men of the patrician and senatorial classes at Rome, and also wealthy equestrians.
27 On challenges to the gender binary, see Connell 1995; Herdt 1994; Butler 1990: 22–33; Hird 2000; see also Foxhall 1998, 4; Overing 1986; Rubin 1975; Threadgold 1990.

Introduction

28 After Foxhall 1998.
29 *Non enim veros videtur habere visus effectus, sed fallitur saepius iudicio ab eo mens; Arch.* 6.2.2.
30 We have evidence for clothing taken as surety in the *P. Oxy.*, for small as well as large amounts of money, showing that customers came from all kinds of socio-economic backgrounds (see Liu 2009, 72 n. 68). Secondhand clothing (one's own, or stolen) could be taken to the market and sold: Petr. *Satyr.* 12–13.
31 By way of comparison, in the fourth century CE a day's wage for a stonemason was fifty denarii, and pork was twelve denarii per Roman pound. See Wild 1994, 31.
32 See Liu 2009, 74–5 n. 82 for estimates and references.
33 See Pliny (*Nat.* 19.22–4) for descriptions of awnings in the amphitheatre and in private houses.
34 See Holleran 2012, 54–5. Liu (2009, 57) notes that the *-arius* suffix is confusing, as it means maker, user, dealer, or operator of something, and that perhaps the modern distinction between tradesmen and craftsmen is too artificial to be applicable to the ancient world (Liu 2009,70).
35 See Palombi 1990, 66.
36 Holleran 2012, 57 and n. 205. See Pl. *Curc.* 482; Mart. 11.27.11; *purpurarius: CIL* 6.9848, 14.2433 (other mention of *purpurarii* occur at 6.33888, 6.37820, and 6.9844–6). Perfumes: Hor. *S.* 2.3.228. Sellers of perfume and incense were often linked together: *CIL* 6.5638, 6.36819. For inscriptions from sellers on the Vicus Tuscus, see *CIL* 6.33923, 6.37826, 6.9976.
37 Holleran 2012, 250; see also Mart. 9.59 and 10.80.
38 *Purpurarius*: Gregori 1994, 739–43; Holleran 2012, 59; *CIL* 6.9847, (=26217); Horrea Agrippiana: Holleran 2012, 83–4; Mart. 10.87. Some *vestiarii* as well have been recorded in inscriptions as practicing in this area (*CIL* 6.9972, 14.3958).
39 Holleran 2012, 200. On these paintings, see Nappo 1989.
40 Holleran 2012, 203; and see Pl. *Aul.* 512; Juv. 7.221; *Dig.* 14.3.5.4. Street sellers might also hawk seasonal goods such as blankets and coats in the winter time (Holleran 2012, 216; Pliny *Nat.* 18.225, Juv. 7.221).
41 Holleran 2012, 226; Pl. *Epid.* 455, Petr. *Satyr.* 12–15; Juv. 3.147–53; Amm. 15.12.2. On the secondhand clothing trade, see Holleran 2012, 54, 229.
42 Liu (2009, 63–4) gives several definitions of *cento*: patchwork clothing (Col. *Agr.* 59); a rag for patching (Apul. *Met.* 9); and worn, dirty, or shabby garments. Scholars in the past have defined *centonarius* only as a ragman or secondhand clothing dealer; Liu's thesis (2009, 71) is that they were craftsmen and tradesmen in woolen fabrics, both new and used, but also that *centonarii* did not have to be the only businessmen involved with secondhand clothing in the Roman cities (ibid).
43 Holleran 2012, 226; Lucil. 1282; Apul. *Met.* 4.8.27; *Dig.* 18.1.45.
44 See Liu 2009, 71–3 for examples; Pleket 1988.

1 Tunic and toga: clothing and rank

On the basic tablets of the tunic and toga the Romans tried to inscribe information about rank and status. Usually it is the toga that receives attention from modern dress historians (scholars have examined its border, length, symbolism, etc.; see below), and while it is true that the tunic may be called a 'status-free' garment, in the sense that any man of any class may wear a tunic (Kampen 1981, 55), I argue here that it could be a clear indicator of one's place in Roman society too. The toga was of course the Roman garment *par excellence*, although the form was Etruscan (Bonfante 2003, 45). Here I summarize toga varieties from the skimpy Republican toga (the *toga exigua*) to those togas sporting the *balteus* or 'shoulder-*umbo*' in the third century; different toga drapes for different occasions; and the proper cut and draping of an orator's toga. I also examine in detail the high symbolic content of the toga: as a marker of the male citizen, the client, and the urbane sophisticate. Finally, for all its importance as a symbol of rank and refinement, it was also expensive to purchase and maintain, and there are several examples of the omission of the garment.

Some of the references I have collected here are well-known; as are some of the conclusions I draw. But is important to gather and set out instances of the description and use of Roman garments which are visible in the historical and artistic records. Only then may we arrive at an imaginative picture of the spectacle of dress and its and emblematic force.

Tunic

Construction[1]

The tunic (*tunica*) was the simple short-sleeved or sleeveless garment worn by men of all ages and ranks, the basic male garment for both public and private wear (Harlow 2004, 54). The shape of the tunic was a straight slip with a horizontal opening at the top through which the head passed, and vertical openings on each side for arm holes (Wilson 1938, 56; see Fig. 1.1).

Croom has noted a variety of weaving techniques for tunics from Egypt, (2002, 20–1). Some required that the garment be woven all in one piece,

14 *Tunic and toga: clothing and rank*

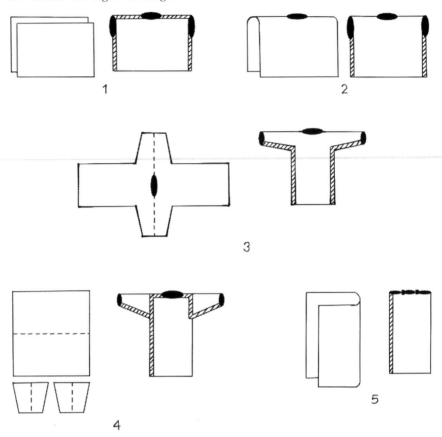

Figure 1.1 Tunic drawing (rendered by K. Olson-Lamari). After Croom 2002, 21 fig. 3

demanding a very wide loom (see Wilson 1938, 56, of garments in the Coptic period).[2] After it was woven the tunic was folded along the neck opening so the two ends met evenly; then it was stitched together with a seam on each side and under each arm (Fig. 1.1 nos. 2 and 3). Varro's description of a tunic with broad stripes (*lati clavi*) makes it clear it could be made of two separate panels of fabric stitched together on the shoulders and up both sides (*L.* 9.79; Fuentes 1987, 43; Pausch 2008, 74–6; Fig. 1.1 no. 1).[3] In some artistic evidence a shoulder seam is clearly shown (Wilson 1938, 57). Or the tunic could be woven sidewards, folded along the vertical seam, and stitched together, with sleeves added afterwards (Croom 2002, 31; Fig. 1.1. no. 4). Granger-Taylor (1982, 10) has noticed that lengths of tunics seem also to have been adjusted by a tuck sewn at the waist; these likely existed at one time on most surviving tunics and may "relate to the need to adjust readymade clothing to individual requirements."[4] Fuentes (1987, 44) notes a fresco from Pompeii (shop of Verecundus) which "has on the right hand side a worker coming

Figure 1.2 Sign from the shop of Verecundus the *vestiarius*. Pompeii (IX,7,5). First century CE
Art Resource: ART39105

forward with what appears to be a tunic panel, or perhaps a complete tunic" (Maiuri 1953, 147; Fig. 1.2. It may also be a rug).

Interestingly, on surviving fragments of tunics scholars have detected evidence of tailoring and sewing, and it is obvious that the Romans were familiar with scissors, needles, and thread. Italy is often regarded as the area of 'woven-to-shape' textiles, but many finds indicate the needle was in use both for structural and decorative purposes.[5] In addition, there is archaeological, literary, and epigraphical evidence for the mending of garments. Mannering has noted that a third of the recorded textiles from Mons Claudianus (most dating 104–155 CE) show characteristics like hemming, patching, and darning: textiles "were too costly just to throw away"[6] (2000b, 14). Not only were garments mended again and again, but in many cases likely refashioned into other garments: one discovery at Mons Claudianus was a portion of a natural-colored tunic with several haphazard 'woven-in' gammas, an ornament which, to judge from other finds at this site, usually belonged to the Roman *pallium* (the Greek-style cloak; Mannering 2000a, 289; see also Yadin 1963, 219–23; Bogensperger 2014). There is no doubt this tunic was remade from a mantle.

Literary sources also provide some evidence of darning and sewing. Pliny (*Nat.* 8.191) mentions that mending clothes makes them last longer; at Juvenal 3.254, a mended tunic is ripped. Clothing repair could be done at home (Cato *Agr.* 2.3), but there is also evidence for paid professional menders. Thus the *Edict* of Diocletian records a number of different tailoring and finishing services (VII, 48–51; how they differ is often unclear). The *vestificus/a* (a clothing maker),[7] the *vestiarius/a*,[8] and the *sarcinator/sarcinatrix* (a mender) are also found in various inscriptions.[9] Liu remarks that since garments were kept and mended for a long time, this might have slowed the need for new garments; still, as there were so many lower-class people the aggregate demand must have been massive (2009, 74).

Sleeves and cincture

Tunic sleeves were usually incidental.[10] Aulus Gellius states "at first" (*primo*) tunics were close and short, having sleeves which ended below the shoulders.[11]

16 *Tunic and toga: clothing and rank*

But by the last years of the Republic the tunic seems to have grown wider, and covered the upper arm (Wilson 1938, 56); this was the form of the imperial tunic as well.[12] From a cursory glance at the literary sources, it is clear that a long-sleeved tunic was not something Roman male citizens ought habitually to wear: perhaps long sleeves were considered undesirable not only because of their association with women (see below, Chapter 5) but also because of their connection to servility. A slave wears a long-sleeved tunic in Plautus (*manuleatam tunicam; Ps.* 738). Columella thought that slaves who worked out of doors in bad weather should wear long-sleeved tunics.[13] But sometimes long sleeves were considered necessary even for men of the upper classes: Pliny the Elder wore a long-sleeved tunic to write in during the winter (Pliny *Epp.* 3.5.15).

The 'girt-up' tunic (i.e., one that was tucked up high into the belt or *semicinctium*)[14] could be a sign of energy: persons whose tunics were girded were more fit for action.[15] The girt tunic was also worn by ship's captains (Pl. *Mil.* 1181); serving slaves (Hor. *S.* 2.8.70); and soldiers.[16] In more practical terms, the bloused material of a tunic which was girded could be used as a pocket (Sen. *Ben.* 7.19.3). But usually, wearing the tunic with no belt indicated an effeminate nature (see below, Chapter 5), or some other moral failing. Thus in Horace, the adulterer caught in the act must run off with tunic ungirded and with bare feet (*discincta tunica fugiendum est et pede nudo; S.* 1.2.132), and the stereotypical wastrel is unbelted (*discinctus aut perdam nepos; Epod.* 1.34), epitomizing his lack of financial self-control. Idleness is described as 'ungirt' at Ov. *Am.* 1.9.41 (*discinctaque in otia*); Juvenal uses *discingo* to mean 'conquering utterly' (*nuper Marius discinxerit Afros*; 8.120). Several authors tell us that standing in front of the general's tent all day in ungirded tunics was a humiliating punishment for soldiers.[17]

Number of tunics

The toga and tunic were supposed to be worn together, but Romans in the regal period allegedly wore the toga with no inner tunic. Aulus Gellius references this practice (6.12.3), and Pliny (*Nat.* 34.23) mentions statues of Romulus and Tatius erected in the time of Tarquinius Priscus, togate and without tunics.[18] Cato the Younger reportedly went out in public in warm weather with a *campestre* or loincloth under his toga instead of an undertunic, citing the habits of regal Romans as an illustrious precedent.[19] Possibly if the tunic was omitted for the sake of decency a *campestre* or similar was required under the toga. Stone (1994, 38–9, n. 5) has observed that on the southwest panel of the Ara Pacis, Aeneas (or Numa: see Rehak 2001) is portrayed togate but without a tunic (Fig. 1.3).

Croom notes (on the strength of artistic evidence) that the fashion of wearing two tunics under the toga began in the late third or early fourth century: the inner one reaching to mid-calf or ankle, with wrist-length sleeves, and the outer slightly shorter with baggy, elbow-length sleeves.[20]

Figure 1.3 South-west panel of the Ara Pacis Augustae, Aeneas or Numa. Rome. 13–9 BCE
Source: DAI B. Malter Mal2267-0

Discussion of this fashion is generally outside the chronological limits of this paper. But Augustus was said to have worn several tunics against the cold (Suet. *Aug.* 82).

Tunics and age

In keeping with the Roman ideal of visible social stratification, certain features of the toga and the tunic were ideally supposed to differentiate rank and age. A young Roman boy of the upper classes in the central period was supposed to wear an unstriped tunic[21] (but see however the striped child's tunic from Dura-Europos from the first half of the third century CE: Granger-Taylor 1982, 7). Sons in wealthier families would have owned more than one tunic and toga, as the younger Cato (by way of Varro) implies when speaking of his unpretentious boyhood: "to me as a boy there was one modest tunic and toga (*modica una... tunica et toga*), shoes without ties (*sine fasceis calciamenta*), a horse without a horse-cloth, no daily bath, rare gaming-board" (Varro *Cato vel de liberis educandis* [19]: Non. 155L).

The tunic could also indicate that a sexual status or stage of life had been attained by a young man. The 'straight tunic' (*tunica recta*) or 'kingly tunic' (*tunica regilla*) was worn by *tirones*, young men who had just come of age and were celebrating the ceremony of the *toga virilis* (see below). Possibly more voluminous than a regular tunic (see Fig. 1.1, no. 5),

Festus tells us this garment was woven on an archaic upright loom.[22] Varro mentions a *tunica regilla* dyed purple (*regillae tunicae purpura distinguitur; Men.* 372).[23]

Slave tunics

As George has noted, "ascertaining what real slaves wore is difficult since references to slave clothing in Roman texts are rare and those that do exist are frustratingly vague" (2002, 43). The lack of material expression in Roman art is likewise perhaps predictable.[24] Still, some evidence may be gleaned from ancient sources. Cato has a section on clothing for slaves (*vestimenta familiae; Agr.* 59), recommending the owner allot "a tunic 3.5' long and a cloak every second year for each slave. When you give a new tunic or cloak, take back the old ones to make patches of them."[25] Columella recommends slave clothing be made right on the estate, but slave clothes were often bought from second-hand patchers or clothing dealers, the *centonarii*.[26] Slave tunics ran the gamut from decorated and expensive (a practice which called attention to the fact that their master or mistress was wealthy; see below, Chapter 4), to thin and tattered. But most slave tunics were likely simple, a style "characterized by plain utility, not elaborate ornamentation."[27] In the late second/early third century CE, Ulpian specifically mentions tunics and hooded cloaks (*paenulae*) in a list of slave clothing (*Dig.* 34.2.23.2).

Vestes clavatae[28]

That tunics could carry signs of juridical rank – the stripes down either side – is well known. Such stripes on statuary rendered in paint have now of course disappeared, but are still visible in wall paintings and mosaics. The stripes were either woven in during the construction of the tunic, or added afterwards: Granger-Taylor has noted that the paired stripes on a child's wool tunic from Dura-Europos were produced simply by changing the color of the weft from white to purple without any alteration in the weave (200–250 CE; 1982, 7; see also Wild 1994, 17). On the other hand, the *Digest* states that "Pomponius [second century CE], in his *Letters,* also holds that even if the stripes have not been sewn together with the garments (*etsi non sunt clavi vestimentis consuti*), they nevertheless are contained in a legacy of clothing" (*veste legata; Dig.* 34.2.19.5; 34.2.23.1).

As the broad stripe (the *latus clavus*) and the narrow (the *angustus clavus*) are usually referred to in the singular, there has been some scholarly confusion over whether the *clavus* was one band down the centre of the tunic or two bands on the shoulders (see Bender-Jørgensen 2011, 75–6). Wilson actually disproved the former notion in 1938; still, the idea "lives happily on in re-enactors' websites, and among costume designers of movies and current TV series" (Bender-Jørgensen 2011, 75–6; Pausch 2008, 26; Wilson 1938, 64).

The stripes were likely referred to in the singular because only one stripe was visible after the toga was donned: perhaps another instance of the idealizing nature of references to clothing in the literary sources.

Senatorial clavi[29]

Tunicae of the senatorial class had wide purple stripes (scholars estimate perhaps 7.5–10 cm) which extended to the lower edge of the tunic on both sides of the shoulders.[30] We do not know when this sartorial custom began: Pliny (*Nat.* 9.39) states that Tullius Hostilius wore a striped tunic, but elsewhere that many distinctions in male dress (the wide-striped tunic distinguishing senators from equestrians, for instance) were introduced "at a late date" (*quamquam et hoc sero*; 33.29; and see *HA* Alex. Sev. 27.4). By Quintilian's day the tunic with the *latus clavus* hung a little longer than the ordinary tunic, which hung to just below the knees (*Inst.* 11.3.139, on which see below, Chapter 5). Care needed to be taken that the purple stripe fell in the correct way, "since negligence sometimes is noted."[31]

The right to wear the *latus clavus* was in the empire bestowed by law; it was "not a question of mere decoration."[32] In 203 BCE Scipio presented Masinissa with a tunic with *lati clavi* (Livy 30.17.13); Julius Caesar was said to have granted this to the Gauls (Suet. *Iul.* 80.2).[33] Augustus allowed sons of senators to assume the *latus clavus* immediately after they had received the *toga virilis* in order to encourage them to choose a career in politics (they are called *laticlavii*; Suet. *Aug.* 38.2).[34] Suetonius reports that Augustus himself assumed the *latus clavus* even before he had assumed the *toga virilis* (*Aug.* 94.10). Caligula granted this right to equestrians (Cass. Dio 59.9.5). Claudius bestowed the broad stripe on a freedman's son (Suet. *Claud.* 24). By the time of Vespasian, holding the right to don the *latus clavus* was equivalent to receiving permission to stand for office; the stripes therefore emphasized the wealth and connections needed to do so (Vespasian himself had waited "a long time" [*diu*] to seek it).[35] Statius speaks of a youth assuming the *latus clavus* together with the *toga praetexta*, the bordered toga (*Silv.* 5.2.29; cf. 4.8.59–62).

The 'wide stripe' became metonymy for the senatorial order. At Sen. *Epp.* 98.13 the elder Sextius refuses the broad stripe offered to him by Julius Caesar.[36] Petronius' Trimalchio wears a napkin with a *latus clavus* around his neck, to give the impression of being able to wear the broad-striped tunic (*Satyr.* 32; Mart. 4.46.17). The wide-striped tunic was termed "powerful" by Statius (*tunica potens*; *Silv.* 5.2.29); in Suetonius a tribune of senatorial rank is a *tribunum laticlavium* (*Dom.* 10.5; cf. *Otho* 10.1). He also reported that Tiberius deprived a senator of his *latus clavus*, i.e., removed him from the Senate (Suet. *Tib.* 35). Juvenal called the *latus clavus* the *purpura maior* (Juv. 1.106). The younger Pliny asked Apollinaris to advance "the wide stripe," i.e., the senatorial candidacy of his friend Sextus Erucius (*Epp.* 2.9.2; *BNP* Erucius 1).

Equestrian clavi[37]

The *angusti clavi* were the narrow stripes worn by equestrians (perhaps about 2.5 cm wide, although we do not know for certain).[38] Granger-Taylor (1982, 7) has noted a vertical stripe about 2.4 cm wide running downwards from the edge of the neck of the Arringatore's tunic, of a different alloy than the rest of the statue. Like the wide stripe, the term 'narrow stripe' similarly became metonymy for the equestrian order: in one source Maecenas is described as living content with the *angustus clavus* (Vell. 2.88). Statius refers to the *angustus clavus* rather bitingly as the "pauper's stripe" (*paupere clavo; Silv.* 5.2.18). Suetonius describes his father as *angusticlavus*, "of the equestrian order" (*Otho* 10.1). When Ovid states at *Tr.* 4.10.27–9 that he and his brother took up the *latus clavus*, he means they meant to seek senatorial office. And indeed, Ovid held his first pre-senatorial office of *tresvir* (*Tr.* 4.10.33–4), but then for unknown reasons "fled ambition" and re-assumed the narrow-striped tunic (*Tr.* 4.10.35–8; Rowe 2002, 67).

There may have been some leeway anyway in the width of one's stripe, or perhaps there was in certain periods: Suetonius intriguingly states that Augustus' stripe was neither broad nor narrow (*clavo nec lato nec angusto; Aug.* 73), and lets us know that the width of *clavi* was not regulated in any way at that time (Pausch 2008, 113). Horace tells of one Priscus, a *moechus* or adulterer who was so fickle that he would "change his stripe every hour" (*vixit inaequalis, clavum ut mutaret in horas; S.* 2.7.10. This may in fact refer to color). The relatively few literary references to equestrian *clavi* (as opposed to senatorial) may well betray senatorial writers' disinterest in the clothing of men in the class beneath them.

Clavate garments on lower-class men

Bender-Jorgensen has noted that the specific descriptions of *lati clavi* and *angusti clavi* and the insistence of the written sources on the class distinctions visualized by the width of the stripes "have led to many classicists and others believing that clavate tunics were only used by these two ranks" (2010, 75). Art-historical and archaeological evidence can correct this impression. Wilson (1938, 61) attests to the fact that extant wall paintings are evidence that by the first century CE, and probably earlier, "stripes of some width were worn by almost everyone".[39] Evidence such as the painted advertisement of Verecundus the *vestiarius* or clothing-seller, in which Verecundus advertises the purple-striped cloth in a colony of Rome (where, as Petersen notes, there were no senators and probably few equestrians and a local elite probably severely limited in terms of numbers) meant that there was a market for *clavi* outside the two juridical ranks of senator and *eques* (2009, 200; Fig. 1.2). Pompeiian wall-paintings from the *caupona* or tavern in the Street of Mercury show tunics of customers and servers adorned with stripes (ibid., 200–2); likewise slaves in the banquet scene from Pompeii (Fig. 1.4).

Tunic and toga: clothing and rank 21

Figure 1.4 Banquet scene from Pompeii. Museo Archeologico Nazionale, Naples. First century CE
Art Resource: ART7952

The elder Pliny laments that in his day the wide stripe was even worn by public criers (*Nat.* 33.29). Clavate tunics are also observable in mummy portraits from Roman Egypt (Fig. 1.5), which show all classes (even women) wearing tunics with *clavi*.

Archaeological remains of tunics at Mons Claudianus are identified by the presence of *clavi*: to date, 240 clavate fragments have been found and recorded. The majority are between 1 and 4 cm wide and are predominantly purple, but other colors have been found as well (red, blue, brown; Bender-Jørgensen 2010, 79; Mannering 2000b, fig 10 is a fragment of a green tunic with a pink *clavus*). Some tunic fragments have two or more stripes set next to one another (Bender-Jørgensen 2010, 79). Tunic fragments from the Cave of

22 Tunic and toga: clothing and rank

Figure 1.5 Painted wooden funerary portrait of a man in encaustic, from Thebes, Greco-Roman period. Fourth century CE
Art Resource: AA384315

Letters (on the western shore of the Dead Sea, dating 132–135 CE) also show a great variety of widths of stripes, which Yadin split up into several groups: 2 cm or less, 3–4 cm, 4–5 cm, 5–6 cm, 6–7 cm, and 8 cm (1963, 212–19). Clearly, at these locations, "the signaling of rank must have lodged in something else than width" (Bender-Jørgensen 2011, 76). Bender-Jørgensen has concluded that "*clavi* in different widths were commonly used by all kinds of people. That *clavi* did hold some kind of meaning is obvious from the remains of a tunic found at Mons Claudianus where the *clavi* had been meticulously preserved throughout multiple repairs," even removing them from the original garment and sewing them onto the patching fabric (ibid., 76; Mannering 2000a, 283).

Some tunics had no stripes at all. A plain unstriped tunic is possibly what is meant by the phrase *vestis domestica*, "house-clothing" (cf. *vestis forensis* or *forensia*, clothing for use in public). In Cicero a man has one set of clothing (*vestis*) for when he is at home, another when he goes out (*aliam domesticam, aliam forensem; Fin.* 2.77). Generally, Augustus always wore "common clothes for the house" (*veste non temere alia quam domestica usus est*; Suet. *Aug.* 73) produced (naturally) by his female relations. Seneca purportedly liked clothing which was homely and cheap (*domestica et vilis; Dial.* 9.1.5). The soldiers in lower Germany took Vitellius from his bedroom in the camp (*cubiculum*) in the evening, and made him emperor "in his common house-clothes" (*in veste domestica;* Suet. *Vitell.* 8.1), possibly meaning a plain tunic.

Toga[40]

Construction and material

It is unclear whether the toga was made all in one piece, or in several. Wilson calculated that the imperial toga was about 9'10" in width, and there was likely a seam through it, as the weaving of such a huge web might not have been possible (Wilson 1924, 71). If a toga were woven in two sections the width of each would be 5', "not an unusual width for ancient textiles" (Wilson 1924, 72). Granger-Taylor (1982, 19) however has estimated that the Arringatore's toga was twelve feet wide (Fig. 1.6), and that the larger togas of the imperial period were possibly up to eighteen feet wide.[41] She believes as there is no sign of a seam on the Arringatore's toga that the toga continued to be woven to shape widthways; in other words, in one piece (Granger-Taylor 1982, 10).

The shape of the toga is a matter of some debate. Quintilian thought the toga should be "rounded and cut to fit," otherwise, "there are many ways in which it will be unshapely" (*ipsam togam rotundam esse et apte caesam velim, aliter enim multis modis fiet enormis; Inst.* 11.3.139). Dion. Halic. 3.61 describes the toga as *hemikuklion*, semi-circular.[42] Isidore says of the toga that "it is a plain *pallium* with a round, rather flowing shape, and with rippling folds, as it were...."[43] Goldman believes that based on her modern reconstructions the early toga (such as that worn by the Arringatore statue; Fig. 1.6) was a semicircle, while the fuller toga of Augustan times was more of an ellipse (1994a, 228–9).

Quintilian's statement is however puzzling. There is no indication in other literary sources that the toga was "cut" (*caesam*) in any way; rather, scholars have assumed that it was woven to shape for the wearer.[44] Another meaning of *rotundus* however is "smooth and finished, well-rounded," of a speaker, his writing, or his oratorical style.[45] Encouraging the Roman nobleman to wear a toga which is "finished and well-cut" would accord nicely with Quintilian's emphasis on clothing and appearance as indicative of personal character.

The toga was usually of undyed light wool.[46] We know however that different weights of cloth were used for summer and winter (Goette 1990, 4, 6–7; and see below, Chapter 4). Wilson (1924, 34) claimed if it was to hang properly the toga could not have been made of heavy material – probably no heavier than flannel – and that the larger the toga the lighter the material must have been. New or newly-laundered togas were described as *pexae*, with their wool neatly combed (Mart. 2.44; Williams 2004, 197).

24 Tunic and toga: clothing and rank

Figure 1.6 The Arringatore (Aulus Metellus). Museo Archeologico, Florence. Not before 100 BCE
Bestand-Microfiche-D-DAI-ROM-0483_A08.jpg

Putting on a toga likely required assistance, and Tertullian (*Pall.* 5.1.3–4) is eloquent on the garment's tedious arrangement. First, an entire side of the garment was rolled loosely into folds. One end of the side with these folds was placed against the lower left leg of the wearer, then passed up the left side and over the shoulder. The other side of the toga was then wrapped loosely around the back and placed beneath the right arm in order to facilitate the use of the arm. Then the remainder of the garment was brought around the chest and thrown back over the left shoulder, concealing the end of the toga from which the drapery started (Stone 1994, 16). It was worn, most scholars believe, without a fastening (although see Wilson 1924, 48–9), and the wearer had to keep his left arm bent to support the drapery. While unwieldy, "the Romans were accustomed to wearing draped garments, and naturally managed them with less difficulty than is conceivable to us" (Wilson 1924, 49).

Tunic and toga: clothing and rank 25

Figure 1.7 North frieze, Ara Pacis Augustae, Rome. 13–9 BCE
Art Resource: AA385350

Toga weights, that is, what appear to be weights attached to the bottom edge of the toga to help keep it in place, are shown on the north frieze of the Ara Pacis (Fig. 1.7) but there is no mention of them in literary sources (the weights are the small teardrop-shapes attached to the corners of the togas).

Changes in drape

The toga was subject to numerous changes in shape, size, and manner of draping,[47] "the results of efforts to make the garment, first, more elaborate, and then less cumbersome, and at the same time to retain certain features which were apparently considered essential characteristics" (Wilson 1924, 20). Due to space considerations, I have set out only the broadest changes in the toga here.

Accounts of transformations in the style and manner of draping of togas naturally attempt to utilize Roman art to track the differences. There are problems however in trying to date (or sometimes even identify) clothing in statuary and reliefs. Artistic evidence is not always precisely dateable, for several reasons. *Togati* often had new portrait heads inserted into old bodies, for instance, which makes it difficult for scholars to classify the statues chronologically (Stone 1994, 42 n. 50). In addition, there were usually several different toga drapes in use at any one time, and varying sizes of togas during all periods, presumably because such huge lengths of cloth were expensive

26 *Tunic and toga: clothing and rank*

Figure 1.8 Relief from the Ara dei Vicomagistri. Museo Gregoriano Profano, Vatican Museums, Rome. 20–40 CE
D-DAI-ROM-57.1004

and one could not afford to get a different one every time fashions in draping changed. On the Vicomagistri relief (dated to about 20–40 CE; Fig. 1.8) there are several different styles of toga drapes.[48]

The toga's strength as an ideological symbol may mean that the garment was also employed in art as a kind of visual shorthand. Because the toga was the immediately recognizable and unmistakable mark of a citizen, the toga in visual sources could have functioned as ideogram rather than as an indication of what men actually wore. Thus a togate man who appears on a relief of a commercial scene from Ostia and is obviously not a customer is described by Kampen probably correctly as the manager or owner (1981, 97–8; Fig. 1.9).

The fact that he is togate represents an artistic convention: the man in question may not be in the habit of always wearing the toga, and/or the other workers, who are pictured in tunics, may in fact be free or freed workers and may have the right to wear the toga themselves. Clothing is employed in these instances to visualize status distinctions, not as sociological description. In other words, the owner/manager is above the others in employment status, though perhaps not in juridical status, and the toga is the sign chosen to represent that fact. This shows the toga's strength as an sociopolitical icon, and in fact we can identify many examples of clothing, both male and female, employed as literary or visual shorthand for both moral characteristics or legal status.[49]

Tunic and toga: clothing and rank 27

Figure 1.9 Commercial scene of knife-sellers. Vatican Museums, Galleria Lapidaria 147, Rome
Bestand-Microfiche D-DAI-ROM 1020

A related though surmountable problem is that sometimes the clothing depicted on reliefs is rather unexpected. For example, on the tombstone of Quintus Sulpicius Maximus, an accomplished Greek poet who died in 94 CE at the age of eleven (apparently of exhaustion from scholarly overwork), the boy is depicted in the toga and *bulla*, not the *himation* we might envisage,

28 *Tunic and toga: clothing and rank*

even though the tombstone itself is covered in Greek writing and the Latin epitaph is supplemented by personal details in Greek.[50] Or garments are proleptic, that is, representing or assuming a future status as if presently existing or accomplished: thus one tombstone from the early second century CE depicts two small boys, one a citizen (?), one a *verna* (a home-born slave; Fig. 1.10), both in togas.[51]

The boys each died when they were about one year of age, and the tombstone was erected by Publicia Glypte, probably the mother of one and owner of the other. The depiction shows the *verna* in the costume of a citizen,

Figure 1.10 Tombstone erected by Publicia Glypte to two young boys (rendered by K. Olson-Lamari). Museo di Villa Albani, Rome. Early second century CE

presumably what he would have attained had he lived long enough to be freed by his mistress. But this might also have been the case for the son: although a citizen, he may not have been have been wearing the toga so early, and thus the garment was meant to display his future status.[52]

Lastly, some scholars believe that the toga has perhaps been overemphasized as the 'typical' dress of the Roman male (Harlow 2004, 49; Stone 1994, 13). The garment is of course often represented in Roman statuary and on gravestones, but in fact the formal, ceremonial nature of Roman art (where Romans are represented as they want to be seen) perhaps misleads the viewer as to its use as an everyday garment. Thus the problems of utilizing art as evidence for Roman clothing are rife: the demands of artistic convention and the use of proleptic garments mean it is difficult to determine how often the garment was actually worn, and by whom. The problems of dating, and that some styles of togas were worn or depicted for centuries means that it is challenging to determine change over time. (The symbolic resonances of different garments in ancient literature are perhaps easier to trace). Nonetheless, in what follows I broadly sketch the well-known history of the toga.

Etruscan and Republican togas

Ancient authors believed the toga was of Etruscan origin (Livy 1.8.3; Tert. *Pall.* 1.1; Serv. *A.* 2.781).[53] The distinction of the Etruscan *tebenna* or wrapped cloak (from which the toga may have been derived) was that it had a rounded form, as distinct from the rectangular Greek *himation*. Although that distinction only emerged gradually after the middle of the sixth century during a heavily hellenising phase, "it suited the Romans to point to the [*tebenna*] for a 'native,' and by implication non-hellenic, origin" of the toga (Wallace-Hadrill 2008, 43). The elder Pliny states that the (bordered) toga was worn by the kings Hostilius and Servius Tullius after their conquest of the Etruscans (*Nat.* 8.197 and 9.136), and that the Tullius' *toga praetexta* could still be viewed in Rome in Sejanus' day 560 years later (*Nat.* 8.197).

Literary mention of styles of Republican togas are scattered and vague. There is a reference to Cato's "skimpy toga" at Hor. *Epp.* 1.19.12–14 (the *toga exigua*, on which see Chapter 3 below); Quintilian remarks of togas that "in olden times there were no *sinus* (overfolds); after that they were very short" (*Inst.* 11.3.137). As he does not however give dates Quintilian's statement is not very helpful. Artistic evidence can be more useful, used with caution. On the figures from the Census relief on the altar of Domitius Ahenobarbus (Rome, ca. 100 BCE)[54] as well as on the Arringatore (Fig. 1.6),[55] the togas are sparser and shorter than later incarnations of the toga.[56] Nor do they sport an overfold (the *sinus*) or a knot (the *umbo*), Augustan features of the toga.

In the mid-first century BCE and later the toga was often draped and the arm held as though the man were in a *pallium*, the rectangular Greek mantle (Fig. 1.11).[57]

30 *Tunic and toga: clothing and rank*

Figure 1.11 Roman funerary relief from the Via Statilia. Centrale Montremartini, Rome. 80–50 BCE
Source: DAI B. Malter Mal766

The *pallium*-drape toga is marked by the tight *sinus* in which the arm is held high and close to the chest, and the length of the garment, which almost reaches the shoes. The pose had a long history in Greece on statues of *himation* – clad men (from the fourth century BCE onward), and also found its way into Etruscan statuary.[58] This type of drape is mentioned by Quintilian:

> There are some features of dress which have themselves changed somewhat with the changing times. The ancients wore no *sinus*, and their successors very short ones (*perquam breves post illos fuerunt*). Accordingly, as their arms according to Greek custom were kept within their clothes (*veste continebatur*),

they must have used different gestures from ours in the *prooemium*... [143] The ancients used to let the toga fall right down to the heels, like a Greek *pallium* (*togam veteres ad calceos usque demittebant, ut Graeci pallium*) and this is recommended by Plotius and Nigridius, who wrote on gesture in that period [100–50 BCE]... [the younger Pliny]... says that Cicero used to wear his toga like this to conceal his varicose veins, although this fashion is to be seen also in statues of persons who lived after Cicero's time.

(*Inst.* 11.3.137–8, 143).

What was the reasoning behind this odd fashion of wearing the toga, in which it was often difficult to distinguish toga from *pallium*? Wallace-Hadrill's thesis (2008, 47) is that intense imitation by Roman orators of Attic models in the first century BCE produced a sort of sartorial copying in toga drape. My own conviction (Olson 2014b: 442) is that the *pallium* drape developed as a way of showing one's erudition yet not leaving off the badge of Roman citizenship – the perfect blend of Roman imperialism and Greek learning. (On the *pallium*, see below, Chapter 2.)

Togas on the Ara Pacis

Another form of the toga appeared in the late Republic/early empire and is illustrated on the Ara Pacis (Fig. 1.7). Part of the enormous value of this monument comes from the fact that it displays "a large number of slightly varying ways of wearing the toga," and proves that in its minor details the arrangement of the toga varied with each wearer and at each time it was put on (Wilson 1924, 43). The monument therefore is a "good general statement" of the senatorial toga of this time (ibid.), giving evidence of earlier styles of toga alongside more recent ones.[59]

The most noticeable changes on this new toga were the introduction of the *sinus* (the curving overfold produced by an excess of material),[60] and the *umbo* (a decorative clump of drapery pulled up from the folds of the toga which ran up the left side of the wearer and helped hold the drapery together; Wilson 1924, 49; Stone 1994, 17). These features meant that by loosening the *umbo* the toga could be drawn over the head in a religious sacrifice or to give protection from the weather.[61] A veiled head could also be achieved without loosening the *umbo*, however, if the toga were large enough, as seen in the statue of Augustus in the Terme Museum, Rome (Fig. 1.12).[62] From the Ara Pacis it is easy to see that "the toga of the imperial age was neither suited to much movement nor easy to maintain in its fashionable draping" (Stone 1994, 21).

There is also literary mention of togas from this period. The *toga exigua* may have been worn in the empire by individuals as a deliberate evocation of earlier Republican days (thus Hor. *Epp.* 1.19.13, below, Chapter 3, and Pausch 2008, 26). Augustus reportedly had a policy of moderation in dress, and wore togas "neither scanty nor full," possibly to avoid accusations of either miserliness or ostentation in his costume (*togis neque restrictis neque fusis*; Suet. *Aug.* 73).

32 *Tunic and toga: clothing and rank*

Figure 1.12 Statue of Augustus from the Via Labicana. Museo Nazionale Romano (Palazzo Massimo alle Terme), Rome. First century CE
Source: D-DAI-ROM-65.1112

Persius speaks of his *candidus umbo* which was part of his manly toga (*Sat.* 5.33); Horace similarly doesn't like over-wide togas: "a narrow toga befits a client of sense" (*arta decet sanum comitem toga; Epp.* 1.18.30). Elsewhere he excoriates a wealthy freedman for wearing a voluminous nine-foot toga (*Epod.* 4.8). Ovid hints that wearing a roomy *sinus* is attractive to women (*Rem.* 680), presumably not only because it was the fashion, but also because a voluminous toga indicated one's wealth. At Suet. *Calig.* 35.3, Caligula trips over the hem of his (presumably wide/long) toga in his haste and falls down some stairs. Interestingly,

Tunic and toga: clothing and rank

the Augustan toga represented prosperity by the very method of its construction: that is, in the amount of fabric needed to create it, in contrast to the skimpy Republican garment. McGinn's suggestion however that men were "encouraged" to don the fuller Augustan toga because "the republican type was now reserved for prostitutes and adulteresses" is unsupported by ancient evidence and must be dismissed (2014, 96).

Late first- and second-century CE togas

Over the next century or so, the toga became shorter and narrower, and its method of draping different. The draping of togas of the Flavian period (69–96 CE) appear shorter and rather more securely fastened (Wilson 1924, 74). It is in the late first century that we first see the feature called the *balteus* or 'shoulder umbo,' that is; a method of draping whereby the rolls of folds extend diagonally across the chest, like a *balteus* or sword-belt, and are tightly twisted together and higher up on the chest than previously (as on the Arch of Titus; Fig. 1.13; Stone 1994, 24).

Wilson believed that the *balteus* style of toga needed to be secured in some way, as it would not have responded to a mere slight readjustment of the drapery (1924, 79). Around this time, Quintilian recommends that a toga not

Figure 1.13 Relief, arch of Titus. Rome. 70 CE
Art Resource: ART20199

34 Tunic and toga: clothing and rank

be draped too tightly (88 CE; *Inst.* 11.3.141). Nonetheless, individuals continued to be depicted in the voluminous Augustan toga, including Vespasian and Titus (Fig. 1.14, and Goette 1990, pls 12–14).

A new, short style of toga was introduced in Trajanic and Hadrianic times: this one fell above the shoe-top (Wilson 1924, 75) and featured the *balteus*. But again, there were exceptions to the prevailing style: several of the second-century CE emperors assumed (or at least were depicted in) the enormous Augustan toga. In other reliefs the emperor appears in the toga with the *balteus*, such as the figure of Trajan in a relief from his forum (the *extispicium* relief, early Hadrianic date; Fig. 15). Hadrian as well sometimes is portrayed in the second-century drape (Fig. 1.16), and at other times in the large Augustan garment (Fig. 1.17).

Figure 1.14 Statue of Vespasian. Museo Pio Clementino, Vatican Museums, Rome. 69–79 CE
Art Resource: ART424733

Figure 1.15 Extispicium relief with Trajan. Forum of Trajan, Rome. 120/130 CE
Art Resource: ART70058

The Antonine toga[63]

In the period of the Antonine emperors (138–193 CE) the popularity of the Augustan toga continued to be strong. Although Antonine togas generally followed their predecessors in being short (Wilson 1924, 75) and featuring a *balteus*, examples of the early imperial toga are also very much in evidence. On a panel relief of M. Aurelius, the emperor is shown draped in early imperial style while behind him the *genius Senatus* sports the *balteus* (Fig. 1.18).

The panels from the Arch of Marcus Aurelius (with Constantine's replacement head, now on the Arch of Constantine; Fig. 1.19) also show this style of toga. Those surrounding him wear the usual type of second-century toga.[64] (Interestingly, when the panels of Marcus Aurelius were re-used in the Arch of Constantine in the early fourth century, there is no indication the togas were re-cut to match the prevailing fashion; only new portrait heads were inserted.) The wide imperial toga appears in art which depicts the upper and upper-middling classes as well. Biographical sarcophagi of this period show the style, usually in depictions of weddings,[65] a relief of a freedman and freedwoman,[66] and in the reliefs at the theatre in Sabratha, Libya, where more modern styles of toga also appear (early third century CE; Fig. 1.20).[67]

Why did the late first- and second-century emperors sport the Augustan toga on occasion, when the fashion in togas seems to have comprised a shorter, possibly more convenient size and drape? There are at least three possibilities. Firstly, it may be that portraying the emperor in a grand toga, unlike those the rest of the men in the scene are wearing, may only be a way of visually distinguishing him from others. Secondly, perhaps the Augustan toga represented the peace, prosperity, abundance, and spiritual recovery associated with his reign (visualized on monuments such as the Ara Pacis);[68]

Figure 1.16 Statue of Hadrian; Musei Capitolini, Rome. 120–8 CE
Source: D-DAI-ROM-55.212

the Flavian and adoptive emperors' periods of rule also sought to appropriate this imagery. The use of the large Augustan toga perhaps also symbolized ongoing attempts to legitimate a reign or a dynasty through a resurrection of Augustan cultural and political ideologies. (We might note that the style of the Augustan toga would be familiar, as it had physically remained in evidence in the intervening century through statuary and reliefs which could still be seen around the city of Rome, such as the *togati* in the Forum of Augustus; the resurgent fashion thus alluded directly to material evidence of the Augustan-era toga.)

Tunic and toga: clothing and rank 37

Figure 1.17 Great Antonine altar, dynastic scene, from Ephesus. Vienna, Kunsthistorisches Museum. After 169 CE
Source: D-DAI-ROM-51.201R

For those not of the ruling dynasty it may be that such togas were hand-me-downs (and one could not afford to get a new toga made every time fashions in style and size changed). Or perhaps such a large garment, which used so much fabric, showed one's prosperity.

Figure 1.18 Panel relief of M. Aurelius. Musei Capitolini, Rome. 176–80 CE
Source: B. Malter Mal772-12

Tunic and toga: clothing and rank 39

Figure 1.19 Panel from the Arch of Marcus Aurelius (now on the Arch of Constantine). Rome. 176–80 CE
Art Resource: ART157286

Later forms of the toga

The toga style which became popular in the third century is called the banded toga or *toga contabulata* by modern scholars, likely a development from the toga with the *balteus*, and first appearing on busts from Tripoli.[69] In this style,

Figure 1.20 Decorative element from the base of the stage, Roman theatre at Sabratha, Libya. Early third century CE
Source: DAI FA7090-11

three bands of stacked folds adorn the toga (Goette 1990, 57–9, 71–4; Stone 1994, 24–5; Fig. 1.21).

Probably the folds were held together by being placed in a press beforehand, but perhaps also by concealed stitching (Wilson 1924, 79). In the frieze

Tunic and toga: clothing and rank 41

Figure 1.21 Toga contabulata. Palazzo Doria-Pamphili. Rome. 260s CE
Source: D-DAI-ROM-8158

at Leptis Magna, Severus (?) appears in an early imperial toga, while other *togati* mostly wear the newer style (Stone 1994, 24 and 32, fig. 1.15).[70] On a later monument, the Acilia sarcophagus (ca. 260 CE; Fig. 1.22), we can see *four* distinct styles of draping: the *toga contabulata*, the toga with no tunic, the toga with *balteus*, and the wide first-century toga,[71] perhaps showing the staying power of different toga drapes.

The orator's toga[72]

Quintilian has many cautions and recommendations on the proper cut and draping of an orator's toga, since the Romans equated oddities in dress with oddities of behavior: improper draping could harm a career (Stone 1994, 17), and the physical appearance of the advocate was acknowledged as an effective

42 Tunic and toga: clothing and rank

Figure 1.22 Acilia Sarcophagus, from Acilia. Museo Nazionale Romano (Palazzo Massimo alle Terme), Rome. 238 CE
Art Resource: ART389345

tool (Bablitz 2007, 191). Quintilian makes it clear that the toga is the most appropriate garment for orating,[73] although there is no special garb peculiar to the rhetorical profession. In the orator's case however his clothing "is noticed more" (*sed magis in oratore conspicitur; Inst.* 11.3.137), and should be "distinguished and masculine" (*splendidus et virilis*) as with all men of standing (*ut in omnibus honestis; Inst.* 11.3.137). An extreme case of an orator's concern with his appearance is found in Macrobius, who reports that the orator Q. Hortensius Hortalus (114–49 BCE; *BNP* Hortenisus 7) was extremely particular about the arrangement of folds on his toga:

> He was clothed to the height of elegance (*vestitu ad munditiem*), and so that he might go out well-draped (*ut bene amictus iret*), he looked at himself in a mirror and placed the toga on his body so that a graceful knot (*nodus*) drew up the folds, arranging them not by chance but by design, and to make sure that the fold of the garment as it fell followed the contours of his upper body (*sinus ex conposito defluens modum lateris ambiret*). Once when he had arranged it with great care, he brought charges against his colleague who brushed against him in a narrow passage and destroyed the arrangement of his toga (*structuram togae destruxerat*); he thought it a crime that the folds should be moved from their place on his shoulder.
>
> (Macr. 3.13.4–5; trans. Wilson 1924, 73–4)

Other authors also mention the orator's toga. Tacitus believed a rhetor should "wear a rough toga" (*hirta toga*) rather than glitter in "the many-colored dress of whores" (*quam fucatis et meretriciis vestibus insignire; Orat.* 26.1). Juvenal however was of the opinion that "eloquence rarely goes with a cheap garment" (7.145–7).

There were also (at least in the late first century CE) recommendations about methods of wearing and using the toga during an oration. Quintilian believed that for the orator to wrap the toga about himself in the heat of speaking was a sign "almost of madness,"[74] to throw it over the right shoulder effeminate, but to neglect to rearrange a slipped toga near the beginning of one's speech was a sign of "carelessness, or laziness, or ignorance of the way in which clothes ought to be worn" (11.3.149: *non reponere eam prorsus neglegentis aut pigri aut quo modo debeat amiciri nescientis est*).[75] In fact, Quintilian advocates adjustment of the toga or even putting it on anew before beginning a speech (11.3.156). By contrast, at the end of a speech the orator's sweaty and disheveled appearance, with clothes in disarray and toga slipping off (*neglegentior amictus et soluta ac velut labens undique toga; Inst.* 11.3.147) is laudable, the visual sign of impassioned and engaged oratory.

Special toga drapes

The *cinctus Gabinus* was a method of tying the toga which produced a firm stable garment (Wilson 1924, 87), leaving the left arm practically free.[76] In this drape, Wilson believes that the *sinus* was brought up over the head; the folds which normally lay on the left shoulder were drawn under the left arm, around the waist, and then tucked in (1924, 86–7; see fig. 47A and 88 n. 38). Servius states (quoting Cato) that the *cinctus Gabinus* meant "girt in the Gabine manner, that is, with part of the toga drawn over the head, and with part girded" (*et incincti ritu Gabino, id est togae parte caput velati, parte succincti: A.* 5.755; and see 7.612).[77] Sometimes associated with war (Fest. 251L; Livy 8.9.5–9), Dubourdieu believes it was a drape for religious rituals involving crossings ("au tracé ou au franchissement des frontières;" 1986, 16. See Livy 5.46.2, 10.7.3; Val. Max. 1.1.11; Lucan 1.596; *CIL* 11.1420.25).[78] Thus the consul wore it when he unbarred the gates of war (Virg. *A.* 7.610–15).[79]

The toga *ad cohibendum bracchium* (as Cicero calls it) was a drape in which one arm was tightly wound up in the cloth.[80] "It used to be, when I was young, that a single year was set for keeping the arm confined in the toga (*ad cohibendum brachium toga*) and for exercise and field sports in the tunic (*ludoque campestri tunicati*), and the same provision obtained in the camp and in operations if we embarked immediately on a military career" (Cic. *Cael.* 5.11). This may be a reference to a fashion in toga drape which was current when Cicero was young, or a metaphorical reference to a restrained style of oratory appropriate for the *tiro* (see Richardson and Richardson 1966, 254). But it is more likely that this style was an ideal confining drape of the young citizen when he had no need to engage in strenuous physical or oratorical activity (Richardson and Richardson 1966, 267; Goette 1990, 27 and pl. 4, 1–3), and perhaps the phrase *ad cohibendum brachium* was a kind of literary shorthand for 'apprenticeship.' Seneca confirms that *tirones* were draped in this manner (*Contr. Excerpt.* 5.6), and Quintilian mentions it as well, of toga styles of the past (*Inst.* 11.3137, above. See also Val. Max. 6.9. ext. 1). There seems to be no artistic evidence of this drape (*pace* Richardson and Richardson 1966, 258–9), and scholars believe it may in fact have been what we call the *pallium*-drape (above; Christ 1997, 29).

Toga praetexta

Significance of wool and purple

In Roman society much everyday clothing was made of wool (although other fabrics were also known, such as linen, silk, and cotton), but the fabric was in certain instances endowed with apotropaic significance and used for religious garments and those worn in rites of passage (Sebesta 1994a, 47). The toga of the *flamen dialis* was of wool, for instance, and he wore a skein of wool from a sacrificial victim.[81] The Roman bride wore a special woolen tunic woven on an upright loom, and the belt of her tunic was also woolen, woven from the fleece of a ewe.[82]

Some colours were considered apotropaic as well. The purple stripe on the *toga praetexta* or bordered toga, for instance, was thought to give protection to the wearer (Sebesta 1994a, 47). Many men in Roman wore the *toga praetexta*, but as Linderski states (2002, 351) "it is important to ask when they wore it." Thus tribunes, aediles (Pliny *Nat.* 9.137), praetors (Hor. *S.* 1.5.34–6; Val. Max. 9.12.7), consuls (Livy 8.95; *HA* Alex. Sev. 40.8), consul designates (*CIL* I [2]. 582), censors, *triumviri, vicomagistri* (at the Compitalia; Cic. *Pis.* 8; Livy 34.7.2), *magistri* of *collegia*, and magistrates of *coloniae* (Livy 34.7.2), wore the garment. The *decemviri* of the early Republic also wore the *toga praetexta* (Sebesta 2005, 119 n. 15) as had the Roman kings (Pliny *Nat.* 9.136), generals celebrating the *ovatio*, those committing *devotio*, and the male populace when celebrating the Ludi (Cic. *Phil.* 2.110). Other wearers of the garment were emperors, augurs (Cic. *Sest.* 144), *flamines* (Gell. 10.15.16); and "*popae* and *servi publici* assisting in public sacrifices wore around their waists the *limus*, a long rectangular 'skirt' with a praetextate lower border" (Sebesta 2005, 116–17). *Fratres Arvales* and the Pontifex Maximus wore the toga praetexta at their sacrifices (Linderski 2002, 351 n. 50, with references), as did the *epulones* and the *quindecemviri*. Non-senatorial officials had the right to appear praetextate at their public functions (Linderski 2002, 359).

Why exactly purple was apotropaic is unknown. It was an expensive color and had connotations of royalty and nobility, but we should note as well that scarlets and purples were not strongly differentiated in antiquity: purple was closer to red than to blue. Perhaps it was the color's similarity to blood that gave it this special meaning (Pliny in fact states the most highly-prized sea purple had a color like that of congealed blood; 9.135). The *toga praetexta* did have a general apotropaic significance: Ps-Quintilian writes of "the very sacredness of togas bordered with purple, which envelops priests, magistrates, and by which we render the tenderness of childhood sacred and inviolate" (*ipsum illud sacrum praetextarum quo sacerdotes velantur, quo magistratus, quo infirmitatem pueritiae sacram facimus ac venerabilem; Decl. Min.* 340.13; and see Pliny *Nat.* 9.127). Sebesta (2005, 116) notes that *praetexere* by extension also meant 'to protect or defend.'

The location of the border on the *toga praetexta* has been the subject of some scholarly difference. Fittschen (1970) maintains the border is on the lower edge of the toga; Granger-Taylor (1982, 10) believes it was on the upper edge; Stone (1994, 13–15) and Wilson (1924, 54) state the border moved from the lower to the upper edge sometime in the early empire; Linderski (2002, 359–60) that there were two types of bordered togas, one with the border on the upper edge and one with the border on the lower. Literary evidence is generally of no help here, as the authors assume their audience knows where the border is and so do not trouble to explain it (e.g., Livy 34.7.2; Pers. *Sat.* 5.30). Granger-Taylor (1982, 10) cites etymology in support of her argument for the placement of the border on the upper edge: *praetexta* means 'woven first,' and "indicates that weaving began at the upper straight edge with the warp running vertically;" thus the border would have been on the upper edge of the toga.

There is also limited artistic evidence for the location of the border. While the Romans certainly believed that their bordered toga was Etruscan in origin (Livy 1.8.3; Pliny *Nat.* 8.195; Bonfante-Warren 1973, 611), comparative evidence from Etruria is not very helpful. Borders were "a typical and constant feature of Etruscan dress" (Bonfante 2003, 15), yet their placement varies. The *praetexta* border on the Roman toga would have been applied with paint on ancient statues, paint which has since worn off; garments were even made praetextate on bronzes.[83] One example usually adduced to prove the placement of the border on the lower edge of the toga is the Arringatore statue (Figs 1.6 and 1.23; e.g., Wilson 1924, 35, 52–3; see also Goette 1990, pl. 13).

Granger-Taylor (1982, 10) states that not only is this inconsistent with the meaning of *praetexta*, but also points out that the border is never actually seen here in other artistic evidence (although certain late Republican paintings from Delos do seem to show a border on the lower edge).[84] She believes the Arringatore's 'border,' which contains an inscription (Fig. 1.23) and in fact does not go entirely round the toga, may be evidence of a weaving technique called 'twining,' which is used to give reinforcement and strength to a part of a garment which suffered strain (in this case, perhaps this was the part of the toga that suffered the most damage during walking). So the Arringatore's toga probably does not show the location of the border at all.

Other artistic evidence is somewhat more useful in locating the toga's border. Paintings from *lararia* in Pompeii (one in the house of the Vetii, Fig. 1.24; and one in the Thermopolium of Asellina) show the border on the upper edge, as

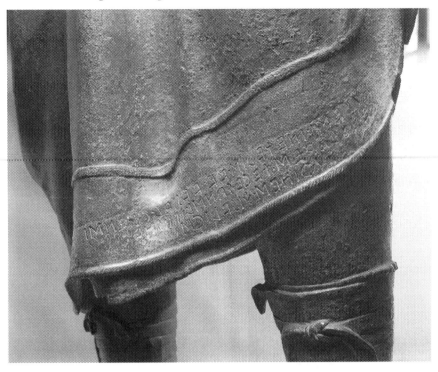

Figure 1.23 The Arringatore (Aulus Metellus). Museo Archeologico, Florence. Not before 100 BCE
Source: Bestand-Microfiche-D-DAI-ROM-0483_C14.jpg

does a mosaic rondel from the fifth-century CE basilica of Santa Maria Assunta in Aquileia (Fig. 1.25). Having an expensive purple stripe on the *upper* border would be more practical, as the lower border would come in for more wear and tear.[85] Whatever its placement, the border does seem to have been woven into the garment, and not added afterwards.[86]

As is well-known, the bordered toga was also children's wear. There are many literary references to children's bordered togas, presumably worn by those of the upper or upper-middling classes, as poor boys and girls would likely be clad only in the tunic.[87] The costume was supposed to mark off those children who were to be shielded from obscenity or sexual contact (Sebesta 1994a, 47). The unpleasant Valerius Valentinus boasted that he had seduced a *puer praetextatus* (Val. Max. 8.1; *RE* Valerius 372). Persius describes purple as the 'guardian' of a boy (*custos; Sat.* 5.30); Juvenal speaks sarcastically of a hostage who will go home "with praetextate morals" (*praetextatos... mores*; 2.170). Festus reports that impure words were not to be uttered in the presence of a child clad in the *toga praetexta* (282–4L). Macrobius notes that the "blush of the purple" might induce a boy to live his life with modesty (*ut ex purpurae rubore ingenuitatis pudore regerentur,* 1.6.17), and that praetextate boys used to

Figure 1.24 Painting from a *lararium*. House of the Vettii, Pompeii (VI, 15,1). First century CE
Art Resource: ART41022

Figure 1.25 Mosaic rondel, Basilica of Santa Maria Assunta. Aquileia. Fifth century CE
Art Resource: ART 524538

attend the Senate with their fathers (1.6.18–25). Val. Max. 3.1.1 tells of M. Aemilius Lepidus (cos. 187 and 175 BCE; *BNP* Aemilius I 10) who went into battle as a boy and saved a countryman's life; for this deed a statue was set up in Rome showing him in the boy's *toga praetexta* and the locket or *bulla*.

Did males of other ranks wear the *toga praetexta*? Macrobius (quoting Laelius) states that the right to wear the *toga praetexta* was granted even to the sons of freedmen during the Second Punic War (though only those born in a legitimate marriage: *S.* 1.6.13–14). On the other hand, Cicero paints a picture of the non-Roman Archias (*Arch.* 5) received into the home of the Luculli while still wearing his *toga praetexta*.[88] Slave boys did not wear the garment: at Suet. *de Rhet.* 1.2 a handsome and high-priced slave boy is dressed in a toga and *bulla* for the purposes of disguise (and fools everyone; see also Stat. *Silv.* 2.1.135–6).

Toga virilis/libera/pura[89]

When the Roman boy was in his mid-teens (although there are attested cases of as low as 13 [Nero] and as old as 18 [Caligula]),[90] he dedicated his *toga praetexta* and *bulla* or amulet to the household *lares* and donned the woolen *toga virilis*.[91] His change of clothing, as well as perhaps the physical inspection of the boy's genitalia,[92] happened in private at the young man's home, often but not always coinciding with the Liberalia festival on 17th March.[93]

Thus formally assuming the *toga virilis* took place in two ceremonies: the private one in which the youth actually assumed the manly toga; and the public one which happened at the Liberalia. In this last the youth took part in a procession through the city into the forum where he performed sacrifices (App. *BC.* 4.5.30, probably at the temple to Jupiter Optimus Maximus), and perhaps also deposited a small coin in Juventas' small shrine in the Capitoline temple or the one at the Circus Maximus (Dion. Hal. *Ant. Rom.* 4.15.5; Dolansky 2008, 51). The boy may also have registered his name at the *tabularium* (Dolansky 2008, 51). We must keep in mind however that plenty of boys would have donned the *toga virilis* outside Rome (Dolansky 2008, 52) and thus this precise part of the ceremony would not be performed. In addition, poorer boys would not necessarily have owned or worn a toga, since such lengths of cloth were expensive to buy and cumbersome to wear. After the ceremony, *sportulae* would be distributed to the crowds of well-wishers (Dolansky 2008, 52; and 65 n. 27 with references). The ceremony was observed by family members, friends, possibly even slaves,[94] and links the male body with "place, dress, and male bonding" (Richlin 1997, 92; Christ 1997, 25).

The youth's new toga was unstriped and undyed, and symbolized the young man's freedom from paternal control. It was therefore also referred to as the *toga pura* or *toga libera*.[95] The *toga virilis* was thus a visual symbol of the young man's process of socialization: in many pre-industrial societies, "changes in one's appearance mark passages and symbolize conditions that are socially recognized... accepted and legitimate clothing... induces the individual to merge with the group, participate in its rituals and ceremonies, share its norms and values, properly occupy his or her position" (Perrot 1994, 13). Tacitus tells us that Claudius turned the language of juvenile clothing to good advantage when he arrayed his stepson Nero in the robes of triumph (*triumphali veste*), and his own son Britannicus in the juvenile white and purple (*in praetexta*), so that the people "could speculate on the probable fortune of each" (Tac. *Ann.* 12.41). Seneca speaks of the joy a young man felt when laying aside his *praetexta* and taking up the *toga virilis* (*Epp.* 4.2; Stat. *Silv.* 5.2.68–9).

Tunica palmata *and* toga picta/purpurea[96]

The *tunica palmata* and *toga picta/purpurea* were worn in the Republic by triumphing generals (Livy 10.7.9, 30.15.11–12) and other persons of distinction.[97] In the imperial period, the garments were worn by the emperor (Tac. *Ann.* 4.26). Purple in color, with designs picked out in gold wire, the costume was heavy, sumptuous, expensive, and laden with connotations of rank and status.

The *tunica palmata*, perhaps purple, originally had a border the width of a *palma* or handspan, the reason for its name,[98] although as Bonfante-Warren notes (1973, 610), *clavus* means 'stripe,' not 'border.' This tunic may have been long-sleeved.[99] At some point it came to have a palmette design embroidered in gold wire.[100] Numa Pompilius granted to the twelve Salii, priests of Mars Gravidas, embroidered tunics (*tunicae pictae*; Livy 1.20.4).

At first, the toga worn with the *tunica palmata* was the *toga purpurea* (Livy 31.11.11). This garment was worn by kings in Rome's regal period (Livy 30.15.11, 31.11.11; Plut. *Rom.* 25). Festus reports seeing portraits of generals in the *toga purpurea* in temples of the third century BCE (228L). Polybius states that the body of a censor was clothed in a purple toga at his funeral (6.53); and Caesar wore a purple toga while he was alive (Cic. *Phil.* 2.85–6; Reinhold 1970, 45 with n. 5). Cassius Dio wrote that the all-purple toga was permitted by Augustus only to those holding public office (49.16). Stone is correct in stating that no source outside the *HA* mentions the Roman emperor in a *toga purpurea* (1994, 39 n. 12; Alföldi 1935). Togate statues exist in which the toga is made of purple porphyry.[101]

After the third century BCE however the *toga purpurea* was replaced by the *toga picta* which was also purple but had designs in gold wire (Fest. 228L).[102] Bonfante believes the form may have derived from Etruscan dress. In the François Tomb, Vel Sathies wears a *vestis picta* (Fig. 1.26), a *himation*, dark wine-red in color with a scrollwork border. It is decorated with naked soldiers carrying shields, dancing the Pyrrhic dance.[103] Although not a *toga picta*, perhaps in color and decoration it is not dissimilar. The decoration of the Roman *toga picta* itself may have been palmettes or various small figures, embroidered in gold wire; hence Wilson has noted that it is sometimes

50 *Tunic and toga: clothing and rank*

Figure 1.26 Fresco from the François Tomb, Vulci. Museo di Villa Albani, Rome. Fourth century BCE
Source: Bestand-Microfiche-D-DAI-ROM-1095_F14.jpg

misnamed the *toga palmata*.[104] Dionysius of Halicarnassus (3.61) describes the garment of the Roman kings, essentially a *toga picta*. Isidore of Seville states that "a toga earned by those who had brought back the palm of victory from an enemy was called a *toga palmata*. This was also called a decorated toga (*toga picta*) because it had the victories woven into it with a display of palm leaves" (*eo quod victorias cum palmis intextas haberet; Orig.* 19.24.5). A coin of Augustus, minted perhaps at Cordoba, shows a visual depiction of the toga and tunic (see Fig. 1.27).[105]

Figure 1.27 Coin of Augustus. Roman denarius. Cordoba. Muenzkabinett, Staatliche Museen, Berlin, Germany. ca. 18 BCE
Art Resource: ART502631

In early times triumphal dress appears to have been the property of the state, housed in the Capitoline temple of Jupiter (*HA* Alex. Sev. 40.8), but the garments were sometimes owned by private men. In 200 BCE the Senate gave to Masinissa the *toga purpurea* and *tunica palmata* when asking him for assistance against Philip (Livy 31.11.12). Alexander Severus never assumed the *toga picta* except when consul (40.8), "and then it was always the one which was brought out from the temple of Jupiter and assumed by all the other praetors and consuls." The emperor Gordianus was allegedly the first Roman to own a *toga picta* and *tunica palmata* as private property (*HA* Gord. Tres. 4.4; 224–5 CE).

Toga as symbol[106]

The toga had a high symbolic content, and as a visual text could denote several things. Firstly, of course, the toga was an immediate marker of the Roman citizen. The word *togatus* was often used by itself to designate such men,[107] and the Romans were described in literature as the "togate race," *gens togata*.[108] The emperor Claudius reportedly wished to see the Greeks, Gauls, Spaniards, and Britons in togas (*togatos videre*; Sen. *Apol.* 3). That for centuries there was little real change in the garment is due to the fact that the toga was one of the means by which Romans divided themselves off from the barbarians, who wore stitched clothing. Citizens in the provinces wore the toga to proclaim their status as such (Sen. *Apol.* 3 and Tac. *Agr.* 21); non-citizens were forbidden to wear it (Suet. *Claud.* 15.2; Pliny *Epp.* 4.11.3),[109] as were hostages and exiles (Pliny *Epp.* 4.11.3, *Dig.* 49.14.32). Thus the quality of *Romanitas*, of being Roman, was made known and in part generated by the garment.

In addition to transmitting information about one's rank as citizen, the toga had other resonances. Outside the *cinctus Gabinus* drape, which was sometimes associated with war, the toga on the whole represented peace, and was a symbol of harmony and repose (Cic. *Pis.* 30.72: *sed quia pacis est insigne et otii toga*). Thus the orator employing metonymy might elegantly substitute the words "Ceres" for corn, "Liber" for wine, and "toga" for peace (Cic. *de Orat.* 3.167). The toga as a symbol of peace was often naturally contrasted with *arma*, symbol of war. Thus one could write of weapons "yielding to the toga" (*cedant arma togae*; Cic. *Cons. Fr.* 8; see also *Off.* 1.77, *Pis.* 72; Livy 3.10.13). Authors contrasted *bellum* and *toga* (Vell. Pat. 1.12.3) or *castra* and *togae* (Ov. *Rem.* 152). Valerius Maximus described civil strife as *violentiae togatae* (9.7.1), while ready courage in peace was *togata praesentia* (3.7.5). At Stat. *Silv.* 5.2.58 a governor rules justly, his imperium tempered by the toga (*imperium mulcente toga*). Tacitus wrote of Tiberius' excellent work "in the toga," that is, in civil affairs, in contrast to his *victoriae* (*Ann.* 1.12; see also Val. Max. 8.15.1; Juv. 10.8).

'Toga' could also be used to refer metaphorically to urbanity, sophistication, and the city.[110] Cicero praised Caesar as one who was *clarus in toga*, illustrious in civil life (*Fam.* 6.6.5; cf. Liv. 22.26.2; Luc. *BC* 5.382). To be forgetful of Rome and city existence was *oblitus togae* (Hor. *Carm.* 3.5.10–11); an urbane manner of speaking *verba togae* (Pers. *S.* 5.14). Martial termed sophisticated epigrams *urbanae togae*, in contrast to scurrilous verses (11.16.2); one Quintilian is the "glory of the Roman gown" (*gloria Romanae... togae*; 2.90.2). At Val. Max. 3.2.17 *togae fortitudo* is bravery in the Forum or in politics; at Quint. *Inst.* 2.16.7 the phrase *in toga* is used to mean "in civilian life." In the Empire, the term *togatus* became synonymous with client status since clients greeted and accompanied their patrons in the toga (above).[111] The toga could also serve to hearken back to times of past glory, and to visually legitimate a dynasty's power, as in the case of the first- and second-century CE emperors (above).

As Hunink notes, the toga could have positive associations (formal dress, peace, Roman culture) or negative ones (dress of clients or prostitutes).[112] The longevity of the toga and its multi-faceted imagery shows how visual form "can have its own authority, its own self-perpetuating symbolic and emotional force" (Hollander 1994, 4). Despite its seeming omnipresence in Roman society, however, there were at the same time frequent complaints of omission of the toga, surprising in such a status-conscious culture.

Omission

There are several practical reasons for the fact that those men entitled to wear the toga left it off on occasion (George 2008, 95–6). New togas were costly: at

Mart. 2.44.1–4 three woolen togas (a *togam pexam*) cost as much as a slave boy or four pounds of plate. In addition, cleaning and caring for the garment was expensive (see Chapter 4 below on fulling and washing; and George 2008, 99). And the toga was uncomfortable: cumbersome and hot (see Mart. 12.18.5: *sudatrix toga*).[113] Tertullian is adamant that togas needed tedious arrangement and that men "do not feel that they are wearing the garment but laden or carrying it."[114] He further claims that men hasten immediately after arriving home to discard the garment (5.2.1–2). Rhetoric aside, togas must have "severely limited, if not physically prevented" big movement, (Petersen 2009, 186; and see Christ 1997, 28). But those very things which made the toga inconvenient – its expense and cumbersomeness – also made it a marker of status. Thus the cost of purchasing and maintaining a toga, along with its inconvenient nature (especially for those involved in manual labor), may have meant that it was out of the reach of many.[115]

There are however several examples in literature of the omission of the toga even amongst the politically active classes. Augustus reportedly enacted legislation forcing men to assume the toga in the Forum and the surrounding area, and in the theatres, perhaps as part of his programme to reform public and private morality.[116] He himself always kept a toga in his bedroom at the ready to assume if he were suddenly called out on public business (Suet. *Aug.* 73). Claudius decreed the garment mandatory for the tribunal where cases involving Roman citizens were involved (Suet. *Claud.* 15.2). Mart. 14.124 (the gift of a toga) has been interpreted by scholars as Domitian enjoining the use of the toga at spectacles (Leary 1996, 189, 199). Hadrian reportedly ordered senators and equestrians to wear the toga whenever they appeared in public except when they were returning from a banquet (implying some men did not).[117] Such commands indicate that the toga was not being worn by those who had a right to wear it.

Martial states the toga was required at formal occasions: the *salutatio* or morning greeting (14.125), the spectacles (14.135) and the law courts (14.136).[118] Thus a *toga rara* was a great pleasure, in part because it meant one did not have public business (10.47.5). Juvenal relates that men in rustic parts of Italy wear only tunics until they are laid out for burial in their togas (3.171–9). Here too are aediles "content with white tunics" as vesture for their high office, rather than togas (*sufficiunt tunicae summis aedilibus albae*; 3.179). Elsewhere, an old man wants to let his skin drink in the sun and "escape the toga" (*effugiatque togam*; 11.203–4). Pliny the Younger rejoiced that he need never put on the toga at his Tuscan villa (*nulla necessitas togae; Epp.* 5.6.45), and described his friend assuming the toga only on holy days (*toga feriata*), and leaving off his *calcei* (shoe-boots: see below; 7.3.2) while out of Rome. Possibly poor men would own just one toga: Martial (4.66) tells us of a provincial man who lives a frugal life with one toga and one *synthesis* or dinner-costume (on the dress of poor men, see below, Chapter 3). Elsewhere, Martial himself wears out four togas per summer in Rome, yet in the country one toga lasts him four autumns (10.96.11–12). And of course Romans removed their togas during the festival of Saturnalia, which Seneca noted with disapproval (*Epp.* 18.2).[119]

Leaving off the toga, while comfortable, may have led to a certain amount of sartorial confusion. There was ideally a natural correlation between the clothing of the slave and his low social position, but no clothes associated with slavery particularly. Thus if a man did not assume his toga when he went out in public he ran the risk of being mistaken for a slave (or a foreigner). Thus at Pl. *Am.* 343 the question is asked of a character making an entrance *servosne es an liber?* – "are you slave or free?" (see also Sen. *de Clem.* 1.24.1; App. *BC.* 2.120; Artem. *Oneir.* 2.3; Paul *Sent.* 18.1.5). Nor was the toga effective in distinguishing *libertini* from *ingenuii:* both free and freed could wear the toga, as scholars have noted (Petersen 2009, 207; Hor. *Epod.* 4.8). In Petronius' *Satyricon,* Hermeros states he was a slave for forty years, "but no one could now tell whether I was slave or free" (57.9; *nemo tamen sciit, utrum servus essem an liber*). Croom (2002, 49) points out that when a respectable Roman left the house he would wear something over his tunic – a toga or a cloak – not because he necessarily needed protection from the elements but because it was the proper thing to do.

Intriguingly, the toga is never overtly characterized in ancient literature as masculine or manly clothing. It only fully reveals itself as a masculine garment when its *absence* is spoken of: on foreigners, slaves, and women. The toga then was quintessential Roman male attire because it was the garb of the citizen, who was also ideally a sexually dominant male. If ancient sexuality was about control and supremacy, then the toga-less person was disenfranchised, powerless, and penetrated. Persons who did not wear the toga were located outside traditional power structures.[120]

Conclusions

This chapter has tried to collect some of the literary and artistic evidence for the Roman tunic and toga. Ancient sources suggest the ways in which the symbolism of the tunic was ideally supposed to indicate one's juridical rank (through stripes, length, and thickness); one's age or sexual status (the *tunica recta*); and physical activity or moral laxity (through sleeve length and cincture; and see below, Chapter 5). The tunic was a classless garment however, in that all males wore a tunic, whatever their rank, status, or age.

The toga similarly could cross economic and social boundaries and confines of age, and a border was often put on (or left off) the toga to denote these specifics. Special toga-drapes delineated activity (the *cinctus* Gabinus) or age (*ad brachium cohibendum*). The toga was a ritual garment as well, symbolizing a condition that was socially recognized: the boy who assumed the toga also adopted a body that was politically and sexually capable.

"There is really no garment the doffing of which congratulates a man more than that of the toga," wrote Tertullian in the late second century CE (*nullius profecto alterius indumenti expositio quam togae gratulatur; Pall.* 5.2.2). The toga is a "classic example of 'emblemic style,'" an artifact marked with a distinctive form that "transmits a clear message to a defined target about conscious affiliation or identity."[121] The voluminous Augustan toga reappears again and again throughout the Roman draped centuries, in imperial and private portraiture, despite the fact that the toga was undergoing changes in style during those times. This large toga with its *sinus* and *umbo* may have symbolized peace, prosperity, and wealth. Although cumbersome, social boundaries were often reinforced "through matrices of dress, undress, action, and inaction" (Petersen 2009, 195, of reliefs).

Notes

1. On the tunic, see Croom 2002, 31–40; Fuentes 1987; Goette 1990, 8–10; Goldman 1994a, 221–3; Pausch 2008 (a masterful study); Wild 1994; and Wilson 1938, 55–71.
2. On weaving clothes to shape in the ancient world, see Granger-Taylor 1982; Gleba 2008b, 84; Wilson 1938, 25. On tunic production see Pausch 2008, 71–89; Wild 1994.
3. Tunics from the Cave of Letters constructed in this manner are narrower in the body than the one-piece tunics and are assumed to be children's. See Yadin 1963, 204–9 and 212 no. 6, fig. 70. The lengths of the tunics here range from 2′ 4″ to 3′ 8″ with an average of 3′ 1″. Widths are 2′ to 3′ 3″, with an average of 2′ 7″ (Yadin 1963, 205, 212–19).
4. Granger-Taylor (1982: 10). Granger-Taylor (ibid., 24 n. 31) has noted that "it is feared that these tucks are sometimes removed during conservation," although Wild (1994, 10–11, 28–9) believes that the tucks were often opened out before the body was placed in the grave.
5. Archaeological evidence for sewing implements is limited: needles made of various materials, for instance, are not always mentioned in excavation reports as they are small and easily lost (Gleba 2008b, 84, 156–7). See however the finds at Vindolanda (Birley 2009, e.g. 55–7, 74, 78). Goldman 1994a states (217) that needles in antiquity were not as sharp or pointed as they are today, and that the thread used was probably one of the weft threads.
6. A late antique tunic in Abegg-Stiftung collection in Riggisberg, Switzerland shows signs of heavy wear and repair in places (Wild 1994, 29–30): the spots where the wearer's hands projected from the folds of the garment were mended, and the neck opening tore through at some point and was darned.
7. *CIL* 6.8554 (in the imperial *familia*: freedman of Claudius, and described as *vestificus Caesar*[*is*]), 6.9979, 6.37724. *Vestificae: CIL* 6.964 (imperial family), 6.5206, 6.9744, 6.9980 (of scarlet clothes). See Liu 2009, 80.
8. There are dozens of inscriptions commemorating *vestiarii* and *vestiariae*. See for example *CIL* 4.3130, 6.3680, 6.4476, 6.8556; Liu 2009, 75–83.
9. *Sarcinator: CIL* 6.3051, 6.6348, 5.7568; *sarcinatrix: CIL* 6.4029, 6.4030, 6.4031, etc. See Liu 2009, 73 n. 76 for further examples.
10. On tunic sleeves, see Pausch 2008, 84–9.
11. No date for the fashion is given: *postea substrictas et breves tunicas citra umerum desinentis habebant; NA* 6.12.3. See the Arringatore statue, Fig. 1.6.
12. Croom has noted that very often the width of the tunic was widened towards the armholes without making the body of the tunic generally more voluminous (Croom 2002, 31).
13. *pellibus manicatis: R.* 1.8.9. Pausch (2008, 86–9) writes of long-sleeved tunics as a negative *topos*.

Tunic and toga: clothing and rank

14 On the *semicinctium* (sometimes translated as 'apron' instead of 'belt/girdle'), see Mart. 14.153; Petr. *Satyr*. 94.8; Leary 1996, 215–16, and Leary 1990.
15 Hor. *S.* 1.5.5, of travellers; Petr. *Satyr*. 19.5; Apul. *Met*. 9.6; Serv. Aen 8.724; *TLL* s.v. '*praecingo*' col. 436–7. See Pausch 2008, 89–96.
16 On the military tunic, see Pausch 2008, 197–9; Speidel 1997, 235 and 2012, 3–4, 7, 10–11; Sumner 2002, 3–12 and 2009, 17–70.
17 *tunicatos discinctosque*: Suet. *Aug*. 24.2. See also Livy 27.13.9, 35.11.7; Val. Max. 2.7.9; Fron. *Str*. 4.1.43; Tert. *Idol.* 19.
18 On these statues, see Palmer 1998, 60.
19 Asc. *ad Cic. In Scaurianam: Cato praetor iudicium, quia aestate agebatur, sine tunica exercuit campestri sub toga cinctus* (Clark [1907] 1956); Wilson 1924, 26. Plut. *Coriol*. 14 and *Cat. Min*. 6. For the *campestre*, see Olson 2003, 206–7.
20 Croom 2002, 39; Stone 1994, 35, 38 with fig. 1.20 (400 CE); Wilson 1924, 104.
21 Contra Wilson 1938, 63–4.
22 "woven from the top, by those standing" (342L; see also Pliny *Nat*. 8.194; Fest. 364L). The upright loom was reportedly first used by Tanaquil wife of Tarquinius Priscus, who wove the earliest *tunica recta* (Plin. *Nat*. 8.194; Fest. 364L). On the *tunica recta*, see Pausch 2008, 191–3. Fraschetti (1996, 78) envisions the boy sleeping in the *tunica recta* the night before as brides did. Néraudau (1979, 148) believes the youth donned it immediately before assuming the *toga virilis*.
23 The dalmatic, worn in the late second and early third century CE, was a loose, wide, possibly long-sleeved tunic with tight sleeves usually held by a belt, made of expensive fabric, normally a sign of luxury and effeminacy; see Croom 2002, 34; Harlow 2004, 54; Pausch 2008, 180–7; and Dio 72.17.2; *HA Comm*. 8.8; HA *Eleg*. 26.2.
24 On slave clothing, see Bradley 1994, 95–9, with references; George 2002.
25 *tunicam P. III S, saga alternis annis. Quotiens cuique tunicam aut sagum dabis, prius veterem accipito, unde centones fiant*. The elder Cato reportedly boasted that his own clothing never cost over 100 drachmas (Plut. *Cato* 4.3).
26 Slave women could of course be kept on estates to work wool and make clothing (Liu 2009, 74–5; Cato *Agr*. 2.3; *Dig*. 33.7.12.5). See above, Introduction.
27 Bradley 1994, 88–9; although, as he notes (101), living in an opulent household brought no promise of material ease to slaves.
28 On *clavi*, see Pausch 2008, 104–18.
29 See Pausch 2008, 108–11 (origin and meaning of *clavi* as status symbols). On the differences between *lati* and *angusti* clavi, and *clavi* in art, see Pausch 2008, 112–18.
30 Granger-Taylor (1982, 20) claims the purple stripes gradually moved towards the centre of the tunic, and compares the stripes on the tunic of the slave Arnza on the Francois tomb to those of the Arringatore (her fig. 1). This conclusion is not borne out by the encaustic paintings from Roman Egypt of clavate men, however.
31 Quint. *Inst*. 11.3.139: *ut purpurae recte descendant, levis cura est; notatur interim neglegentia*.
32 The evidence for the grant of the broad stripe in the reigns of Augustus and Tiberius is "very slight," but by the reign of Claudius was established practice (Millar 1977, 291). Mentions of it occur in literature and inscriptions up to the early third century (Millar 1977, 292). See Chastagnol 1975 and 1976; Jones 1955; Levick 1991, 240; Millar 1977, 290–2; Saller 1982, 50–1 and n. 58. See also *HA Sev*. 1.5; *CIL* 12.1783; Tac. *Dial*. 7 (a *novus homo*).
33 See *ILS* 6998 in which the *latus clavus* is offered to an *eques* (a Gaul) who refuses it.
34 There may have been a special ceremony for boys assuming the broad stripe: see Pliny *Epp*. 8.23.6.

35 Suet. *Vesp.* 2.2. On Vespasian's hesitation in assuming the *latus clavus*, surely incorrect, see Levick 1991, 241. Vespasian reportedly charged a young man HS 200,000 for obtaining the *latus clavus* for him, against the father's wishes (Suet. *Vesp.* 4.3).
36 Sextius was a Stoic with Pythagorean leanings; *BNP* Sextius I 1.
37 On equestrian status, see Brunt 1969 and 1983; Rowe 2002, 67–84; Wiseman 1970. Rowe correctly points out (2002, 73) that definitions of 'the equestrian *ordo*' have differed greatly amongst modern scholars, but that rather than a single definition, "there was a tangled set of overlapping categories and definitions" including pedigree, military service, wealth, status symbols, perquisites, public function, and participation in ceremony.
38 Wilson (1938, 62–3) believes the narrow stripes were worn by Roman *boys* as well and cites a variety of artistic evidence.
39 See Granger-Taylor 2008 for changes in *clavi* on tunics in the third century CE. Croom 2002, 32 gives some artistic examples of lower-class men in clavate tunics.
40 On the toga generally, see Bieber 1959; Croom 2002, 41–9; Christ 1997; Davies 2005; Dyck 2001; Goette 1990; Kleiner and Kleiner 1980–81; Kleiner 1991; Rothfus 2010; Stone 1994; Vout 1996; Wilson 1924 and 1938, 36–54.
41 Isidore wrote that "the proper measurement for the toga is six ells" (*mensura togae iusta si sex ulnas habeat; Orig.* 19.24.5). Wilson 1924, 82 takes this to mean about 18″ per ell, or about 9 feet.
42 Although see Wilson 1924, 29–30 and fig. 7.
43 *est autem pallium purum forma rotunda et fusiore, et quasi inundante sinu...; Orig.* 19.24.3.
44 Granger-Taylor (1982, 19) takes *caesam* here as meaning "shaped," as this statement follows a long section in the *Institutes* on the proper draping of a toga. But there are no parallels for this meaning of *caedo* elsewhere in Latin literature.
45 e.g., Cic. *Orat.* 40, *Brut* 272; Hor. *Ars* 323; Gell. 11.13.4, 16.1.1, 17.20.4; Granger-Taylor 1982, 20.
46 Granger-Taylor (1982, 5) has noted evidence of closing cords and a starting border or transverse selvedge on the Arringatore's tunic. This strongly suggests (ibid., 7) the garment was of wool, as such corded edgings are found on wool textiles. Gleba (2008b, 98) lists factors affecting quality of wool: which part of the animal it comes from, if the animal is male or female, its age and physiological state, which type of food it consumes. For togas of other materials, see below, Chapter 4.
47 Goethert (1939, 202–4) and Stone (1994, 41 n. 46) assume all changes in toga drape started in Rome and spread out to the provinces; but see Bonanno 1988 on imperial and private portraiture styles.
48 On this relief, see Stone 1994, 41 n. 47, with references.
49 See e.g., Cic. *Phil.* 13.28; Livy 6.41; Juv. 13.33; Suet. *Aug.* 38.2.
50 *CIL* 6.33976. See Kleiner 1987, 162–5, no. 45, with references; Rawson 2003, 17–20. There is a strong probability that his parents (Q. Sulpicius Eugramus and Licinia Ianuaria) were freed slaves, of Greek extraction.
51 *CIL* 6.22972. On this panel, see Kleiner 1987, 195–6, no. 68, with references; Rawson 2003, 259–61.
52 George has noted (2001, 183) that many boys on reliefs are usually shown "lifted up to the same height as their parents" so that both the toga and *bulla* are visible. Since freed persons could wear the toga but only freeborn could wear the toga *praetexta* and the *bulla*, "the sons on these reliefs are hence conspicuously dressed in the badges of civic honour which had been inaccessible to their fathers in their own servile childhoods."
53 Wilson (1924, 18–19) believes "the evidence from existing [Etruscan] monuments is wholly negative," and that the Roman toga was, in fact, a purely Roman

invention. See Hafner 1969 for a discussion of Etruscan *togati* (although he does not always recognize the difference between *palliati* and *togati*; see Bonfante 2003, 125 n. 20); Dion. Hal. 3.60.
54 On the Census relief, see now Goette 1990, 20–1, 106 A a 4; Meyer 1993; Stilp 2001; Torelli 1982, 5–25; Zanker 1988, 12–14.
55 Granger-Taylor 1982, 20. On the Arringatore, see Dohrn 1968; Goette 1990, 21, 106 A a 2; Stone 1994, 39 n. 15; Wilson 1924, 25–34. Granger-Taylor believes that the Arringatore does *not* in fact wear the toga and tunic worn by upper-class Romans, and therefore the dating of the statue to *after* the *Lex Julia* of 89 BCE is inaccurate (1982, 20). The length of the upper edge of the toga indicates the Arringatore was not made after 100 BCE (ibid).
56 Republican/early imperial togas: Goette 1990, 20–8; Stone 1994, 15–17; Wilson 1924, 17–42.
57 Bieber 1959, 388 and fig. 22; Christ 1997, 25; Olson 2014b; Stone 1994, 16 and 40 n. 30; Wallace-Hadrill 2008, 45.
58 Bieber 1959, 377–85; Hafner 1969.
59 Rothfus 2010, while an intriguing article on the change from the Republican to the Augustan toga (she posits the fuller toga became fashionable because Roman nobles were trying to distance themselves from lower-class wearers of the toga: the new style was thus "an elite assertion of identity and status;" 426), does not account for the existence of earlier styles alongside the new form of toga. Thus on the Ara Pacis, for instance, I note two senators (at least) who do not sport the *sinus* and *umbo* style of toga. Nor does her study take into account the possibility of the fashion beginning in the non-senatorial classes and spreading upwards (427; for an example, see Bonanno 1988).
60 Stone believes that while the evolution of the *sinus* is unknown, "it may represent observation of a similar use of an overfold over the torso on the *himatia* on some Greek statues" (Stone 1994, 17). Goette (1990, 102) believes Augustus himself was responsible for this new style, and that it may have been inspired by the priestly *laena* worn by the *flamines*.
61 Wilson 1924, 44–5; Stone 1994, 20 fig. 1.6. On veiling in Roman sacrifice, see now Huet 2012, with references.
62 See Stone 1994, 41 n. 45; Wilson 1924, 61; Zanker 1988, 127–9 and fig. 104.
63 See Goette 1990, 54–63; Stone 1994, 25, 34–5, 38; Wilson 1924, 89–115.
64 On these reliefs, see Angelicoussis 1984; Goette 1990, 137 B b no. 124; Ryberg 1967.
65 See the examples in Birk 2013, 61–6.
66 Portrait of a freedman and woman, 160–190 CE. Rome. See Kleiner 1992, 283 fig. 250.
67 See Caputo 1959, 19–23.
68 On this see e.g., Zanker 1988, 172–83.
69 Stone 1994, 25 and 43 n. 66, with references.
70 On this frieze, see Kampen 2009, 82–103, with references.
71 On this sarcophagus, see Birk 2013, 72–3 and n. 294, with references.
72 On the garb of orators see Bablitz 2007, 191–2; Gunderson 1998 and 2000, 71, 77.
73 As Bablitz notes, it seems advocates from the provinces could appear before the court in their native dress (2007, 250 n. 182: *Acta Isidori* rec. B., col. ii, 1.37. See Musurillo 1954, appendix III. It is difficult however to determine the historical accuracy of the *Acta*).
74 Sempronius Tuditanus' tendency to drag his toga is mentioned in connection with his *insania* (Val. Max. 7.8.1; *BNP* Sempronius I 22).
75 See Quint. *Inst.* 11.3.144–6. Quintilian even discourses upon the use of the eyes, eyebrows, lips, nostrils, neck (11.3.75, 78, 80, 82). "Each time Quintilian

turns his eyes upon the body it is invested with both significance and risk" (Gunderson 1998, 181). On the orator's body, see Fögen 2009, 23–43; Gunderson 2000, 59–86.
76 On the *cinctus Gabinus,* see Bonfante-Warren 1973, 596–7, 606–7; Dubourdieu 1986; Goette 1990, 7; Linderski 2002, 343 n. 16; Stone 1994, 39 n. 6; Wilson 1924, 86–8.
77 Isidore (*Orig.* 19.24.7) provides a somewhat confused description.
78 On the toga wound around one's head as a 'helmet,' a sign of battle: see Linderski 2002, 343 n. 17; Amm. 18.6.13, 25.6.14.
79 Dubourdieu 1986, 18 concludes that *Quirinale trabea cinctuque Gabino* (*A.* 7.612) is a hendiadys and that the *trabea* and the Gabian cincture would not be found together. On the *trabea,* see below, Chapter 4.
80 See Richardson and Richardson 1966, 267; and Goette 1990, 27 and pl. 4, 1–3.
81 On the clothing of the *flamen dialis,* see Vanggaard 1988, 40–5.
82 On the costume of the Roman bride, see Hersch 2010, 69–114; La Follette 1994; Olson 2008, 21–5.
83 Pliny reports that "the addition of lead to Cyprus copper produces the purple color seen in the bordered robes of statues" (*colos purpurae fit in statuarum praetextis; Nat.* 34.98).
84 Paintings from Delos: see Bulard 1926, 46, 82–3, 141–2 and pls VII.2 and XIX.
85 Wilson believed the purple edge moved from lower to upper edge for a similar reason: the lengthening of the toga in this period and the consequent dragging of the purple border along the ground (Wilson 1924, 54).
86 Gleba 2008b, 200; Goette 1990, 4–5; Wilson 1924, 55; but see *Dig.* 34.2.19.5 and 34.2.23.1, above.
87 For girls in the *toga praetexta,* see Olson 2008, 141–2. On boys' clothing generally see Croom 2002, 120–2; Gabelmann 1985, 497–517; Goette 1990, 96–7 with plates; Wilson 1924, 51–2 and 1938, 130–2.
88 "The clothing term... serves to plant a subtle suggestion of Archias' Romanness" (Dyck 2001, 123).
89 On the *toga virilis,* see Amiotti 1981; Dolansky 2008; Néraudau 1979, 147–63; Pausch 2008, 31–3; Rawson 2003, 142–4, 325–6; Wiedemann 1989, 113–42.
90 See Dolansky 2008, 49 with references. Isid. *Orig.* 19.24.16 tells us boys were in the bordered toga until age sixteen.
91 See Ov. *F.* 3.771; also Cic. *Phil* 2. 44, *de Amicit.* 1.1, *Pro Sest.* 144; Livy 26.19.5, 42.34.4; Suet. *Claud.* 2.2; Sen. *Epp.* 4.2. (a young boy escorted to the Forum); Pliny *Epp.* 1.9.2 (regularly invited to these ceremonies). After donning the *toga virilis,* the youth was a *iuventus* for one year, during which he underwent an apprenticeship or *tirocinium,* receiving military training and serving as a reserve soldier. For the elite, public military training took place in the Campus Martius (McDonnell 2006, 183).
92 See Dolansky 2008, 49, with references.
93 Cic. *Att.* 5.20.9; Ovid *Fast.* 3.771–2; on dates see Dolansky 2008, 49–50.
94 See Dolansky 2008, 50–1; Hor. *Carm.* 1.36.9; App. *BC* 4.5.30; Pliny *Epp.* 1.9.1–3, 10.116.
95 Ov. *F.* 3.771; Prop. 4 (5) 1.132; Cic. *Amic.* 1.1; Cic. *Att.* 5.20.9, 6.1.12, 9.17.1 and 9.19.1; Cat. 68.15; Pliny *Nat.* 8.194. Stat. *Silv.* 5.2.66–7 refers to it as 'the white garment" (*albenti ... amictu*).
96 On these items, see Bonfante-Warren 1970, 59–61, 1973, 610–11; Goette 1990, 6, 9–10; Reinhold 1970, 59; Wilson 1924, 84–6, 1938, 67.
97 The Romans also referred to triumphal dress as the *ornatus* of Jupiter Optimus Maximus (Livy 10.7.10; Juv. 10.38; Serv. *Ad Ecl.* 10.27: *triumphantes, qui habent,*

60 *Tunic and toga: clothing and rank*

omnia Jovis insignia, sceptrum, palmatum). See Bonfante 2003, 53, 122, n. 51; Bonfante-Warren 1970, 59–61.
98 Bonfante-Warren 1973, 610; 1970, 64–5. See Fest. 228L: *tunica autem palmata a latitudine clavorum dicebatur, quae nunc a genere picturae appellatur.*
99 From the evidence of a Latin triumph on a Praeneste *cista* of 100 BCE: see Bonfante-Warren 1964, 37.
100 Bonfante-Warren 1970, 64; Fest. 228L.
101 These statues have recently been divided into the early second century CE and the Tetrarchic period. Goette 1990, 45–9; Stone 1994, 39 n. 12. See also Delbrueck 1932, 49, 54–8, 96–100.
102 See Dion. Hal. 3.61; Florus 1.5.6 (Tarquinius); Bonfante-Warren 1970, 61–2, 64–5; Goette 1990, 6.
103 On this fresco, Bonfante 2003, 201 fig. 135; Gleba 2008b, 26, 81.
104 Wilson 1924, 85. The first mention of it occurs at Mart. 7.2.8; perhaps this is a transferred epithet. See also Isid. 19.24.5; Bonfante-Warren 1970, 64–5.
105 Bergmann 2010, 88, fig. 31a, 385–6 (cat. no. 58a–b); for a similar coin see *RIC¹* 99; *BMC* 397.
106 On the symbolism of the toga, see Galinier 2012; Rothfus 2010; Stone 1994; Vout 1996; Wallace Hadrill 2008, 41–3.
107 *Togatus*: see Cic. *Phil.* 5.14, *Sull.* 85, *de Orat.* 1.111, *Rosc.* 135, *Rab. Post.* 27; Sall. *Jug.* 21.2; Livy 3.52.7.
108 *Gens togata*: Virg. *A.* 1.282. In Athen. *Deip.* 5.213 the togate Romans are easily picked out by assassins. Roman historical dramas were called *fabulae praetextae* (Cic. *Ad Fam.* 10.32.3 and 5). See also Pausch 2008, 23–38; Stone 1994, 38 n 1.
109 A Tarentine reportedly defecated on L. Postumius Megellus' toga to show his contempt for Rome; this leads to Rome declaring war on Tarentum (cos. 291 BCE: *BNP* Postumius I 16. See Dion. Hal. 19.5.1–6.1; App. *Samn.* 7.2). Granger-Taylor (1982, 10) believes the toga was not much worn outside Italy. Wallace-Hadrill (2008, 45) notes that in one of the earliest usages of the word 'toga,' it refers to Italian allies supplying troops to Rome, not Roman citizens (this in the agrarian law of 111 BCE: *ex formula togatorum: CIL* 1².585).
110 The toga marked a man as civic being, who embodied *gravitas* and *pietas* (Harlow 2004, 51).
111 Mart. 1.108, 2.74, 3.46, 6.48, 9.100, 10.18, 10.47, 10.74.3, 10.82, 11.24.11; 14.125; Juv. 1.96, 7.142.
112 Hunink 2001, 109. On the toga as the "dress of prostitutes," see Olson 2002 (with references), and McGinn's pointed critique of this article (2014).
113 On the discomfort of the toga, see George 2008; Wilson 1924, 82.
114 *Pall.* 5: *quid te prius in toga sentias indutum, anne onustum*? See Hunink 2005, 250–1.
115 On the other hand, the elder Pliny tells of a severe and dignified fresco artist called Famulus who used to paint dressed in his toga, even while on scaffolding (*Nat.* 35.120).
116 Suet. *Aug.* 40.5: *negotium aedilibus dedit,* 44.2: *praetextatis cuneum suum… sanxitque* There is however nothing in the extant *Leges Juliae* on any such clothing legislation. Compare Commodus, who reportedly "contrary to custom… ordered the spectators to attend his gladiatorial shows clad not in togas but in cloaks (*paenulatos*), a practice usual at funerals, while he himself presided in dark vestments" (*in pullis vestimentis praesidens; HA* Comm. 16).
117 Hadrian himself allegedly wore the toga when in Italy and at banquets always reclined at table dressed either in a *pallium* or a toga (*HA Hadr.* 22.2).
118 Nonius writes: "the toga is so called from *tegendo*. And it is a toga with which we are covered in the forum, as is customary" (*sicut in consuetudine habetur, vestimentum quo in foro amicimur;* 653L).

119 Dewar notes that sending togas as Saturnalia presents was a Roman custom (2008, 219). For togas as gifts, see Mart. 2.39, 7.36, 7.86, 8.28, 10.15, 13.1, 13.48, 14.124, 14.125.
120 Richlin (1993, 532) has noted that "the highly class-stratified nature of Roman society is an essential component in the construction of Roman sexuality – the two systems can hardly be understood independently." On Roman sexual categories, see below, Chapter 5.
121 Wallace-Hadrill 2008, 41–2, with references.

2 Other aspects of costume

This chapter is a continuation of the description of basic items of clothing worn by Roman men: different types of jewelry which indicate rank, for instance (such as the *bulla* of the Roman citizen boy and the rings of senators and *equites*), hats and leggings, and the different types of cloaks and capes which were worn by all members of Roman society. Such items could of course indicate status by their dye or other ornamentation; examples of these may be found below in Chapter 4. Details of Roman dress such as these described here may seem to some to veer dangerously close to the antiquarian, but they need to be provided if we are to understand the kinds of ways in which clothing could be significant in Roman society.

Jewelry and rank

The bulla

Freeborn sons of citizens could wear the *bulla,* the bubble-shaped amulet (Macr. 1.6.9–10).[1] Sons of freedmen (that is, born while their parents were still slaves) and slaves were forbidden to wear it (Palmer 1998, 15 and 69; Suet. *Rhet.* 25). The story of the *bulla*'s origin is a bit unclear; like so many other pieces of Roman costume, Romans believed the piece had an Etruscan source (*bulla aurea, quo cultu reges soliti sunt esse E<trus>corum*; Fest. 430L; Juv. 5.164: *Etruscum aurum*; Plut. *Rom* 25). Tarquinius Priscus is said to have been the first to present his son with a *bulla*, as a token of bravery, since the boy had killed an enemy in battle when still of an age to wear the bordered robe (Pliny *Nat.* 33.10; Plut. *QR* 101). Macrobius gives an alternate version: that Priscus decreed sons of patricians should wear the *toga praetexta* and the golden *bulla* (1.6.11); then at 1.6.16 that the first son born to a Sabine woman had the distinction of wearing the *bulla*.

It is true that the earliest archaeological example of a bronze bulla dates from a tomb in Etruria, first half of the eighth century BCE (Warden 1983, 69). Bonfante-Warren notes that examples have been found in Etruscan tombs from the seventh and sixth centuries BCE, and is represented in art on heroes, dancers, and divinities, worn about the neck or upper arm (1973, 605;

2003, 77, 143–4 n. 95). The latest artistic example of a *bulla* is on a boy from the late third century CE (Croom 2002, 72).

Different shapes and materials were known. *Bullae* were normally circular or ovoid (or had "a figure of a heart attached;" Macr. 1.6.17; Warden 1983, 71 figs. 2–5) and were made of various materials. Calpurnius speaks of glass *bullae* (*vitreas ... bullas; Ecl.* 6.41 [39]). Bronze *bullae* remained popular over a long period of time beginning in the eighth century BCE (Warden 1983, 69). Gold *bullae* appear in the sixth century BCE (Warden 1983, 69; Fig. 2.1), and were the prerogative of children of wealthy families (Fig. 2.2).

They of course were valuable. In 210 BCE when the Romans needed to equip a fleet, austerity measures were introduced: among the small amounts of gold allowed to private citizens, one item was a *bulla* for each son (Livy 26.36.5). Cicero suggested that Verres' nephew Junius had to sell his *bulla aurea* because his uncle had reduced him to poverty (Verr. 2.1.152). Suetonius reported that wealthy women threw the *bullae* and *togae praetextae* of their children into Caesar's funeral pyre – expensive items, perhaps

Figure 2.1 Gold *bulla* from the Casa del Menandro, Pompeii. Museo Archeologico Nazionale, Naples. First century CE
Art Resource: AA354885

64 Other aspects of costume

Figure 2.2 Statue of a togate boy wearing the bulla. The head is of Nero as a young child. Rome. 41–54 CE
Art Resource: ART181893

signifying the loss of Caesar's protection, and as well part of the Roman practice of self-abasement in mourning (Suet. *Iul.* 84.4. See below, Chapter 3). Pliny states lower-class boys wore a leather strap (*lorum*; *Nat.* 33.10); Juvenal too states that poor boys wore a knot in a thong of leather around the neck (*nodus tantum et signum de paupere loro*; 5.165). Macrobius states this was originally a right granted to freedmen's sons born of legitimate marriages (1.6.14).

The *bulla* may have held "cures" (*remedia* or *praebia*), effective against the Evil Eye but never explicitly described,[2] reportedly invented by Tanaquil, wife of Tarquinius Priscus.[3] One pre-Roman example from Terni is decorated with a Bes figure and is filled with reddish earth (Warden 1983, 72 and n. 53). Triumphing generals also carried golden *bullae* with *remedia* before them in the procession (Macr. 1.6.9). But *bullae*, empty or not, were items of general apotropaic significance: in pre-Roman Italy, hung as ornaments from tripods (Warden 1983, 74) and on horses as ornaments (*phalerae*; ibid., 73).

The locket or leather thong, like the *toga praetexta*, signified the boy was not to be approached by men for sexual purposes (Plut. *QR* 101; here the *bulla* is worn by boys even when they are unclad). Paul ex Fest. writes that

> the golden *bulla* is the insignia of praetextate children/boys (*puerorum praetextatorum*), which hangs down on the chest, as it signifies that age needing to be regulated (*aetatem... regendam*) with *consilium*, the judgment, of another. It is thus either called the *bulla* from the Greek word *boulē*, which is called *consilium* in Latin, or because the *bulla* touches a part of the body, that is the chest, in which *consilium* naturally lies.
>
> (32L)

The *bulla* was laid aside, perhaps dedicated to the Lares of the household, when the boy assumed the *toga virilis* (Prop. 4.1.131; Pers. 5.31). The clothing and ornaments of Tiberius given to him as a child by Pompeia sister of Sextus Pompeius – a *chlamys* and *fibula* and gold *bullae* – were apparently kept and exhibited near Baiae (Suet. *Tib.* 6). In yet another example of Roman metonymy using clothing terms, Juvenal uses the phrase *bulla dignus* to mean "childish" (13.33).

Rings of senators and equites[4]

Men of many ranks also wore a ring as a marker of juridical category (for rings as status markers, see below, Chapter 4). The elder Pliny gives a detailed moral history of the material of rings. While his censorious tone clearly disapproves of flashy rings worn by persons in his own day,[5] his history contains much that is valuable, even though it is often confusing and convoluted.

Pliny tells us that rings for men do not appear to have been in common use until about 305/304 BCE (*Nat.* 33.17; at 33.10 he remarks that the statue of Tarquin on the Capitoline had no ring). Pliny believed that the fashion for wearing rings came from Greece (*Nat.* 33.9); Florus that rings as a mark of status were taken over from the Etruscans (1.1.5). The earliest Roman rings were of iron, with no stone (Pliny *Nat.* 33.9, 33.12; Marshall 1907, xviii). By the second century BCE, an iron ring was associated with men who had attained the high office of praetor (Pliny *Nat.* 33.21), but gold rings were also worn: Pliny tells us that men who had held curule office and their descendants held the right to wear the gold ring from 321 BCE, although they laid them aside on occasions of state mourning or disaster.[6] But he also contended that in the Republican period "for a long time" (*longo certe tempore*; 33.11) senators did not wear the gold ring unless granted one as a foreign ambassador. The custom had been for senators at home "to wear an iron ring as an emblem of warlike valour" (*Nat.* 33.9; see also 33.30); apparently not even a triumphing general would have considered exchanging his iron ring for a gold one (33.11–12). *Equites* were granted the right to wear a gold ring by 216 BCE (Livy 23.12.2). In the Republic, the right to wear the gold ring was also conferred on persons of military distinction. Military tribunes perhaps possessed the *ius anuli aurei* by the third Punic War: Appian states that in 149 BCE Scipio requested Hasdrubal to bury the tribunes killed in battle; these he would recognize by their gold rings (*BC* 8.104). Gaius Marius himself did not assume a gold ring until his third consulship (104/103 BCE). Not even by the time of the Social War were all senators wearing gold rings; most still wore iron (33.21). We must exercise caution here, however, as Pliny is giving us a highly-colored moralistic history to accord with his theories of decline and decadence.

In the late Republic the gold ring began to be bestowed on persons who were neither *equites* nor had participated in any significant military victories. Sulla granted it to the actor Q. Roscius Gallus,[7] and Verres publicly conferred the gold ring on his clerk, much to Cicero's disgust (Cic. *Verr.* 2.3.185–7). When Caesar reinstated D. Laberius' lost equestrian rank in 46 BCE, he restored as well as his symbols of rank including his gold ring (Suet. *Iul.* 39.2; *BNP* Laberius I 4).

Under the Empire "the gold ring was much more freely bestowed" (Marshall 1907, xx), or at least perceived in this way by upper-class authors; in addition, fashions in ring materials were changing in bewildering ways. By the early first century it seems senators were regularly wearing gold rings: at Augustus' funeral some senators decreed that gold rings should be laid aside and iron ones worn (Suet. *Aug.* 100.2). Augustus granted the right to wear the iron ring to a certain stratum of *equites*/jurors (Pliny *Nat.* 33.30), and to all physicians (Dio 53.30.3). In 22 CE, a *senatusconsultum* made it illegal for anyone to wear gold rings except those who 1) held equestrian status or higher; 2) possessed the right to sit in the first fourteen rows of theatre seats reserved for equestrians; and 3) had been free-born for three generations (Pliny *Nat.* 33.32; Pliny *Epp.* 8.6.4; Reinhold 1971, 280–2). The free birth requirement meant a rush to acquire fictive *ingenuitas*, which could be granted by imperial favor; Pliny noted that even freedmen were assuming it.[8] To combat this, the *lex Visellia de libertinis*, passed in 24 CE, "promised certain penalties to those who abused the *ius anuli aurei*, available only to senators and *equites*" (Schmeling 2011, 115).[9] The practice of bestowing special gold rings as a sign of military distinction continued under the empire (Marshall 1907, xx), and in 197 CE Septimius Severus granted the right to wear the gold ring to all soldiers (Herodian 3.8.4).

The question of rank, status, and ring material is further complicated by the fact that in the first century CE iron rings plated with gold were popular among those who did not have the *ius anuli aurei*: the elder Pliny reported with disgust that in his day slaves wore iron rings "encircled with gold" (*ferrum auro cingunt*; *Nat.* 33.23). In the *Satyricon*, Trimalchio has a gold ring on the little finger of his left hand; on the top joint next to it he has a gold ring which appeared to be made entirely of gold but was set round with iron stars (*Satyr.* 32.3). Perhaps freedmen at that time were supposed to wear iron rings: again in Petronius, the freedman Hermeros wears an iron ring (*Satyr.* 58.11; Leary 1996, 186–8; cf. Schmeling 2011, 115). But the practice of wearing rings not one's own by rank continued: Martial (2.29, 11.37) complained of ex-slaves wearing inappropriately elaborate rings. The younger Pliny (*Epp.* 8.6.4) stated that gold rings were the badges of equestrian rank, and that slaves wore iron rings.[10] And in fact, the many extant gilded bronze rings from the imperial period show that many who did not have the *ius anuli aurei* strove to give the impression of free birth while evading the law (Marshall 1907, xx). While there was change in ring materials over time, it seems rank and status also combined in interesting ways, to make usurpation of symbols of rank a matter of status.

Usurpation[11]

Consumption is a process of communication, not just a simple function of income, and competition for luxury goods a visualization of the struggle for power (Bourdieu 1984: 2). Roman male clothing especially was intended to indicate the social hierarchy, and there were specific sartorial signals meant to designate each *ordo* (senators, equestrians, the free poor, and slaves). Social mobility within particular boundaries was the underlying cause of the usurpation of symbols of rank, although interestingly, the privileges marked by these insignia were privileges of prestige and status only: no money or political benefits accrued to the wearers. Rank brought with it status.

The most common type of usurpation of symbols of rank was that of the *eques* or knight, because membership in the equestrian *ordo* was personal, not hereditary (see Reinhold 1971, 281, 285). Usurpation of these symbols seems to have been widespread in the Imperial period, and ancient sources tell of men illegally wearing tunics with the narrow stripe (*angustus clavus*), and the gold ring: clearly, the Romans understood that the right to wear certain distinctive symbols was inherent in the attainment of rank. The illegal acquisition through distinctive clothing of seats in the fourteen rows designated for equestrians is a common complaint in Martial (3.95, 5.23, 5.25, 5.27, 5.35, 5.41). The attendant in the theatre might remove those he knew were not equestrians from the reserved seats (Mart. 5.8); but the casual observer would not be able to tell who was a *iustus eques* and who was not. Equestrian status symbols (including rings) were a subject of legislation both by Augustus (Pliny *Nat.* 33.30) and Tiberius (*Nat.* 33.32).

Usurpation of symbols of senatorial rank was rarer, but we do hear through Horace of a man who assumes the broad-striped tunic and "binds the black thongs halfway up his legs" (*nigris medium impediit crus/ pellibus; S.* 1.6.27–8) and as a result has his parentage called into doubt.

Martial writes of a freedman who sits in the front row of seats sporting garments of Tyrian purple, red *calcei,* and the *luna* (the crescent-shaped shoe decoration of the patrician; 2.29) and (through Juvenal) of one enterprising

68 *Other aspects of costume*

man who sewed the *luna* onto his black shoe, an odd *faux pas* (*adpositam nigrae lunam subtexit alutae;* 7.192, and see Reinhold 1971, 284). These two examples may only be evidence of the authors' disgust for the undeserving who rise to social prominence; still, perhaps this scenario was believable to a Roman audience.

Other male clothing

Cloaks and capes[12]

Cloaks on the whole were classless garments and did not usually visualize rank, but they could denote status (see below, Chapter 4). Some were sexless as well: Ulpian in the late second/early third century CE states that there are clothes adapted to the use of either sex, "which women and men may share in common such as a *paenula* or *pallium* of a type which a man or his wife may use without criticism" (*communia sunt, quibus promiscue utitur mulier cum viro, veluti si eiusmodi penula palliumve est et reliqua huiusmodi, quibus sine reprehensione vel vir vel uxor utatur; Dig.* 34.2.23.2). A problem faced by the modern scholar is that different names were applied to cloaks which closely resembled each other (Wilson 1938, 78), the details of which are unclear.[13] In addition, cloaks appear in Roman art mainly on pictorial reliefs (such as the columns of Trajan and Marcus Aurelius and sarcophagi; Wilson 1938, 78), but usually lack any detail of colour or texture. Thus I have included here no photos of the different kinds of Roman cloaks and capes (except the *cucullus* or hood), as I am convinced we can neither identify these with certainty in artistic evidence nor distinguish between the different types.

Croom helpfully defines various types of wraps worn in Roman antiquity. A 'mantle' was an outer garment draped around the body, with no fastening (such as the *pallium, abolla,* or *endromis*; 2002, 51). A 'cloak' at its simplest was a rectangle of cloth fastened by a separate brooch almost always on the right shoulder, leaving both hands free, and could be of any length (*sagum, chlamys, lacerna, laena*).[14] A 'cape' was sewn up the front, usually had a hood, and afforded better protection from the elements than a cloak (*bardocucullus; paenula*; Croom 2002, 52, 54). Like tunics, mantles and cloaks were "woven to shape" in antiquity (Cardon et al. 2011, 210), although they were available as well in the secondhand clothing markets and were taken in to be mended (*P. Oxy.* IV.736).

Cloaks and capes are on the whole not a literary subject. While there are some positive texts regarding wraps, these garments tended to be associated with the poorer classes (Juv. 3.168–70, on which see below, Chapter 3), slavery (Col. *R.* 1.8.9), and disguise (Juv. 6.116–21, 8.144–5; *HA* Lucius Verus 4.6, Elag. 32.9).[15] Enveloping cloaks are frowned on at times in ancient literature probably because although comfortable and warm, such garments cover up distinctive signs of rank (the border on a *toga praetexta*, for example), or are worn instead of a toga. The often prescriptive nature of the literary sources on Roman clothing meant that everyone is imagined in their ideal costume.

Abolla

The *abolla*, (the name may have been derived from the Greek: see Wilson 1938, 84), was a mantle associated with philosophers or soldiers. Horace (*Epp.* 1.17.25) mentions a *duplex pannus* on a philosopher which may be the *abolla;* Martial (4.53.5) gives the name to the mantle adopted by philosophers. Juvenal uses the garment proverbially when he asks his readers to "listen to a crime of a greater abolla" (*audi facinus maioris abollae*; 3.115: the crime being the murder of a pupil by his philosophy teacher). At Juv. 4.76 a praefect wears it. Tertullian mentions the *pallium duplex* of the philosopher Crates (*Pall.* 5.3.1). Nonius (863L) names it as a military cloak; Servius describes it as "double," and also akin to the *chlamys* (*duplicem amictum: id est abollam quae duplex est; sicut chalmys; A.* 5.421. On *duplex,* see below). The *abolla* however was not fastened by a brooch and the *chalmys* was, and there is no hint in the classical sources that the *chalmys* was ever 'double' (Wilson 1938, 86).

Bardocucullus/cucullus

The *bardocucullus* was a coarse, heavy cloak, perhaps originating with the Bardaei, an Illyrian tribe (Wilson 1938, 95; Mart. 14.128), and was close-fitting, of various lengths. While resembling the *paenula*, the hood on the *bardocucullus* seems to have been smaller and the point less elongated than the hood on the former (Wilson 1938, 93).

The *cucullus* was a hood.[16] Columella (*R.* 1.8.9–10; 11.1.21) recommended that it be worn with *saga*, cloaks, to protect farm laborers in bad weather. This hood is often employed by persons in light verse as a device for disguise: a man watches the games with his hood pulled down so ushers will not move him, for instance (Mart 5.14), or to prevent people trying to kiss him (Mart. 11.98.10). It is also used as concealment going into a forbidden festival (the Bona Dea; Juv. 6.330), or for creeping out at night for adulterous liaisons (here it is a Gallic hood: *Santonico... cucullo*; Juv. 8.145).

Artistic examples of *cuculli* and *bardoculli* occur mainly on sarcophagi of hunters and shepherds (see Wilson 1938, 92–3 with fig. 56); as in (Fig. 2.3).[17]

Chlamys[18]

The *chlamys* was technically a Greek military cloak, but many Roman sources name it as a luxury item (see below, Chapter 4). It had four corners and a rounded lower edge (Tarbell 1906, 283–4); Pliny states that the shape of Alexandria is like a Macedonian *chlamys,* with indentations in its circumference and projecting corners on its right and left sides (*Nat.* 5.62; and see Strabo *C.* 793; Plut. *Alex.* 26). Isidore states "the *chlamys* is a garment

70 Other aspects of costume

Figure 2.3 Sarcophagus, man in hood. Centrale Montremartini, Rome. Late third–early fourth century CE

that is put on from one side, and not sewn together, but fastened with a brooch" (*chlamys est qui ex una parte induitur, neque consuitur, sed fibula infrenatur; Orig.* 19.24.2). It was shorter than the *pallium* and draped differently, placed over both shoulders and pinned on one.

The earliest mention of this cloak in Latin literature occurs in Pacuvius *Hermiona* 186 (early second century BCE: see Non. 124L). Plautus names it as soldier's clothing (*Epid.* 436), as foreign clothing (*Pers.* 155), and simply as male clothing (*Pseud.* 735 and 1184, *Merc.* 921, *Men.* 658). At *Curc.* 611 a *chlamys* is used as a prize in a dicing game. Cicero mentions that Sulla wore a *chlamys*, and that the statue of Lucius Scipio on the capitol bore a *chlamys* and *crepidae* (Greek sandals; *Pro Rab. Post.* 27). In Statius (*Silv.* 1.1.43), an equestrian statue of Domitian sports the garment. A man in costume as a huntsman wears a tucked-up *chalmys* in Apuleius' *Metamorphoses* (*succinctum*; 11.8).

The cloak is also spoken of several times in literary sources as the clothing of boys (Lucil. 9.71; see Non. 93L). Andromache's gift to Ascanius is a Phrygian *chlamys* (Virg. *A*. 3.484). A *chlamys* and a *fibula* were given to the young Tiberius by Pompeia, sister of Sextus Pompeius, in Sicily, and the articles were kept and exhibited at Baiae (above, Suet. *Tib.* 6.3). By the late second/early third century CE, Ulpian named the *chlamys* as an article of children's clothing: "children's garments (*puerilia*) are clothes used only for this purpose, such as *togae praetextae, aliculae,*[19] *chlamydes,* and *pallia,* in which we are accustomed to dress our children" (*Dig.* 34.2.23.2).

The garment was also the clothing of citharodes (Cic. *Rhet. Ad Her.* 4. 60; Hor. *Epp.* 1.6.40; Sen *Epp.* 76.31), and the subject of metonymy: in Juvenal *Satires* 6.73 and 379 women try to make an actor /musician "undo his *fibula*" (likely of his *chlamys*); in other words, have sex. The *chlamys* was a Greek battle (?) garment and hence likely had the ambiguous status of other Greek garments (see below, on the *pallium*).

Endromis[20]

At Mart. 4.19.4 the garment is described as a mantle to put on during or between athletic activities, as it will protect from the cold or the rain. An "uncouth" present here (*sordida*; or perhaps this means "unfulled;" see Bradley 2002, 22), it is greasy (*pinguis*; that is, water-resistant) and warm. At 14.126 Martial writes: "a poor man's gift it is, but not a poor man's wear/this wrap I send you in lieu of a *laena*" (Leary 1996, 191); presumably then the *endromis* used less material than the *laena.* Because the *endromis* was not fastened it was not a very practical garment (Croom 2002, 51). Juvenal mentions one in Tyrian purple (worn by a female athlete; 6.246), at 3.103 as a wrap simply giving protection from cold. Tertullian (*Pall.* 4.4.1) refers to the garment as "coarse" (*solox*).

Lacerna[21]

The *lacerna* was a probably originally a military cloak (Prop. 3.12.7; 4.3.18; Vell. Pater. 2.70; Ov. *Fast.* 2.746; Kolb 1973, 130–1), adopted in time by civilians (Vell. Pater. 2.80.3–4). It seems not to have come into use until the last century of the Republic, as the name does not appear in Varro, Livy, Plautus, or Terence. The literary passages give no detailed description of the *lacerna*, but it seems to have been a cloak "for all classes and for different occasions" (Wilson 1938, 118; Kolb 1973, 125–7). Sometimes it was worn over a tunic only, or over a toga in cool or inclement weather (Pliny *Nat.* 18.225; Mart. 8.28.22, 12.29.10–11; Kolb 1973, 124–5). It was used as late as the fourth century CE (*HA Carin.* 20.4). Sulpicius (Sev. *Dialog.* 1.21.4) describes it as "flowing." Isidore writes that the *lacerna* was "a fringed *pallium* at one time worn by soldiers" (*pallium fimbriatum quod olim soli milites utebantur*; 19.24.14; there is no evidence from the central period however for the statement that the *lacerna* was fringed). The *lacerna* did not have a hood (Prop 3.12.7; Fest. 105L), and thus a *cucullus* was sometimes worn along with it (Mart. 14.139). Martial's remark at 14.132 (that he sends a present of a *pilleum* [a cap] instead of a whole *lacerna*) is explained by Statius, who speaks of *pillea* stitched from *lacernae*; that is, caps made of pieces cut from an old cloak or from the leftover pieces of a new one (*caesis pillea suta de lacernis; Silv.* 4.9.24; and Wilson 1938, 118).

72 Other aspects of costume

The *lacerna* may have had at one point connotations of a lower-class garment; Cicero professes revulsion for this particular cloak (*Phil.* 2.76). The proper costume for a Roman senator was a toga and *calcei*, not "Gaulish slippers and a *lacerna*" (*nullis nec gallicis nec lacerna*; Cic. *Phil.* 2.76). Horace's adulterer casts off his usual equestrian insignia and hides his perfumed head in a *lacerna* when visiting his married mistress (*S.* 2.7.55). Titus Castricius, while berating his former pupils for their unconventional dress of tunics, *lacernae*, and Gallic shoes admits the tunic and *lacerna* is customary by this time, the first half of the second century CE (Gell. 13.22.1; he references Cicero as well). Suetonius mentions it was worn by *equites* who used to take it off as a show of honor to Claudius (*Claud.* 6). At Juv. 16.45 a *iudex* wears one. *Lacernae* could be thick (Mart. 8.58.1); and rich young men had them in different colors (see below, Chapter 4). On the other hand, *lacernae* were a common present from patron to client: at Pers. 1.54 a *trita lacerna*, a worn-out *lacerna*, is given to a client, and Martial at 6.82.9–12 begs his patron to send him a good *lacerna* so he will not be teased (and see 7.92.7–8). On the *lacernae* of poor men, see below (Chapter 3).

Laena

The *laena* was described by Varro (*L.* 5.133) as the most ancient male garment. Fastened by a *fibula*, it hung from both shoulders, and was circular in shape (Wilson 1938, 113). It was worn as a wrap over clothes when going out to dinner (Mart. 8.59.10; here *laena* is used as a synonym for *pallium*) or worn for protection against the cold. At Mart. 14.138 it is a cloak with a shag: "in wintertime smooth cloth is not much use. My shag makes your mantles warm" (*tempore brumali non multum levia prosunt:/ calfaciunt villi pallia vestra mei*). As a cloak for inclement weather, however, a cloak with a hood offered much more protection. Mart. 12.36 names a short *laena* from a cheap patron (*brevis laena*), even worse at keeping the cold out, although Varro (*L.* 5.133) and Festus (104L), among others, describe the *laena* as "double," perhaps indicating a double thickness of wool, or its size.[22] In Statius, a favorite young slave boy shall not wear a tight *laena* or a narrow *lacerna* (*brevibus constringere laenis /pectora et angusta nolens artare lacerna; Silv.* 2.1.129); presumably voluminous cloaks made with a wealth of material could show status. Non. 868L states the *laena* was a military cloak, an assertion not borne out by other authors. The garment is mentioned as late as the fifth century (Prud. *Hymn Cath.* 7.157).

The *laena* is sometimes equated with other Greek cloaks. According to Festus (104L) the *laena* is the Greek *chlaina*, a small rectangular scarf worn so that the ends were placed over the shoulders, and the rounded section hung over the front in a horseshoe-shape (Bonfante 2003, 50, 102; the *chlaina* is not a garment found in Latin literature, to my knowledge). In addition, we might be tempted to say that the *chlaina* and the *pallium* were the same thing, but in addition to having different shapes, the "*laena* and *pallium* eventually represented two very different garments, after a long process of specialization had taken place: the *laena* became a religious costume, and the *pallium* became the Roman name for the Greek *himation*" (Bonfante 2003, 102; see also 126–7 n. 29). As a ritual garment, the *laena* was worn by the *flamines* and other religious officials (Cic. *Brut.* 56; Serv. *A.* 4.262).

Paenula[23]

The *paenula* was a large, all-enveloping cape (Artem. 2.3) with a hood (Pliny *Nat.* 24.138), designed for cold or wet weather, and worn all over the Western empire (Kolb 1973, 90–3). Seneca (*Ben.* 3.28.5, 5.24.2) infers the *paenula* is the cloak of a soldier (see also Suet. *Nero* 49.4, *Galba* 6.2),[24] but we often hear about the garment in regard to private citizens.

The *paenula* is mentioned as early as Plautus as a protective garment (*Most.* 991; Varr. in Non. 861L). It must therefore have been made of "heavy rain-proof material" (Wilson 1938, 87; Kolb 1973, 89–90; Quint. *Inst.* 6.3.66; Juv. 5.79 – although here the cloak is dripping wet), such as leather (Mart. 14.130 with Leary 1996, 194–5) or *gausapa* (Mart. 14.145; on which see below, Chapter 4). Tacitus (*Orat.* 39) infers that it fitted closely enough about the body to confine the arms.[25] Because it was made of heavy material Wilson was of the opinion that it could not have been fastened with a *fibula* but must have been fastened with strings, thongs, or a clasp (1938, 89). Wilson (1938, 88) also believed that the hood must have had "a recognized and uniform shape."

There is other literary mention as well. At Cic. *Pro Milo.* 54 it is a travelling cloak, and Milo is muffled or entangled in it (*inretitus*); he must fling it back when he starts fighting Clodius' men (29; and see Suet. *Nero* 48.4). To "tear the *paenula*"of a visitor (Cic. *Att.* 13.33.4) meant to beg him to stay, to twist his arm. It is a warm garment at Hor. *Epp.* 1.11.18, and the cape of both a muleteer and a litter-bearer at Sen. *de Ben.* 3.28.5. The perverse Commodus reportedly ordered the populace to come to public shows in the *paenula* instead of the toga (*HA Comm.* 16.6); Alexander Severus allowed old men to assume it in cold weather (formerly it had been only in rainy weather; *HA Alex. Sev* 27.4; see Kolb 1973, 103–6). By the early third century CE the *paenula* was worn by women as well (see *Dig.* 34.2.23.2, above, and Kolb 1973, 107–09). Slaves wear the garment at *Dig.* 34.2.23.2 (*penulae*); makers of *paenulae* (*paenularii*) are mentioned in inscriptional evidence (*CIL* 9.3444, 10.1945).

We hear of the garment in late antiquity as well. The *CT* 14.10.1 (382 CE) states that men who appeared in any public official capacity had to wear the toga; otherwise they were forbidden to assume military dress and did not have to assume the *chalmys*, but they could wear a *paenula* and a tunic (see Kolb 1973, 97–105). By Isidore's time, it was a fringed cloak (*paenula est pallium cum fimbriis longis*; 19.24.14).[26]

Pallium[27]

A common substitution for the toga was the *pallium*, Greek-style cloak. *Pallium* is a Latin word without a Greek derivation.[28] The word the Greeks often used for the *pallium* is *himation*, "but so little loading does the word carry in Greek that authors like Plutarch are happy to use it to refer to the Roman toga."[29] Baroin and Valette-Cagnac are of the opinion however that the *pallium* is a purely Roman invention and in fact can reference any number of different Greek cloaks (*himation, tribon*, etc.). Because of this, they maintain, it is impossible to either reconstruct what the *pallium* looked like or write a history of it (2007, 519). Normally scholars take it as referring to the wide Greek cloak, square-shaped, with four corners and many folds (Bieber 1959, 398). By contrast, the toga was distinguished by the curved edge, *sinus* and *umbo*, and its long end hanging between the feet (ibid., 415).

The *pallium* had the longest history of any of the cloaks worn by the Romans, and Baroin and Valette-Cagnac speak of "cette ambivalence du *pallium*:" it could be male, female, coat, blanket, used instead of the toga or worn overtop it (2007, 524). First mentioned in Plautus and Terence (Pl. *Curc.* 288; Ter. *Phorm.* 844),[30] Greeks are often referred to as *palliati*. It was the characteristic garment of Aesclepius, philosophers, and Christians (Wilson 1938, 80; see Val. Max. 6.9. ext. 1 for a transparent *pallium* on a Greek). Wilson claims Romans always wore a tunic underneath the *pallium* (1938, 81), but Tertullian states that "… this same Cato, by baring his shoulder (*humerum exertus*) at the time of his praetorship, favoured the Greeks no less by his palliate attire" (*haud minus palliato habitu Graecis favit; Pall.* 3.7.3), hinting that Cato at least wore his *pallium* with no tunic underneath. The bronze statue of a boy in a pallium (Fig. 2.4; late first century BC–early first century CE) shows the garment worn with no tunic. The *pallium* is worn with an unbelted tunic at Tert. *Pall.* 5.3.3.

Roman men were excoriated or exonerated for wearing the *pallium*, depending on the circumstances. P. Rutilius Rufus stopped wearing the toga when he fell into the hands of Mithridates at Mytilene and donned a *pallium* and *socci*, as the king showed cruelty to all wearers of the toga.[31] Postumus also had to assume Greek dress upon arriving at Alexandria to take up his position as *dioecetes* (Cic. *Rab. Post.* 28), treasurer of the king's revenues. Rabirius was criticized by his enemies for wearing the *pallium* and "other ornaments not commonly worn by a Roman man" (*aliqua habuisse non Romani hominis insignia*; ibid., 25–6); Cicero points out that he had "to either don the *pallium* at Alexandria in order to wear the toga at Rome, or he had to retain the toga and fling away all his fortunes" (*Rab. Post.* 26). Livy notes that Scipio and his entire troop gave themselves over to *licentia* while in Naples, wearing sandals (*crepidis*) and *pallia* (29.19.11–13; and see Val Max 3.6.1). Decades later, Augustus unreservedly distributed Greek *pallia* to his companions (Suet. *Aug.* 98; Wallace-Hadrill 2008, 38), and his political advisor, the dandiacal Maecenas, seems to have regularly worn it (Sen. *Epp.* 114.6).[32] The

Figure 2.4 Bronze statue of boy in a *pallium*. Late first century BCE–early first century CE. Rome
Art Resource: ART322334

elder Seneca remarked men who declaimed in Latin, went away, changed out of their togas into *pallia*, and came back and declaimed in Greek (*Con.* 9.3.13). Hadrian reportedly only wore the *pallium* to banquets outside Italy (*HA* Hadrian 22.5; Fig. 2.5).[33] When Severus appeared before Marcus Aurelius in a *pallium*, he was given a toga from the emperor's own wardrobe (*HA* Sev. 1.7).

Greek clothing on a Roman man could have had several simultaneous meanings: erudition, culture, effeminacy, wealth, even rejection (for some) of the basic qualities of *Romanitas* or Roman masculinity – conflicting concepts which may have been encapsulated in the *pallium*. An elite Roman could assume the *pallium* occasionally as an outer cloak, but if he entirely discarded

Figure 2.5 Bronze statue of Hadrian in a *himation*. Archaeological Museum, Istanbul. Second century CE
Art Resource: ART405472

the toga for the *pallium*, he was censured no matter where he was living; perhaps this pertained in the middling classes as well. There may well also have been a class resonance. The *pallium* was associated with erudition and effeminacy, but it was also the ordinary rectangular cloak of the regular person; the garment of the non-political and thus the lower classes.[34] Certain authors name it as the dress of slaves (Pl. *fr.* 177, cit. in Isid. *Orig.* 19.24.1; Pl. *Capt.* 779; and see Tert. *Pall.* 5.1.1.1). Perhaps, as Baroin and Valette-Cagnac note, "la signification du pallium n'est pas dissociable du contexte dans lequel il est inséré" (2007, 527), and the most important quality about the *pallium* is that it was not a toga (2007, 550).

Paludamentum[35]

The military cloak called the *paludamentum* was not allowed in the city of Rome except in a triumph or in special rituals, and was the exclusive badge of generals and their staff and later the emperor when on military service (Varro wrote that those wearing *paludamenta* are "conspicuous and well-known;" *L.* 7.37). A garment "of ancient origin" (Florus 1.5.6), the shape of the *paludamentum* was a rectangle, with the lower corners cut away by a diagonal line (Wilson 1938, 103–4). Wilson has noted that all fibula- or brooch-fastened Roman cloaks "have, by one Greek author or another, been called a *chlamys*, Latin authors generally have reserved this comparison for the *paludamentum*, which, in fact, was very like the *chlamys*" (1938, 103; Harlow 2004, 59–60). After the first century CE the garment is less frequently mentioned (Wilson 1938, 101), although the *HA Marc. Aur.* 14 states it was put on by M. Aurelius and Verus in 166 CE when they went out to quell a disturbance in Gaul (this is the sole mention of the *paludamentum* in the *HA*). Amm. 23.3.2 mentions it was worn by Julian in 362 CE.

The *paludamentum* was military garb; something to be laid aside on re-assumption of civic duties (Pliny *Pan.* 56.4). Dyed a deep scarlet or purple, or bleached white (Val. Max. 1.6.11), it was sometimes interwoven with gold, and fell to mid-calf. Isidore states the *paludamentum* was made "distinctive through purple or red and gold" (*paludamentum erat insigne pallium inperatorum cocco purpuraque et auro distinctum; Orig.* 19.24.9).[36] Croom (2002, 52) states the *paludamentum* may be seen on busts of emperors, where it is thickly fringed and pinned with a large circular brooch.

Sagum[37]

At a relatively early date the *sagum* and a smaller version, the *sagulum*,[38] became the cloak of the ordinary Roman soldier (Wilson 1938, 105).[39] Rectangular in shape (App. *Hisp.* 4.42; Suet. *Otho* 2.1; Isid. *Orig.* 19.24.13), it was folded so as to be double for at least a part of its length (Wilson 1938, 106) and could serve as a blanket at night. Both the *sagum* and the *sagulum* may have been of Gallic origin (Polyb. 2.28.7; Var. *L.* 5.167; Caes. *Gall.* 5.42; Diod. 5.30.1; Virg. *A.* 8.660 [in which they are striped]; Strabo 4.6.3; Wilson 1938, 104). Germans (Pomp. Mela 3.3.2; Tac. *Germ.* 17) and Spaniards (Strabo 3.3.4) also wore it.[40] Pliny mentions a Gaetulian shepherd in one (*Nat.* 8.54). Gallic *saga* themselves were rough and flocky (Strabo 4.4.3) and worn with trousers (Tac. *Hist.* 2.20).

Fastened with a *fibula*, the military *sagum* could be quite luxurious. *Saga* and *sagula* are often referred to as glowing, brilliant, or purple in military displays (Sil. Ital. 5.516–17, 17.527; Amm. 29.5.48). We hear of Spanish (Livy 27.19.12; Val. Max. 5.1.7) and purple (Livy 30.17.13,) *sagula*, with gold *fibulae*. Sometimes the *sagum* was also worn by the general (probably purple: Asin. Pollio 57.5; Val. Max. 5.1. ex. 6: a Punic *sagum* is a rich gift). At Sil. Italic. 9.419–22 lictors in the field wear red *sagula*.

Although in the main a piece of military clothing, we occasionally meet with the *sagum* on civilian men. Thus at Tac. *Hist.* 2.20 Caecina (*BNP* Caecina II 1) is criticized for wearing a multi-colored *sagulum* and trousers amidst toga-clad Romans. Martial implies it was worn by poor men (6.11.7–8: a greasy Gallic *sagum*). In the late second/early third century CE, Ulpian states *saga* belong to slaves and men but not women or children (perhaps because of their military origin? *Dig.* 34.2.23.2). And certainly all kinds of people must have worn *saga* in the fourth century CE, given the range of prices in Diocletian's *Edict* (19.60 and 61). As Liu notes, making *saga* and *sagula* was big business in Gaul and elsewhere: there is plenty of inscriptional mention of *sagari, negotiores sagarii,* and *mercatores sagarii* in the *CIL*.[41]

Military dress and armour might be assumed to have had a strong influence on Roman male civilian clothing, but surprisingly this is not so. In fact, it is clear that soldiers were distinguishable from civilians by certain elements of their clothing, such as military sandals (*caligae*; see Goldman 1994b, 122–3), the leather military belt (*cingulum;* Southern 2006, 153), and a shorter tunic (ibid., 154). Most importantly, however, soldiers did not wear the toga (see Sumi 2005, 171). The toga was the garment of Roman civilians, and was in fact the symbol of peace, naturally contrasted with *arma*, the symbol of war. So different was the clothing of Roman soldiers from that of civilians that there were two rituals involving a change of one for the other which were regulated by Roman law.

Military dress ritual: **sagum** *and* **paludamentum**

As a military cloak, the *sagum* became metonymically associated with war (Cic. *Phil.* 5.31, 8.32), and there was ritual connected with it. The *sumere saga*, the formal exchange of the toga for the military cloak, was decreed in the Republican period by the Senate in times of military emergency (Polyb. 2.28.7, 2.30.1; Heskel 1994, 142–3; Wilson 1938, 105), although in some instances an actual announcement is not mentioned, and we are left to wonder whether the Senate directed the change of clothing, or whether the citizens assumed or put off the *sagum* of their own accord. In the Republic, citizens would mourn a defeat by assuming the *sagum*, as when the rebellious Picentes slaughtered the Romans in the town of Asculum in 91 BCE (Livy *Epit.* 72: *saga populus sumpsit*, 73, 118), and celebrate a victory by taking it off (consul L. Julius Caesar's victory over the Samnites in 90 BCE, for example; *ob eam victoriam Romae saga posita sunt*; Livy *Epit.* 73; *BNP* Iulius I 5). Sometimes the garment would be worn continually by senators when there was a war on (Cic. *Phil.* 8.32). Cicero wished that the *sumere saga* be enacted against Anthony: "I say that a state of tumult should be declared, a vacation of the Courts proclaimed, the *sagum* assumed, a levy held" (*tumultum decerni, iustitium edici, saga sumi dico oportere, dilectum haberi...*: Cic. *Phil.* 5.31). In 43 BCE Cicero cautioned against citizens setting aside their *saga*, which they had assumed out of fear for Brutus' life, until Brutus was safely out of Mutina; recommending they reserve "the return to the garb of peace for the completion of victory" (Cic. *Phil.* 14.1: *reditum ad vestitum confectae victoriae reservate*).

Assuming the *sagum* or putting it aside was a visualization of the patriotic solidarity the citizens felt in their fortunes in war (although Dio 41.17 reports that citizens in 49 BCE changed back to the toga out fear of Caesar). Certain types of cloaks "were a distinctive sign of military service, for 'taking the cloak,' as a figure of speech, meant 'going to war,' just as 'wearing the cloak' was an expression for 'being at war'" (Speidel 2012, 9). Thus Vellieus Paterculus states that the Social War of the first century BCE went so badly for the Romans that "the Romans were compelled to resort to the *sagum*, and to remain long in that garb" (*utque ad saga iretur diuque in eo habitu maneretur*; 2.16.4). Cicero in his sixth *Philippic* tells his fellow-citizens "we must come to the *saga*," (i.e., go to war: *ad saga iretur; Phil.* 6.9).

In the empire, citizens no longer donned or doffed this cloak *en masse* as a visualization of Rome's military undertakings, although the symbolism inherent in the *sagum* remained potent. Vitellius and his companions entered Rome in their military cloaks, for which they were not forgiven (Suet. *Vit.* 11.1), while "the emperor Marcus Aurelius was praised because he would not allow his soldiers to wear their military cloaks in Italy" (*HA* Marc. 27.3).

Ritual was also involved in the assumption of the *paludamentum*. In the Republic, before going out to his theatre of war, the consul would offer vows in the Capitol surrounded by lictors in *paludamenta* (Livy 45.39.11). When the consul Gaius Claudius set out from Rome in 177 BCE to take command of the army in Illyricum without having first executed this ceremony, the soldiers reportedly refused to recognize his leadership. Without the ritual formalities, he was thought not to have the legal right to command, and Gaius was forced to return to Rome and perform the rites (Livy 41.10.5–9; *BNP* Claudius I 27). It is not known whether the *paludamentum* was worn into battle, but in death the garment was the badge of the general whether or not his campaign had been successful (thus Antony orders Brutus to be buried in his *paludamentum* at Val. Max. 5.1.11).

Despite this, the symbolic power of the cloak seems to have changed little over first few centuries of the Christian era. The phrase *paludamento mutare praetextam* ('to change the bordered toga for the general's cloak') meant to change civil administration for military command (Isid. *Orig.* 19.24.9). Or conversely, when Sidonius writes *qui invident tunicatis otia stipendia paludatis* (*Epp.* 5.7.3), he means to change to civil life from the military.

Other cloaks

Varro mentions a *gaunaca*, a heavy oriental cloak shaggy on both sides (*in his multa peregrina ut gaunaca et amphimallum graeca; L.* 5.167). In the *CIL* we find a *gaunacarius,* a maker of these cloaks (6.9431). The word may refer to a cloak made of *gausapa* (on which see below, Chapter 4).

Hats

Most men in the central period do not seem to have worn hats regularly, although hoods were known (see above). Several authors refer to the *causea*, a piece of headgear which originated in Macedonia and was a sunhat (Dalby 2000, 156; Leary 1996, 82). In Plautus, such hats are worn for the purposes of disguise: a man masquerading as a sea captain has a rust-colored *causea* at Plaut. *Mil.* 1178; a man posing as a foreign traveler wears one at *Pers.* 155. In Valerius Maximus, the Hellenistic king Antigonus sports a broad-brimmed worn "after the Macedonian fashion" (*more Macedonum*; 5.1.ext.4). A *causea* is a gift at Mart. 14.29, its wide brim standing in for the awnings at Pompey's theatre. It may have been similar in form to the *petasus*, another sunhat (worn by gods at Pl. *Am.* 143, 145; see also *Ps.* 735). Augustus wore one outdoors (Suet. *Aug.* 82). A brimless, tight-fitting cap made of leather, the *galericulum*, was worn by charioteers and wrestlers (Croom 2002, 69; Mart. 14.50; Leary 1996, 106). Hats do not seem to have been worn as a fashion item until the late third century CE (Croom 2002, 68).

The *pilleus* or *pilleum* was a brimless conical hat, of felt or leather, worn by freed slaves in the central period to symbolize their freedom, perhaps shaving their heads first (Pl. *Amph.* 462), and paying a visit to the temple of Feronia (Serv. *A.* 8.564). To judge from artistic evidence, slaves who had been freed by testament wore the *pilleus* at the master or mistress' funeral (as on the relief on the Tomb of the Haterii).[42] Freeborn persons who had been captured also wore the *pilleus* for a short time after recovering their freedom (Livy 30.45; see also 33.23; Val. Max. 5.2.5–6). After the murder of Julius Caesar the *pilleus* was stamped on certain coins of Brutus, to symbolize Rome's new-found freedom from Caesar's tyranny (see also Suet. *Nero* 57).[43] The Roman populace is also said to have worn it during the Saturnalia (Mart. 11.6.4). The Roman habit of conflating rank and articles of dress is seen in the phrase *servos ad pilleum vocare* ('to call slaves to the *pilleus*'): it meant to summon them to freedom (Pl. *Amph.* 462 [in which *pilleum capire* means to gain freedom]; Livy 24.32.9; Sen. *Epp.* 47.18; Suet. *Tib.* 4.2; Macr. 1.11.12; and see Val. Max. 8.6.2). The cap was also the subject of other kinds of metonymy: in a fragment of Plautus a free man addresses a slave as "my cap, my friend, my health" (*pilleum meum, mi sodalis, mea salubritas*; Non 325L, with Ehrman 1993, 277–80).

Undergarments, leggings, and chest coverings[44]

There are some literary references to specifically male 'underclothes' in the form of briefs or loincloths (the *subligaculum*, the *campestre*, the *licium*). Cicero refers to the *subligaculum* ('that which is girded up from below;' probably put on diaper-like) as a loincloth worn by actors (Cic. *Off.* 1.129; Non. 42L). Horace mentions a loincloth/briefs, the *campestre*, which must have been of a skimpy nature, as he states that it would not be comfortable to wear when a snowy wind is blowing (*Epp.* 1.11.18; see also August. *CD* 14.17; Isid. *Orig.* 19.22.5). It was possibly put on under the toga if the tunic was not worn (Plut. *Cat. Min.* 6.3). The mill slaves in Apuleius' *Metamorphoses* are also wearing loincloths, a symbol of their degraded condition: "some had thrown on a tiny cloth that just covered their loins" (Apul. *Met.* 9.12).

The *subligar* may have been equivalent to the *subligaculum* (and in fact the similarity of their etymology may indicate the interrelationship). Pliny states it was worn by workers gathering and refining incense; Juvenal names it as an actor's garment (Pliny *Nat.* 12.59; Juv. 6.70). Unfortunately, due to the paucity of evidence, there is no way to tell if there were any differences between the *subligar, subligaculum, campestre,* and *licium.* The *subligaculum* (and the like) is mentioned only in relation to actors, workers, slaves, and athletes. It seems unlikely that Roman men wore briefs as everyday wear under their tunic.[45]

The usual underwear for men (and women) was the *tunica intima*, or undertunic, called the *subucula*.[46] Horace is indignant that a tattered *subucula* beneath his silky tunic is a subject for ridicule. Besides indicating that it was worn by men, this passage also suggests that it may have been visible.[47] Augustus wore a *subucula* as protection against the cold (Suet. *Aug.* 82).

The *thorax* or *capitium*[48] was a chest-protector, worn under the tunic by men and women in cold weather by Augustus (Suet. *Aug.* 82), and by invalids (see Hopman 2003, 567). The *thorax* given by a man to his client's son at Juv. 5.143 is green in color, perhaps marking it as insultingly effeminate (Hopman 2003, 567).

Feminalia or *fascia/fasciola* refer to bands worn about the thighs due to cold or ill-health (Hor. *S.* 2.3.255; Suet. *Aug.* 82; Quint. *Inst.* 11.3.144) or as military wear,[49] also assumed by athletes (Juv. 6.263) and hunters (Petr. *Satyr.* 40). Although *fascia* in the plural seems usually to mean leg coverings,[50] *fascia/fasciola* is simply the generic Latin term for bandage or wrapping, and thus can refer to such a wrap used as a brassiere, as a head ribbon, or even swaddling bandages (thus Val. Max. 6.2.7; *HA* Clodii Albini 5.9.3; Croom 2002, 93–5). A *tibiale* was similar in form, but protected the lower part of the leg.[51] A possible reference to Pompey's foppish demeanor is found at *Att.* 2.3.1: "I didn't like the look of his *caligae* and white leggings," writes Cicero (*fasciae cretatae*; see Val. Max. 6.2.7). Possibly the Romans associated leggings not only with the barbarian of the northern provinces ('*bracati*') but also with physical and mental weakness (Harlow 2004, 47 n. 7, 48, 64). Trousers did eventually make it into mainstream Roman dress: by the sixth century CE a complete reversal had come about, and long sleeves, fitted tunic, and trousers had become the court dress of the Roman emperor (Harlow 2004, 67).

Footwear[52]

Ideally, shoes reflected Roman ideas of status, rank, trade, and profession: "all wore distinctive dress and footwear, appropriate to their roles in life" (Goldman 1994b, 101). It was also important "for a respectable man to wear the correct form of shoe in the correct circumstances" (Croom 2002, 60). Due to gaps in the evidence there is a serious lack of awareness of the changes which took place in Roman footwear over time, a problem compounded by linguistic challenges. "There are a number of different words for shoes, boots, slippers and socks, not all of which are easy to identify fully, particularly when they are compared to surviving shoes from the archaeological record or indeed the evidence from art" (Croom 2002, 60). The *Edict* lists a number of different shoes and boots, "illustrating some of the available range" (Croom 2002, 63), but often the intended sex of the wearer is often not identified.

Holleran has noted that *tabernae sutrinae* were where shoes were made (Holleran 2012, 123, and Tac. *Ann*. 15.34, Hor. *S*. 1.3.131–2, 2.3.106; Sen. *Ben*. 7.21.1–2). Della Corte identified the *taberna* at VII.1.41–2 in Pompeii as a *taberna sutrina*: it contained a stone bench, knives, hooks for stretching leather, a pair of tongs, three bronze needles, and two small jars of what might be *atramentum*, black shoe dye (see Della Corte 1965, 185). On a wall is scratched: "On the day before the ides of July I repaired the angular chisel and the shoemaker's thonged (?) awl" (*CIL* 4.1712; see Pliny *Nat*. 34.123). Shoes may have been displayed outside the shop: a raven befouls such a display at Pliny *Nat*. 10.121–2 (see Holleran 2012, 124). Cobblers also mended shoes (Mart. 9.73, 12.59).

Shoes were made of vegetable- or alum-tanned leather, and became waterlogged fast. A wet shoe is sometimes used as an example of something loose or baggy (Mart. 11.21.4) and shapeless shoes invited ridicule (Ov. *Ars* 1. 514–16). Some surviving shoes however show fine workmanship and sophistication,[53] and examples from Vindolanda show a comparatively rapid succession of new styles (van Driel-Murray 2001, 191). The adoption of Roman footwear in Roman Britain also "represents an entirely new way of using clothing in social communication, drawing on concept and symbolism which were widely understood at all levels of society" (van Driel-Murray 2001, 186). Roman shoes were often hobnailed on the sole to make them last longer (Croom 2002, 61; Flavius Josephus 6.1.8), and examination of some surviving shoes from Vindolanda reveals the hobnails placed in such a way as to compensate for foot or gait problems.[54]

Calcei[55]

The *calceus* or ankleboot was an Etruscan import to Rome (Bonfante-Warren 2003, 61), and was worn by male citizens of all classes. Croom (2002, 61–2) has excellent descriptions of each of the types of *calcei*, and it is this account I follow here. The first type of *calceus* was a plain close-toed ankle boot, worn by poorer citizens. In artistic evidence, it has a characteristic ridge across the instep (see Fig. 2.6; and Croom 2002, 61) but it is not known how it was put on and fastened (see Goette 1988, 459–64). In the fresco from the bakery at Pompeii (Fig. 2.7), all the customers wear dark-brown *calcei*.

The second type of *calceus* was worn open down the front, often with a tongue, fastened by two straps attached to the side of the shoe which were

Figure 2.6 Patrician, 'equestrian,' and senatorial *calcei* (rendered by D. Fletcher). After Goette 1988, 459.

Figure 2.7 Fresco: distribution of bread in a bakery at Pompeii. Museo Archeologico Nazionale, Naples. Late first century CE
Art Resource: AA325902

wrapped a number of times around the ankle, with the long ends left dangling (see Fig. 2.6; Croom 2002, 61; Goette [1988, 457–9] calls this the *calceus senatorius*). The third form had an extra set of straps tied halfway up the calf so there were two knots at the front; the ends of this knot, often longer than the ends of the lower knot, were often tucked under the other straps (see Figs. 2.6 and 2.8; thus *patricios calceos Romulus reperit IV corrigiarum assutaque luna*; Isid. *Orig.* 19.34.4; Seneca refers to *lora patricia*, patrician shoe-straps; *de Tranq.* 9.11.9). Goette (1988, 452–7) calls this *calceus patricius*; Goldman (1994b, 119) collapses the last two types of shoe-boot into one. In artistic representations of these two types of *calcei*, the leather is depicted as being so soft and fine that the toes are visible through the shoe.

Although scholars give their own labels to different types of footwear, as Croom notes (2002, 62), "the exact distinction between ankle boots for the two ranks [senator and *eques*] is unclear and even the evidence for color is contradictory." Varro complicates the matter, stating that while Romans

Figure 2.8 Detail, statue of Augustus from the Via Labicana. Museo Nazionale Romano (Palazzo Massimo alle Terme), Rome. First century CE
Photo: author

distinguished between men's and women's *calcei,* "we know that women sometimes wear men's shoes, and men women's" (*cum tamen sciamus nonnunquam et mulierem habere calceos viriles et virum muliebris; L.* 9.40). Although ancient literary sources are largely unhelpful, types of *calcei* looked different enough, at least by the fourth century, to be listed separately in Diocletian's *Edict: calcei patricii* were sold at most for 150 *denarii* per pair; *calcei senatorii* cost 100; equestrian *calcei* are listed at 70 *denarii* (*Edict* 9.7–9).

Calcei senatorii were worn by those who had attained magistrate status. They (or at least the straps) appear to have been black in color (Hor. *S.* 1.6.27–8, here the straps of the shoes come halfway up the leg; Juv. *Sat.* 7.191–2). The *calceus* worn by those of patrician descent was called the *mulleus* (see Pliny *Nat.* 9.65; also Paul *ex Fest.* 129L; Dio 43.43.2; Mart. 2.29), perhaps because its purplish-red color was similar to that of the mullet fish.[56] Isidore describes the shoe thus: "*mullei* are similar to *cothurni*, with elevated soles, but the upper part has a small mallet (? – *malleolus*) of bone or brass, to which thongs are fastened. They are named from their red color, the sort of color a mullet fish [*mullus*] has."[57] The costume of the cavalry in early Rome in the regal period is said to have been striped tunics and red *mullei* – insignia which later became adopted by patricians (Alföldy 1985, 7–8). One scholar believes that when men of former equestrian rank began to be enrolled as senators, "the color distinction of the more outstanding red would have provided an excellent way to distinguish the landed gentry from the *nouveaux riches*" (Goldman 1994b, 119). But as with many items of clothing, we must be aware that this may represent an ideal sartorial situation, not quotidian reality.

In addition, the red patrician shoe-boot, not the black senatorial one, was ornamented with the *luna*, a crescent-shaped decoration in one of the ties (Mart. 2.29; *patricia luna*; Stat. *Silv.* 5.2.28).[58] Isidore states that Romulus invented the *luna*, sewn into the four laces of the *calceus*, and that only patricians used to wear them. "The moon on them did not represent the image of the celestial body," he writes, "but a sign of the number 100 [i.e., C], because in the beginning there were one hundred patrician senators" (*Orig.* 19.34.4). Elsewhere, Martial writes of country life: "nowhere will you see a crescent shoebuckle or a toga or clothes that smell of purple dye" (*lunata nusquam pellis et nusquam toga/olidaeque vestes murice*; 1.49.31–2). Juvenal (*S.* 7.192) describes a *luna* on a black senatorial shoe, perhaps an example of someone who did not understand the subtle language of upper-class dress.[59] This shoe ornament unfortunately appears nowhere in the artistic record and perhaps was a comparatively short-lived item (Croom 2002, 62; Goldman 1994b, 119).

Wearing *calcei*, whatever their color, emphasized one's formal and correct Romanness. Thus Scipio Africanus (*BNP* Cornelius I 70) who is at home, puts on his *calcei* to greet his guest Laelius and walk in the garden (Cic. *Rep.* 1.18). Milo changes out of his *calcei* when he returns home from the Senate (Cic. *Pro Mil.* 28). Caesar's tunic is belted and he keeps his *calcei* on even though he is being held prisoner by pirates (Vell. 2.41). A fragment of the

Greek historian Nicolaos recounts a story of Caesar's later life in which he ran shoeless out into the streets on hearing of Octavian's illness, indicating his frantic alarm (*FGrH* 90.127.9; see Kraus 2005, 109). Suetonius criticizes both Caligula (*Calig.* 52) and Nero (who is *discalciatus*; *Nero* 51) for not wearing *calcei*.

Sandals: crepidae *and* soleae

Sandals, or footgear "which cover the bottom of the soles, and are bound on by slender thongs" (Gell. *NA* 13.22) are called by a number of terms in the ancient sources: *gallicae* (translated as 'Gallic slippers;' on which see below, Chapter 4), *soleae*, and *crepidae/crepidulae* (from the Greek word for sandals). The literary sources are not clear on the differences between and amongst these, although Horace does distinguish between *crepidae* and *soleae* (*crepidas sibi numquam nec soleas fecit; S.* 1.3.127–8).

Delicate sandals were indoor shoes and may have marked the wearer out as a man of sophistication, although some thought they were inappropriate for upper-class men if worn out-of-doors (Suet. *Calig.* 52). They were certainly not proper shoes to wear with the toga, as Croom has noted (2002, 60).[60] *Soleae* may have been worn specifically inside the house or at the baths: Trimalchio is also described as *soleatus* at the baths at *Satyr.* 27.2; at Mart. 12.82.6 a man puts on *soleae* after his bath (although the point may be that he came to the bath wearing them). At Seneca *Contr.* 9.2.25 a Roman praetor is improperly shod in *soleae*. Martial (3.50.3) tells us sandals are brought or worn to dinner, and then removed when one reclines at table. He refers elsewhere to sandals lined with wool (*soleae lanatae*; 14.65: Leary 1996, 123–4).

Boots

According to Dio, the footwear which Julius Caesar sometimes used was "high and of a reddish color, after the style of the kings who had once reigned in Alba, for he claimed that he was related to them through Iulus" (Dio 43.43.1). Martial (14.140; with Leary 1996, 204–5) mentions *udones*, socks or moccasins made from felted goat hair.[61] A *pero* was a boot, although how it differed from the *calceus* is unclear. Juvenal (14.186) refers to a *pero* as protection against frost.

Shoe metonymy

The terms for shoes, mainly *calcei*, slipped into common phrases. In Plautus, a character states "now I don't care at all what shoes I wear;" i.e., what unbecoming thing I do (*nec mi adeo est tantillum pensi iam, quos capiam calceos; Truc.* 765). The phrase *calceos mutare* "to change (into) *calcei*" could mean "to become a senator" (Cic. *Phil.* 13.28); to assume the symbols of rank of the office was equivalent to holding the office itself. To call for *calcei* when one was reclining (*calceos poscere*) meant to rise from dinner (Pliny

Epp. 9.17.3). At Hor. *S.* 2.8.77, a rich host "calls for his sandals" (*soleas poscere*; see Pl. *Truc.* 363, 367).

Conclusions

In this chapter I have gathered together evidence for the other elements of male dress. Some of these encapsulated rank: the *bulla*, the gold ring of the *eques*, *calcei*, while some were essentially classless: undergarments, cloaks, mantles, and capes. Far from showing rank, cloaks covered up the distinctive signs of class, which may be one reason they are sometimes frowned upon by the ancient authors, who like to imagine every male in his ideal dress (although of course cloaks could be luxury items depending on fabric, dye, and ornamentation: see below, Chapter 4). Certain items of clothing could even encapsulate rank *and* status in a contradictory manner, such as the *pallium*. The garment of the everyday man, it also marked one's status as an member of the intelligentsia, well-versed in Greek culture and the uses of *otium*. The *pilleus*, worn by freed slaves and by the free population (or some of them) during the Saturnalia, symbolized juridical freedom but also liberty from quotidian social categories and behavior. Even the *anulus aureus*, which was supposed to be assumed by the equestrian alone in the imperial period, was counterfeited in gold and iron and worn by those outside this rank as a mark of status. Rank and status were intertwined in sometimes incongruous ways, and nowhere is this more evident than in a discussion of the clothing of the poor and Roman mourning garments, and the assumption of abasement and humility, the subject of the next chapter.

Notes

1 On the *bulla,* see Isid. *Orig.* 19.31.11; Dolansky 2008, 62–3, nn. 15–16; Goette 1986; Rawson 2003, 28, 29, 44, 45, 50, 51, 144–5; Palmer 1998; Warden 1983.
2 See Var. *L.* 7.107; Macr. 1.6.9–10, 14, 17; Palmer 1998, 19–21.
3 Pliny *Nat.* 8.194; Fest. 276L; Plut. *QR* 271E. Priscus was traditionally the fifth king of Rome (616–579 BCE).
4 On rings in antiquity, see Marshall 1907; Hawley 2007; Reinhold 1971, 284–7; Stout 1994.
5 The elder Pliny grumbled that rings, traditionally worn on the fourth finger of the left hand, were hidden anyway by the voluminous folds of a man's toga (*Nat.* 33.13); but the fashion next was for the first finger, and finally the little finger (*Nat.* 33.24; Pollux 5.100f; see Marshall 1907, xxvii).
6 Such as that at the Caudine Forks: Livy 9.7.8; and see below, Chapter 3. "Hence it is pretty certain that all senators at that date must have had the right of wearing the gold ring, though many conservative persons refused to avail themselves of it" (Marshall 1907, xix).
7 Macr. 3.14.13; *BNP* Roscius I 4; Reinhold 1971, 285–7; and Stout 1994, 78.
8 Pliny *Nat.* 33.33; see also Suet. *Claud.* 25, and Reinhold 1971, 286. Beginning with Commodus, however, bestowing fictive *ingenuitas* became separate from bestowing equestrian rank and was usually done via the *ius anuli aurei* (Reinhold 1971, 287, with references).

88 Other aspects of costume

9. On the *Lex Visellia*, see *Cod. Just.* 9.21, 9.31, and 10.33.1; *Cod Theod.* 9.20; Reinhold 1971, 286.
10. But Courtney asserts: "the iron ring in Juvenal's day was the mark of plebeians; *equites* and senators wore a gold one" (1980, 506–7; cf. Juv. 7.88).
11. On usurpation, see Reinhold 1971.
12. On male capes and cloaks, see Croom 2002, 49–55; Kampen 1981, 54–5; Kolb 1973; Wilson 1938, 76–129.
13. Isidore, writing in the sixth century CE, names as types of cloaks the *birrus, casula, cucullus, lacerna, paenula*, and *reno* (Isid. *Orig.* 19.23.4, 19.24.14–20), many of which I have not covered here due to a) considerations of space and b) the fact that the terms do not occur in classical Latin. Diocletian's *Edict* of 301 CE names the *birrus* (7.42–3, 19.26; 19.33–42 a number of *birri* from different parts of the Roman empire [Brittanic, Numidian, etc.]; "Laodiceian, resembling one from the Nervii" [19.27, and 19.32], and 22.21–3 likewise, the *carcalla* (7.44–5, 26.120–137), the *sagum* (7.60–1, 19.60–1; the prices range from 500 to 8,000 *denarii*), the *chlamys* and *chlanis* (19.1a, 19.57–8, 22.1a, 22.16–17, 22.20), dalmatics (19.8–9, 19.12–14a, 19.14d, and possibly 14b–c and 14e–h, 19.28, 19.30–1, 19.63, 22.5–6, 8, 10–13; 26.39–43, 26.49–53, 26.59–63, 26.72–7, 29.23–37), the *paenula* (19.31), cloaks "with clasps" from different parts of the empire (*fibulatorium* in the Greek, as no Latin has survived: 19.15–16 and 53–6, 22.18–19).
14. Military cloaks other than the *sagum* often had a curved edge so the cloth in the front hung in graceful folds; civilian cloaks seem often to have had a straight edge: Croom 2002, 52.
15. Paper by Clemence Schultze at the 'Addressing Dress' panel, Celtic conference 2010, Edinburgh, UK.
16. The little conical paper containers used by chemists for spices were also called *cuculli* (Mart. 3.2.5). It may be that "Classical authors associated the [*cucullus*]… specifically with the Gauls" (Epstein 1994, 101 n. 2). Courtney states that "*cucullus* is probably a Gallic word" (1980, 406, with references).
17. On evidence for the Celtic *genius cucullatus* (stone altar pieces and small votive figures in rock and bronze which have been discovered at various Romano-British and Gaulish sites and show hooded figures), see Epstein 1994.
18. On the Greek *chlamys*, see Lee 2015, 116–18 and Tarbell 1906. On the Roman *chlamys*, see Croom 2002, 52; Wilson 1938, 86, 103, 125.
19. The *alicula* was also a cloak or short coat of some sort: at Petron. *Satyr.* 40.5 a slave dressed as a hunter wears it (made of silk); at Mart. 12.81.2 it is the gift of a poor man.
20. On the *endromis*, see Croom 2002, 51; Leary 1996, 191.
21. Bonfante (2003, 126 n. 29) states the word *lacerna* was Etruscan (indicated by the suffix – *erna*). On the *lacerna*, see Bonfante-Warren 1973, 608; Croom 2002, 52; Courtney 1980, 430–31; Kolb 1973, 116–35; Wilson 1938, 94, 95, 117–25.
22. On 'double' garments, see Casson 1983. On the *laena* as 'double,' see Varro *L.* 5.133; Hor. *Epp.* 1.17.25; Tert. *Pall.* 5.3.1; Serv. *A.* 4.262; Isid. *Orig.* 19.24.11.
23. On the *paenula*, see Kampen 1981, 55; Kolb 1973, 73–116; Williams 2004, 194; Wilson 1938, 87–92.
24. On the *paenula* in the Roman army, see Kolb 1973, 110–14; Sumner 2009, 73–5.
25. On the shape of the *paenula*, see Kolb 1973, 76–87; on Gallic *paenulae*, 88–9.
26. On the *paenula* as a Christian and ecclesiastical mantle, see Kolb 1973, 114–16.
27. On the *pallium*, see Brennan 2008; Hunink 2005; Olson 2014b (with references); Pausch 2008, 26–8; Wallace-Hadrill 2008, 41–60; Wilson 1938, 78–83.
28. The word *pallium* is found in later Christian Greek writing ("none earlier than the second century CE, overwhelmingly from late antique and Byzantine sources") and is taken to be a derivative of the Latin word (Wallace-Hadrill 2008, 50–1; quote at 51 n. 35).

29 e.g., Plut. *Brutus* 17, *Coriolanus* 14; and see Ter. *Pall.* 3.7.2; Isid. *Orig.* 19.24.1. Quote: Wallace-Hadrill 2008, 51. See also Wilson 1938, 80. On Greek terms for Roman clothing in Dio Cassius, see Freyburger-Galland 1993 (esp. 120).
30 On the *pallium* in comedy, see Baroin and Valette-Cagnac 2007, 530–2.
31 Cic. *Rab. Post.* 27; *BNP* Rutilius I 3.
32 Apparently he wore it wrapped around his head with his ears sticking out, like a mime actor.
33 On the *pallium* and the banquet, see Baroin and Valette-Cagnac 2007, 534–7.
34 See Tert. *Pall.* 5.4.2; Olson 2014b, 432; Turcan 2007, 208–12.
35 On the *paludamentum,* see Livy 1.26.2, 9.5, 25.16.21; Val. Max. 1.6.11; Pliny *Nat.* 22.3, 33.63; Tac. *Ann.* 12.56; Isid. 19.24.9; Heskel 1994, 134; Wilson 1938, 100–4.
36 Agrippina's was purely of gold (Pliny *Nat.* 33.63; cf. Tac. *Ann.* 12.56.5).
37 On the *sagum,* see Bonfante-Warren 1973, 611; Liu 2009, 75–6; Sumner 2009, 81–3; Wilson 1938, 104–9.
38 On the *sagulum,* see Suet. *Vit.* 11, in which the nasty Vitellius' troops enter Rome in *saqula*; Flor. *Verg.* P. 187R: *utrum praeclarius sit sagulis an praetextatis inperare* (Rossbach 1896: 187). See also Cic. *Pis.* 55; Livy 7.34.15.
39 Publius Decius disguises himself by assuming a soldier's *sagulum,* so it must have been different from an officer's cloak (Livy 7.34.15; *BNP* Decius I 2).
40 A garment called a *sagochlamys* is mentioned in a list of military garments/tribute at *HA Claud.* 14.3.
41 *CIL* 4.753 (Pompeii); 6.9864, 9872 (Rome); 9.1872 (Puteoli); 12.1928, 12.1930, 12.4509 (Gallia Narbonensis), 5.5925, 5928, 5929, 6773 (Gallia Transpadana). See Lovén 1998, 76; Liu 2009, 76–7 n. 92. It seems however that *sagarii* formed *collegia* only in Rome (*CIL* 6.339 and 956) and Lugdunum, with perhaps loose groups of them in Pompeii (*CIL* 4.753) and Thuburbo Maius (Africa Proconsularis; Liu 2009, 76–7).
42 On this frieze, see now Leach 2006, with references.
43 See Howgego 1995, no. 107 (43–42 BCE); *RRC* 508/3.
44 On male underwear, see Olson 2003, 205–10.
45 Croom (2002, 59) however links the practice of wearing a *subligaculum* under the tunic to the length of the tunic worn.
46 On the tunic as underwear, see Olson 2003, 210; Pausch 2008, 143–9.
47 *si forte subucula pexae/ trita subest tunicae* (Hor. *Epp.* 1.1.95–6); Croom (2002, 39) notes that the undertunic is not visible in Roman art until the third or fourth century CE.
48 *Capitium*: see Var. *L.* 5.131 and Gell. 16.7.9 (indeterminate).
49 See Wilson 1938, 73; Croom 2002, 56–7. On military leggings, see Wilson 1938, 73–5. Mentioned: Isid. *Orig.* 19.22.29–30.
50 At Pliny *Nat.* 8.221 mice gnaw at the *fascia* which the general Carbo was accustomed to wear inside his *calcei* (*in calceatu utebatur*): an evil omen, as Carbo later lost his life in Africa (*BNP* Papirius I 9).
51 Wilson 1938, 73; Suet. *Aug.* 82. In *Dig.* 49.16.14.1 the *tibiale* is spoken of as part of a soldier's armour.
52 On Roman footwear, see Croom 2002, 59–64; Goette 1988; Goldman 1994b; Greene forthcoming; van Driel-Murray 1987 and 2001.
53 For examples see van Driel-Murray 2001, 188 fig. 1.
54 See Greene forthcoming. My thanks to Prof. Greene for sharing her findings with me.
55 On the *calceus,* see Bonfante 2003, 61, 64, 65; Croom 2002, 61–2; Goldman 1994b, 116–22; Goette 1988, 449–64; Kampen 1981, 54; Cic. *Phil.* 2.76, *Inv.* 1.47; Hor. *Epp.* 1.10.42; Quint. *Inst.* 6.3.74, 11.3.137, 143; Pliny *Epp.* 7.3.2, Suet. *Otho* 6.3, *Aug.* 92.
56 Goette 1988, 444–8 has a different interpretation of the *mulleus*: the lion-boot. Bonfante 2003 (61) has noted that red, high-topped, laced decorated boots are

found on Spartan and Ionian figures in Greek art in the second quarter of the sixth century BCE, and came to Etruria by way of Magna Graecia (perhaps a variant of the Greek *endromides*).
57 19.34.10; intriguingly, Suetonius reports that Augustus' *calcei* were rather high-soled, to make him look taller than he really was (*calciamentis altiusculis; Aug.* 73).
58 Williams 2004, 117; Contra Barié and Schindler 1999 and the *OLD* (s.v. '*lunatus*'). See Citroni 1975 at Mart. 1.49.31 for conflicting allusions to this ornament.
59 Some editors delete this line altogether: e.g., Jahn 1843; Scholte 1873. See Courtney 1980, 374.
60 Women wear *soleae* as well (Prop. 2.29.40; Ovid *Ars* 2.212; Pers. 5.169).
61 *Udones* are among the presents sent to a soldier at Vindolanda: Tablet 38.1–4 (Bowman and Thomas 1983. On ancient felt and felt-making, see Barber 1991, 215–22; Forbes 1964, 90–3. Felt was produced in the *tabernae coactiliariae* (Holleran 2012, 122–3; see HA *Pert.* 3.3). The woven cloth or garment was pounded, stamped on, or kneaded in wet and preferably warm conditions until the surface was matted to the degree required (lightly to heavily felted; Barber 1991, 216). During the process the weave could become obscured (felting is less prevalent in societies which use patterned fabrics, as the procedure tends to muddy the pattern; Barber 1991, 218), but the cloth kept out wind and moisture better. Heavily felted or fulled cloth could matt or felt the wool so thoroughly that the weave could not come undone; and it was possible to cut such cloth without having to hem or bind edges (ibid.; handy for rain capes and such at Rome).

3 Poverty, mourning, and *sordes*

> "But since the fullers were accustomed to wash stains (*maculas*) from white clothing (*albarum vestium*), and there would be no need of their services if people wore black clothing (*atris vestibus*), Varro said very neatly that the fullers feared the owl because mourning drove them to poverty (*luctus eos ad inopiam adigat*)"
>
> (Turnebus, Adversaria 29.27. Varr. Men. 439, in Non. 498L).

Varro's statement encapsulates nicely the myriad of ways in which the Romans thought about 'dark' clothing: as mourning, as stained/dirty, and as the clothing of the poor. In this chapter I look at clothing of the poor, dirt, mourning, courtroom drama, and abjection; the *togula* (little toga), threadbare cloaks, rituals of mourning, and black clothing. All these things are connected in the Roman status hierarchy, and demonstrate well the complexity of ancient visual culture, the polyvalent nature of clothing, and how circumstances and wearer determined sartorial meaning. Roman dress for the upper classes signified at the personal and political level, and the public display of the body in mourning clothing or *sordes* carried a political charge.[1]

Lower class men

Ancient literary sources give us some incidental details of the clothing of the poor. When a tunic was thin or short, as the tunics of poorer men perhaps were, the term used in several authors is *tunicula*.[2] A short tunic could indicate one was a manual laborer: artistic evidence shows artisans and workers wore tunics which fell (or were belted) above the knees.[3] Artemidorus thought that to dream one was wearing a short, indecent costume signified losses and unemployment (*Oneir.* 2.3). Tunics worn off one shoulder, often called the 'knotted tunic' or the *exomis*, are sometimes shown on laborers; it is not known how common this type of tunic was (Croom 2002, 39).[4]

Tunics worn without the toga could indicate men of the lower or middling orders. Tacitus famously referred to the multitude as "the tunic-clad populace" (*Orat.* 7: *tunicatus populus*). Cicero (*Agr.* 2.94) and Horace (*Epp.* 1.7.65) both use *tunicati* as a metaphor for "the common people." Quintus Ennius also seems to have spoken scornfully, reports Aulus Gellius, "of the tunic-clad young men of the Carthaginians" (*Ann.* 325; cit. Gell. 6.12). Croom has noted (2002, 33) that artistic evidence sometimes shows lower-class men wearing unbelted tunics; perhaps an interesting visualization of the moral laxity and folly which the elites thought inherent in the poorer classes anyway.

When the togas of the poor are mentioned, the garment is usually described as 'little' or 'scanty:' the *togula*. The toga of the poor man may also have been short, but the *togula* may also have been a longer toga of worn quality, thin material, or narrow drapery: fabric was expensive in antiquity. If a poor or middling man wore the tunic out in public without a toga overtop, he ran the risk of being mistaken for a slave (see below); still, many poorer citizens may not have owned togas.

There are several references to the *togula* in the lighter works of Latin literature. The early second-century BCE comic playwright Titinius wrote of a character that "he shall be deprived of a perfumed tunic and little toga; he will have foul-smelling rags" (*tunica et togula obunctula adimetur, pannos possidebit fetidos; Com.* 138 in Non. 860L). A man's toga could also be described as *togula* to deride him: thus Cicero described Pompey's triumphal dress as a "little embroidered toga" (*togulam illam pictam; Ad. Att.* 1.18.6; Luc. *BC* 9.175–9).[5] The *togula* is also described as *gelida* or *algens* ('chilly') implying the fabric was thin or the toga short: at Mart. 6.50 one man goes about "shabby in a chilly little gown" (*gelida sordidus in togula*; see also 12.36, 4.66). Poor togas were described in other ways as well. In Horace, a man is laughed at for having a toga that is ill-fitting (*S. 1.*3.31–2). Martial stated that the toga of an impoverished man might wear thin (9.49); and complained of a miser's tattered clothing not in keeping with wealth (1.103; and see 3.30). A poor man's toga might be short (Mart. 11.56.6), threadbare (Mart. 2.46), or riddled with holes (Mart. 2.43). Zoilus in his fine wooly gown (*pexatus*) laughs at Martial's threadbare toga (*trita*) at 2.58. Fabric also tended to deteriorate through washing (see below, Chapter 4): thus a pauper is buried in a yellowing gown, smooth through age (*pallens toga mortui tribulis*; Mart. 9.57.8, with Henriksen 2012). Juvenal's poor man has a soiled little toga (*toga sordidula est*; 3.149).

In Martial, the toga is associated with the clients or philosophers. Clients are described as *togulati* (Mart. 4.66, 9.100.5, 10.74.3, 11.24.11; George 2008, 96–107); at Mart. 4.66 we meet a lucky provincial man who only wears his *togula* on the Ides and Kalends of each month (and see Mart. 12.70.2). At 11.56 Martial's Stoic friend wears a *brevis toga* day and night (implying, incidentally, that most Romans changed clothing to sleep in). At Mart. 12.70 a poor man and moralist wears the *togula*.

Cloaks could visualize poverty as well. Poor men wore shabby cloaks (Mart. 2.43) or thin ones (Mart. 6.59.5, in contrast to another man's thick cloaks, *gausapinae*). Martial is teased about his 'bad cloak' (*mala lacerna*; 6.82.9–12); at 7.92.7–8 his *lacerna* is chilly and threadbare (*gelida* and *trita*; and see 3.38.9). A *lacerna* is worn smooth through use and age at Mart. 9.57

(and see 8.28.22), or is yellowing (*cerea lacerna;* Mart. 1.92.7). The pauper may wear a *Gallica paeda*, a short wrap which covers only half his buttocks (1.92; and see 12.36 for a short *laena*). The Lingonian *bardocucullus* was also a poor garment, of greasy wool which will contaminate more expensive cloaks ("city Tyrianthines;" 1.53.5). Elsewhere, Martial implies the *sagum* was worn by poor men (here it is a greasy/waterproof Gallic one: 6.11.7–8). In Juvenal, a poor man has greasy/waterproof *lacernae* (*pingues* ... *lacernas,* 9.28) which will nonetheless save his toga, "a coarse toga, crude in color, ill-combed by the Gallic weaver."[6] Elsewhere a poor man's *laena* has many holes in it (Juv. 5.131); a poor poet must pawn his play to buy a *laena* (7.73) and a *lacerna* is dirty and torn (*si foeda et scissa lacerna*; 3.147–51).

Other items of (usually) poorly maintained clothing could also indicate poverty. At Mart. 10.76 a poor poet is in a black hood (*pullo cucullo*); and Juvenal mentions a rough *cucullus*, dark blue in color, the clothing of a poor man (3.170; and see below, Chapter 4). Underclothes were ragged as well: Horace is indignant that his tattered undertunic (*subucula*) is a subject for ridicule (*Epp.* 1.1.95–6). Poor men did not own many clothes (Var. *Cato vel de liberis educandis* [19] in Non. 155L; Mart. 4.66), and those they did were patched with coarse thread (Juv. 3.147–51).

Footwear could naturally indicate low status as well. Farmworkers and slaves in rural areas wore wooden-soled shoes, according to Cato (*sculponeae; R.* 135.1). perhaps a form of clog with wooden blocks under the toes and heel (see Croom 2002, 64 fig. 22.3). This type of shoe has been found in the archaeological record[7] and may have been used in bathhouses as well, functioning as a patten (i.e., a type of shoe worn over other footwear to protect it). At Cat. 98.4 a pair of shoes are described as *crepidas ... carpatinas,* "rustic sandals;" in Horace, a man is laughed at for having a country haircut, a toga that slips off, and a loose *calceus* (*S.* 1.3.31–2). Ovid counsels the man aiming to attract women to wear a well-fitting shoe, "and let your feet not float about in shoes too loose" (*nec vagus in laxa pes tibi pelle natet; Ars* 1.515; see also Sen. *Suas.* 2.17). Misers and paupers wore broken shoes (Mart. 12.29), patched ones (Mart. 1.103.6), or ones with the leather splitting in them (*rupta calceus alter/ pelle patet*; Juv. 3.149–50). Leather shoes in antiquity became waterlogged and easily stretched, and the nobleman would be careful about his footwear. Slaves may have gone barefoot, the result of which was likely "pain and disease," as Bradley notes (1994, 88 and n. 11).

The clothing of the poor was also indicated by the adjectives *obsoletus*[8] and *pullus. Pullus/sordes/obsoletus* had a variety of shades, from deep black, blackish-gray, dark-gray, and 'dusky,' to gray-brown, deep brown, even blackish-purple; doubtless, as Wilson states, designating both clothing made of natural undyed dark fleeces and wool dyed black or another dark color (Wilson 1938, 38).[9] *Pullus* could also denote the dirt associated with poverty (Cal. *Ecl.* 7.80); lowness of condition or birth (Cic. *Brut.* 224; Hor. *Epod.* 17.46; Sen. *Con.* 9.1.11); or the meanest element of a population (Cic. *Att.* 1.16.11, *Piso* 62; Petr. 126.5; Pliny *Epp.* 7.29.3; Calp. *Ecl.* 7.26–9).[10] Crowds

94 *Poverty, mourning, and* sordes

are also generally termed *pullati* (Quint. *Inst.* 2.12.10, 6.4.6; Pliny *Epp.* 7.17.9), and dark garments are 'stained' (Isid. *Orig.* 12.7.5). Persius doesn't want to fill his pages with 'dark-robed nonsense' (*pullatis… nugis*; 5.19). Martial mentions a man who is a lover of 'sad-colored' cloaks (*amator ille tristium lacernarum*; 1.96.4), presumably dark. Thus, poverty had a color in ancient Rome – *pullus* – color also associated with mourning clothing and rituals of grief.

In addition, in many places in Latin literature in addition the poor are described as dirty or *sordidi*. Isidore gives the etymology of *pullus* as derived from *pollutus*, stained or dirty (*Orig.* 12.7.5); the clothing of the poor was often inconceivable to the elite without its accompanying dirt (Blonski 2008, 49). Being clean and well-groomed indicated higher status (see Juv. 9.13–15; Artem. *Oneir.* 2.3): one could afford to have one's haircut and beard trimmed on a regular basis and have clean clothes.

Emotional black

By 'emotional black,' I mean passages in which the man so clothed is neither specifically named as poor nor described as in mourning, and thus perhaps black is assumed as a fashionable color.[11] In the first century BCE Cicero was able to speak of noblemen assuming *tunicae pullae* while in Naples (*Rab. Post.* 27; see below, Chapter 5).[12] Augustus directed that no one in dark clothing (*pullator*) could sit in the middle of the amphitheatre (*media cavea; Aug.* 44.2), and that when he saw a throng of men in a *contio* (an assembly) who were *pullati* in cloaks, he directed the aediles to police the forum and be certain everyone was in a toga (*Aug.* 40.5) rather than a dark *lacerna*. Mart. 4.2.2 a man watching the spectacle in a black cloak alone of all the white-clothed crowd is made suddenly white after snow falls (*nigris… lacernis*).

Mourning

In 59 BCE, Publius Vatinius entered the Temple of Castor to attend the funeral feast of the father of Q. Arrius in his mourning garments as a demonstration of political opposition.[13] Cicero was (or pretended to be) outraged at this flouting of common courtesy and religious ritual all in the name of political statement. "Had you ever seen, ever heard, of anyone presenting himself on such an occasion [in such a costume]?" he asked (*Vat.* 30). Vatinius' deliberate *faux pas* serves as a useful springboard for a discussion of Roman mourning garments.

There were no compulsory mourning periods in Roman antiquity for men as there were for women. Indeed, the observance of *luctus,* the formal mourning period, "was both more proper and more practicable for women than for men (who might be involved in public life)."[14] But the limited scope of male mourning also embodied Roman ideals of masculinity: in the case of men, no rules were laid down, because to mourn in a ceremonial sense was not regarded as honorable.[15] "There was a view that men should suppress grief,"[16] as Treggiari notes, and Cicero "did not wish it thought that he was avoiding parties after his daughter Tullia's death," but he "did keep away from people as far as possible for some time, especially the first month."[17] Pliny in mourning his second wife speaks of a period in which it would be unseemly for him to leave the house (*Epp.* 9.13.4–5).[18]

What did male mourning garments look like, and how long were they worn? Oftentimes male mourning clothing is not specifically named: mourners are designated simply by the color of their garments: *ater/atratus, niger, pullus*.[19] *Ater/atratus* was a color André defines as sable black, lusterless or matte black (1949, 44). Unlike *pullus, ater/atratus* was not normally used to describe the clothing of the poor, and may have been a true mourning color, perhaps deep black or dyed wool (and was also an epic word, unlike *pullus*). It was used to describe mourners and suppliants,[20] and thus (for example) Apuleius describes a father is dressed in black for his dead son on the day of the funeral as *atratus* (*Met.* 2.27). *Niger* was a brilliant black, often again used of mourning garments, pallbearers, and mourners (André 1949, 71; this is a word found in epic as well).[21] When he is taken off to be killed on the orders of Hannibal in 216 BCE, Decius Magius' head is swathed in black (*atra/veste*; Sil. 11.257–8; *BNP* Magius I 3). The consul Valerius Poplicola put on a dark toga for Brutus' funeral (Dionys. 5.17; *BNP* Valerius I 44); in Propertius the mourning toga is *atra toga* (4.7.28).

The male garment associated most often with mourning however was the *toga pulla* (Cic. *in Vat.* 30 and 31, above), a toga of grey or black wool, or perhaps one dyed gray or black for mourning.[22] The *toga pulla* could be made *praetexta* with a purple stripe: Festus informs us that this garment was the official costume of magistrates at funerals (272L); Seneca speaks of a young boy's mourning toga which was also *praetexta* (*vagabatur lugubri sordidaque praetexta; Contr.* 9.5.1). Mourning cloaks could perhaps also be had: after Actium Horace writes that the foe has "changed the scarlet cape for black" (*hostis punico/ lugubre mutavit sagum; Epod.* 9.27–8); Seneca writes of a dark *palla* swirling round the feet of an old man (*lugubris imos palla perfundit pedes*; Sen. *Oed.* 553). '*Pullatus*' meant clothed in black or dark-grey garments: Juvenal describes the mourning nobles go into if a wealthy house in Rome is destroyed by fire (*pullati proceres*; 3.213). Sometimes no specific mourning garment is mentioned: thus Ovid in his *Tristia* speaks of the day when he can lay aside his mourning garments (*lugubria*; Ov. *Tris.* 4.2.73; see also Hor. *Epod.* 9.28). At the rumored death of Germanicus, Tacitus reports (*Ann.* 2.82) that "everyone wore the ordinary tokens of bereavement" (*insignia lugentium*) but the "deeper mourning was carried at heart" (*altius animis maerebant*).[23]

How long were male mourning garments assumed? Unlike women in mourning,[24] it seems (at least in the Republic) men only wore the *toga pulla* to the funeral/funeral games itself and took it off immediately afterward. As we have seen, Cicero excoriated Vatinius for wearing the *toga pulla* to the funerary banquet afterward for the father of Quintus Arrius (59 BCE). "Tell me," says Cicero, "who ever took his place at table in mourning?" (*cedo, quis unquam cenarit atratus?; Vat.* 30). "To whom except yourself on leaving the bath has a *toga pulla* ever been handed?" Cicero asks Vatinius (*Vat.* 31).[25] Even Quintus Arrius, son of the deceased, was at the banquet in white (*albatus*). Cicero states that mourning clothes could be worn at the gladiatorial celebrations which were sometimes part of the funeral, "but the banquet itself is in honour of the celebrant" (*Vat.* 30). To us, the correct costume may seem a small or trivial point, but in fact it serves to underline the importance that self-presentation had in Roman society and is at the heart of Vatinius' sartorial demonstration. Cicero is almost certainly exaggerating for rhetorical purposes, but there must be some truth to his assertion that by appearing in mourning clothing after the funeral was over, Vatinius profaned the Temple of Castor and the public festival, violated old customs, and held in contempt the *auctoritas* of the host. Wearing the *toga pulla* outside a funereal context was not only "inappropriate but inauspicious" (Stone 1994, 15).

The fact that mourning clothing could be deliberately assumed to offend someone must be the point of an otherwise puzzling passage in the *Digest* (Ulpian, late second/early third centuries CE):

> The praetor bans generally anything which would be to another's disrepute (*ad infamiam alicuius*). And so whatever one may do or say to bring another into disrepute gives rise to the action for insult (*actio inuriarum*). Here are instances of conduct to another's disrepute: to lower another's reputation, one wears mourning or filthy garments (*veste lugubri utitur aut squalida*) or lets one's beard grow (*barbam demittat*)[26] or lets one's hair down (*capillos submittat*) or writes a lampoon or issues or sings something detrimental to another's honor.
>
> (*Dig.* 47.10.15.27.3)

Sidonius, writing centuries later, complains of arrogant and wealthy men who are clothed in mourning at weddings and white at funerals (*pullati ad nuptias, albati ad exsequias...*; *Epp.* 5.7.4).

Mourning clothing could also be assumed to signify impending misfortune (or it is utilized so in Latin literature). Pompey dreams of his own funeral and appears at headquarters on the morning of the Battle of Pharsalus dressed in a *pallium pullum*, a sign of the doom to come (Flor. *Epit.* 2.13.45). Lepidus, abandoned by his own soldiers, hides dressed in a dark cloak (*pulloque velatus amiculo*; Vell. 2.80.4). On the eve of the Battle of Carrhae, Crassus mistakenly put on a black cloak instead of a purple one, a bad omen (53 BCE; Plut. *Crassus* 23). Anticipating his defeat, we are told that Vitellius put on mourning (*pullo amictu*; Tac. *Hist.* 3.67). Intriguingly, both Varro and Sidonius (below), centuries apart, mention men clothed in half-black or half-mourning (*semiatratus; semipullatus*),[27] but this may be a reference to *sordes*, to which we now turn.

Sordes in the courts[28]

In the central period, if a capital accusation was launched against a man, he and his family and friends put on *vestes sordidae*; sullied or dirty clothing.[29] The defendant also habitually laid aside the insignia of office (Val. Max. 6.4.4; and see below), perhaps grew his hair and beard (Livy 6.16.4; Mart. 2.24, 2.36, 2.74), and let bodily odor and dirt accumulate. These latter practices are probably what the Romans referred to as *squalor*; Bablitz (2007, 226 n. 85) thinks *sordes* refers to clothing; *squalor* to toilette.[30] By far the majority of ancient literary references to men in what has been called by modern authors 'mourning clothing' are actually *vestes sordidae* or *sordes,* not solid gray or black togas but those of ordinary light-colored wool which had been deliberately dirtied or sullied.

Generally, men were castigated if they did not appear unkempt and dirty while on trial; in some cases this was thought to affect the outcome of the trial adversely. In one of his *Controversiae*, Seneca describes *sordes* as "these trappings that are essential for all those on trial" (*haec necessaria omnibus periclitantibus instrumenta*; 10.1.7). Quintilian thought that the assumption of *sordes* and *squalor* by friends and family and the introduction of supporters so arrayed into the courtroom was of great value in saving the accused from condemnation (*Inst.* 6.1.33). Defendants assumed such an appearance as soon as charges were laid; thus spiteful accusers would bring a charge and then let the case stall, forcing the defendants "into mourning attire (and increased humiliation) for an extended period of time."[31] Augustus struck off the records all such cases (Suet. *Aug.* 32.2). But the practice continued under Claudius (Suet. *Cl.* 15.2) and Vitellius (Suet. *Vit.* 8.1). On the other hand, as Hall notes such dress could also stir up sympathy and indignation for an individual, and could shape the coming legal proceedings "quite significantly" (2014, 62).

There are many references to the practice in ancient literature. Appius Claudius refused to don mourning clothes when he was put on trial before the people in 470 BCE (Livy 2.61; Dionys. 9.54; Suet. *Tib.* 2.4; *BNP* Claudius I 5). The practice is especially pronounced in Cicero's speeches:[32] thus Milo did not let his hair grow nor change his toga at his defense, and this some felt contributed to his condemnation (Plut. *Cic.* 35; Dyck 2001, 120; Hall 2014, 60–1). L. Murena on the other hand appeared at his trial quite correctly in squalor and *sordes* (*squalore et sordibus*; Cic. pro *Mur.* 86; *BNP* 'Licinius' I 35) At Cic. *Sul.* 88, if Sulla is acquitted he will assume his former garb (*vestitum pristinum; BNP* Cornelius I 89). At the trial of Verres in 70 BCE, both plaintiff *and* defendant and their supporters were arrayed in *sordes* (Cic. *Verr.* 2.1.152, 2.5.128). At his trial in 66 BCE, Licinius Macer precipitately changed to a white toga and trimmed his hair in the belief that he was acquitted (Plut. *Cic.* 9; *BNP* 'Licinius' I 30; see Bodel 1999, 261). P. Rutilius Rufus as a defendant in 92 BCE neither put on shabby clothes (*obsoletam vestem*) nor lay aside the signs of office: (*nec insignia senatoris deposuit*; Val. Max. 6.4.4;

BNP 'Rutilius' I 3). Libo Drusus, arraigned on a charge of revolution (*res novas*), having changed into *sordes* (*veste mutata*), went around petitioning his wife's relations (escorted *primoribus feminis*; Tac. *Ann.* 2.29; *BNP* Scribonius II 6). Even though under accusation Publius Scipio Africanus, son of Paulus, continued to shave and wear white clothing (*candida veste uti*), nor did he appear "in the usual garb of those under accusation" (*neque fuisse cultu solito reorum*; Gell. 3.4.1; *BNP* Cornelius I 70). As late as the fifth century CE, Sidonius reported that in one trial the accused, Arvandus, was well-groomed (*Epp.* 1.7.11: *exornatus, politus*) while his accusers were *semipullati* (1.7.9) and *atrati* (1.7.11). Sidonius speaks of "the indignation which the sight of men in the garb of *sordes* arouses" (*sub invidia sordidatorum*); because the accused was well-groomed he excited no pity (1.7.9).

The defendant's supporters are also described this way.[33] Thus in 449 BCE G. Claudius begged support in *sordes* in the face of the crime his nephew had committed (Livy 3.58.1, *BNP* Claudius I 32). The tribunes threatened to assume mourning for Gaius Sempronius Atratinus when he was faced with prosecution in 422 BCE (Livy 4.42.8; *BNP* Sempronius I 6). Cicero that the Roman *equites* and supporters of Ligurius appeared *veste mutata* in the courtroom (*pro Lig.* 33, *BNP* Ligurius 1). Appian tells us that Pompey and his followers changed into mourning/*sordes* when his father-in-law Scipio was accused of bribery (*BC* 2.24; *tēn esthēta metabalein; BNP* Caecilius I 32); Martial 2.24.2 describes himself, a friend of an accused man standing beside him at the trial as *squalidus*. By the third century CE, Venuleius Saturninus can state that no one may assume *sordes* for a defendant unless he is so closely related to him that he cannot be obliged to give evidence against him (*Dig.* 47.10.39).

To us this may seem a bit odd, but as Bablitz has pointed out (2007, 84) "clothing could affect perceptions within the courtroom." In a case concerning the citizenship of the defendant, for example, the two advocates appeared before Claudius, squabbling over whether the accused should appear in court in a toga or in a *pallium*. Claudius ruled that he must change back and forth, depending on whether he was being defended or indicted (Suet. *Claud.* 15.2). Suetonius presents this anecdote to show the emperor's eccentricities, but we can instead see in Claudius' solution his real understanding of what a powerful charge clothing could carry. "At least one of the advocates believed that the litigant's adoption of clothing that could either support or refute his case was a real threat" (Bablitz 2007, 84).[34]

Sordes as a form of public protest

Vestes sordidae could also be donned by citizens in times of political crisis, national emergency, or to show opposition to what they felt were unjust political decrees or actions, as could mourning garments. The opposition to Tiberius Gracchus' tribunician edict in 133 BCE was visualized by a protest in the Forum with men arrayed in *sordes*.[35] Metellus Pius wore *sordes* for two years (100–98 BCE) in protest at the exile of his father.[36] The practice is frequently mentioned in the works of Cicero.[37] In the face of his impending exile (58 BCE) many *equites* gathered on the Capitol in *sordes* (*vestem mutandam; Sest.* 26–7) "to defend me also in every possible way by measures of their own," Cicero claimed. "More innovative… was the coordination of this stunt with a motion initiated in Senate [by L. Ninnius] that all its members should likewise adopt *sordes.*"[38] But the proposal did not have the support of the consuls. Cicero was naturally outraged:

> were you even bold enough to issue an edict that the people should not lament my, their own, the public calamity, that they should not show their sorrow by their dress? (*ne hunc suum dolorem veste significarent*)… Are not men in the habit of changing their dress (*vestitum mutare non solent*) by their own wish (*sua sponte*) when their friends are in danger?
> (*Sest.* 32–33)

While all other citizens had assumed *sordes* in protest of Cicero's exile, Cicero asserted that in order to demonstrate his own stance the consul Aulus Gabinius not only remained in the *toga praetexta* but also reeked of perfume (*Red. Sen.* 12; *BNP* Gabinius I 2). Political solidarity and support were thus immediately recognizable in a powerful visual display, and dissidents could express their disapproval of sentiments or events by refusing to change their clothes.

Citizens made their situation known by other bodily and sartorial signs as well: letting bodily dirt accumulate, for example, and letting beard and hair grow. Thus after Manlius was cast into jail in 385 BCE, Livy states that a large part of the people (*plebs*) changed their clothing and "many" (*multos*) permitted their hair and beards to grow. "And now the Manlian party were more conspicuous than before, both for their sordid dress and for the sorrowful countenances of defendants" (*et iam magis insignis et sordibus et facie reorum turba Manliana erat…*; 6.16.8). Dressing in *sordes* not only called attention to a victim's plight but also roused public indignation on his behalf (Hall 2014, 43).[39]

But the most interesting references to *vestem mutare* and the assumption of *sordes* claim that the practice in the Republic also involved the omission of insignia of rank and office (Val. Max. 6.4.4). Thus after the Samnite victory over Rome in 320 BCE senators and knights discarded their signs of rank:

> immediately, without official sanction of any sort, betook themselves with one mind to every form of mourning (*extemploque sine ulla publica auctoritate consensum in omnem formam luctus est*). The booths round the Forum were shut up; all public business in the Forum ceased spontaneously before the proclamation closing it was made; the senators laid aside their purple striped tunics and gold rings (*lati claui, anuli aurei positi*); the depression amongst the citizens was almost greater than that in the army…
> (Livy 9.7.8)

100 *Poverty, mourning, and* sordes

Pliny notes that in 305/304 BCE when the son of a freedman was appointed curule aedile, the nobility laid their rings aside as a political gesture (*Nat.* 33.17–18; Livy 9.46.12). Even officials who normally were praetextate donned *sordes* in this case (Cic. *Red. Sen.* 12); this also incidentally implies that *sordes* were unlike the mourning toga, which as we have seen could be made *praetexta*. In 53 BCE Cassius Dio claimed that the consuls named by Pompey did not themselves name any successors, but laid aside their clothing to put on the dress of *equites*, as if there was some great calamity (40.46.1). If we can believe Dio, in the face of Clodius' attempts to drive him into exile, Cicero petitioned Roman aristocrats in the dress of an *eques* (38.14.7) and later in *sordes* (Cic. *Att.* 3.15.5; see App. *BC* 2.15; Plut. *Cic.* 30.4–5).

Mourning, poverty, and *sordes*

As we have seen, the clothing of the poor is often described as *pullus* ('grey,' 'black,' or 'dark') in a variety of genres. Heskel believes that *sordes* and mourning clothing were two different things: the one a deliberately dirtied toga assumed in the face of an (often) capital charge (either of oneself or a loved one), along with the omission of insignia; the other a dark toga (sometimes *praetexta*) assumed only on the day of a funeral, and removed immediately afterward. It may be that *sordes* were meant to imitate *pullae* which could not be worn in court because the clothing was reserved for funerals and broke social and religious rules worn outside this occasion, and that is perhaps true. (I also note here that the toga of the poor man and the mourning toga of a Roman senator may have looked very different: finer wool, a darker, more uniform color, a purple border.)

I would argue however that there were close and complicated links between mourning, poverty, and *sordes*. We saw that one could grow one's hair and beard as a sign of mourning or when one was arraigned on a capital charge, and furthermore, that *pulla*, the color of the garment of mourning, is also described as the color of poverty. The elder Seneca demonstrates these intriguing, if puzzling, links:

> A man who had a son and a rich enemy was found killed though not robbed. The youth dressed in *sordes* (*adulescens sordidatus*) and began to follow the rich man about. The rich man took him to court, and demanded that if he had any suspicions he should accuse him. The poor man said, "I shall accuse when I can," and continued to follow the rich man in *sordes* just the same (*sordidatus*). The rich man stood for office, but was rejected; he accuses the poor man of *inuria*.
> (*Contr.* 10.1.1).

Here, a poor man mourning for his father is in *sordes;* but he is also in *sordes* because he is a defendant (*Contr.* 10.1.2; cf. Cic. *Verr.* 2.1.152); this particular *Controversia* also links *sordidatus* with poverty: "when," a poor man later asks, "are we not *sordidati* in the eyes of these rich men?" (*quando autem istis divitibus sordidati sumus?*; 10.2): therefore, poverty, mourning, and *sordes* look the same. Conversely, later in the passage the young man is made to say, "it was out of respect for him [the dead father] that I changed my clothes," i.e., into *sordes* (*in honorem eius vestem mutavi*; 10.1.5): therefore, *sordes* and the clothing of the poor do not look the same, but mourning and *sordes* do. The clothing of poverty, grief, and arraignment all intertwine in a complicated fashion.

Why did the status-obsessed upper-class Roman citizen male think it appropriate on certain occasions to assume elements of the costume of the poor man: the *toga pulla*, the dirt (*sordes*) and squalor of poverty, and/or omit his insignia of rank? Perhaps the connection amongst mourning, poverty, *sordes* is that they all involve abjection: poverty was a low, humiliating state, at least according to the upper classes. *Sordes* involved humility and self-abasement in order to move the jury to sympathy; mourning assumed the form it did because in some sense this is also a form of humility (that is, the neglect of personal appearance through extreme grief). This would also explain the removal of insignia – this meant further degradation on the part of the senatorial man or *eques* (although, as we have seen, the mourning toga could be made *praetexta*).[40] Mourning is, moreover, a period in which things are uncertain, fluctuating, contradictory; temporarily chaotic (Blonski 2008, 54).[41]

Blonski believes men assumed *sordes* when their integration into the city/ political life was placed into question, and that this partially evoked the position of those who were in mourning (i.e., mourners are temporarily not in the world, and must rejoin progressively; Blonski 2008, 51). The man who is in *sordes* or in mourning no longer lives in the civilized world. Blonski notes furthermore that men in *sordes* are not described in the literary sources as dirty or disgusting, as the poor often are (Blonski 2008, 52): such a man is *sordidatus* rather than *sordidus*. Blonski calls this "socialized dirt" or "work dirt," that is, squalor assumed in civic life as an administrative outfit (2008, 53). An old man in mourning in Seneca's *Oedipus*, dressed in black, is however "squalid in his appearance" (*squalente cultu maestus ingreditur senex; Oed.* 554; and see Sen. *Contr.* 9.5.1).

The *toga perversa*

There is one other sign the sources mention as a sign of 'mourning,'/personal anguish/ distress: the *toga perversa,* or reversed toga: a magistrate wore his toga reversed when he had to pronounce a capital sentence. When C. Licinius Macer (*BNP* Licinius I 30) was on trial for extortion, he saw Cicero take off his magistrate's toga while the jury deliberated (*praetextam ponentem vidisset*), and committed suicide anticipating a guilty verdict. He believed Cicero removed his toga in preparation for reversing it, although Cicero may have simply been in need of a redraping (Val. Max. 9.12.7; Plutarch has a different version of this; see above). Seneca recommends that when a magistrate has to assume the reversed toga (*perversa vestis*), he should do so with *gravitas* and solemnity, not in anger (*de Ira* 1.16.5). In Petronius *Satyr.* 58.12 the phrase *toga perversa persequi* means "to hound someone to the bitter end." What exactly 'a reversed toga' means sartorially, and why a magistrate assumed it in these circumstances remains unclear. Linderski conjectures (2002, 363) that *toga perversa* could mean the toga worn a) inside out; b) back to front; or c) upside down. His opinion is that "the first two arrangements could hardly have produced the desired effect," and believes the *toga perversa* meant the toga worn upside down. While certainly possible, I believe this would have carried with it certain impracticalities (how do you drape a toga upside down?) It is more likely that the phrase meant the toga worn back to front, which would have been an obvious reversal of the garment.

Conclusions

In his *Dream-Book* of the late second century, Artemidorus wrote that "for poor men, slaves, prisoners, debtors, and for all those who are in a difficult situation, to dream of losing one's clothes" is auspicious, as it means "that the evils that surround the person will disappear" (*Oneir.* 2.3). This reflects in a small way the fact that clothing in antiquity was a worn world, "a world of social relations put on the wearer's body" (Jones and Stallybrass 2000, 3). A study of Roman mourning and *sordes* underlines the fact that clothes exist without having any intrinsic meaning; they are only given meaning through social construction, through the mental and emotional perception of the self and others. Dressing in *sordes* or mourning by choice – like the son in Seneca – or consciously rejecting such signifiers – such as Aulus Gabinius – makes it clear that vestimentary signals were immediately apparent and consequently effective, especially in a ritual context.

Notes

1 Paulicelli 2014, 4, 12, of Renaissance Italy.
2 Pl. *Rud.* 449; Petr. *Satyr.* 13.3. Under the laws of the XII Tables, only one small purple tunic was permitted at (aristocratic) funerals (*tunicla*; Cic. *Leg.* 2.59).
3 See Fuentes 1987, 43; Petersen 2006, 107 (on the baker Eurysaces' tomb in Rome, the active workers are in short tunics with legs exposed); see also George 2006, 24.
4 See Fuentes 1987, 43–6; Pausch 2008, 158–66.
5 In some instances the term *togula* is clearly derogatory: see Cic. *Piso* 55, in which "little togas" are given to Piso's lictors after they remove their "little cloaks" (*sagula*), clearly creating "a travesty of a triumphal entry" (Dyck 2001, 124 n. 18).
6 [*munimenta togae, duri crassique coloris*]/ *et male percussas textoris pectine Galli/ accipimus*; 9.29–31; del. Ribbeck (1865). Courtney 1980, 430–1 states that these cloaks "were of poor quality, like many Gallic fabrics;" see Mart. 4.19.1; 6.11.7.
7 For examples, see van Driel-Murray 2001, 188 fig. 1.
8 See for example Cic. *Agr.* 2.13; Nep. *Ag.* 8.2; Livy 3.47.1; Apul. *Apol.* 3.
9 Goldman 2013, 65 defines *pullus* as dark, grey, or black only.
10 On dirt see Bradley 2002; Scheidel 2003; Scobie 1986.
11 On the history of fashionable black in Western culture, see Hollander 1978, 365–90; in Roman antiquity, see Olson 2004–5, 110–14.

12 The text here is corrupt: *pulla* is a conjecture by Clark 1909 (*tunica… pulla*) instead of *maeciapella* (unknown).
13 The connection is in fact a bit unclear, as Pocock notes (1967, 118). G. Pomptinus (*BNP* Pomptinus 1) had as propraetor of Gallia Narbonensis quelled the rebellion of the Allobroges in 61. Vatinius and his supporters wished to reserve all the glory for Caesar, and thus opposed this.
14 Treggiari 1991, 494. On mourning in antiquity, see Treggiari 1991, 493–8. Little has been written on mourning for men in antiquity.
15 *Dig.* 3.2.9; see Treggiari 1991, 495–8. At Tac. *Ann.* 3.3, Tiberius and Livia do not appear in public after Drusus' death; see also Cic. *Att.* 12.13.2. Similar customs obtained in Quattrocento Florence: Strocchia speaks of "the restricted scope of men's mourning" and "the sustained complexity of women's mourning" (1992, 173).
16 Treggiari 1991, 493; see Cic *Tusc.* 3.70; Sen. *Contr.* 4 pr. 5; Sen *ad Marc.* 15.3.
17 Treggiari 1991, 493; *Att.* 12.13.2, 12.20.1, 12.21.5, 12.23.1, 12.28.2, 12.38a.1, 12.40.2–3.
18 Treggiari believes that this could refer to the first nine days. Or perhaps fashions had changed: 1991, 493.
19 On colors of black dyes and terminology, see Olson 2004–5, 101. Taylor (1983, 248–62) looks at worldwide colors for mourning. "The negative symbolism of the color black (associated with night, darkness, bad omens, death, evil, sin, disaster, sickness, unpleasantness, the malignant, the dirty, and the undesirable) in contrast with the color white as a symbol of light, virtue, purity, good health, success, the pleasant, and the desirable, has been noted as an almost universal phenomenon" and figures prominently in the areas of religion and the supernatural (Thompson 1989, 110). While sometimes signifying 'dark,' *ferrugineus and caeruleus* are not applied to male mourning garments: see Bradley 2009, 9–11; Edgeworth 1978.
20 Lucr. 2.580; Virg. *A.* 3.64; Hor. *Epp.* 1.7.6; Suet. *Nero* 47.2; Tac. *Ann.* 3.2 (*plebes atrata*); Macrob. *Sat.* 3.15.4; Isid. *Orig.* 10.15.
21 Ov. *Ibis* 102; Juv. 10.245.
22 Contra McGinn (2014, 96) there is no evidence from the central period that states prostitutes wore the dark toga.
23 But after the death of Augustus when the senate convenes the day after the body is brought to Rome Tiberius and Drusus appear in "dark clothing made for use in the forum" (Dio 56.31.3), perhaps a reference to *togae pullae*.
24 On which see Olson 2004–5.
25 This was the ritual bath of purification after the funeral. See Dio 37.51. in which Faustus, son of Sulla, gave gladiatorial games in memory of his father and furnished baths and oil to the people (60 BCE).
26 Bonanno (1988, 159) posits that in the Republic being clean-shaven was the fashion since a beard was associated with mourning; from numismatic evidence it appears that Antony wore a beard for two years in mourning for Caesar (ibid., with references); Octavian wore one until 39 BCE (Dio 48.34.3). Beards for men gained popularity beginning with the Julio-Claudians (Bonanno 1988).
27 Non. 152L, quoting Varro *Bimarco* 47: *ipsum propter vix liberti semiatrati exequiantur*.
28 On *sordes*, see Bablitz 2007, 84–5; Blonski 2014, 27–48; Freyburger-Galland 1993, 125–6; Hall 2014, 40–63; Heskel 1994.
29 Hall (2014, 51) believes that perhaps the practice was not firmly established by 100 BCE, and grew in popularity throughout the first century (going by Cic. *Red. Sen.* 13). The *OLD* translates *sordidatus* as "of mourning garments, usu. as being unfulled," which is puzzling.
30 Blonski believes further that *sordes* often carries with it a moral critique, whereas *squalor* does not (at least until the Christian literature of the fourth century; 2014, 48).

31 Bablitz 2007, 85; and see Hall 2014, 52 on Milo, who was in *sordes* for approximately four months in 56 BCE, having been accused by Clodius (Cic. *Q fr.* 2.3.1–2, 2.6.4; *Att.* 1.16.2).
32 In addition to the examples I have listed here, see also Cic. *de Orat.* 2.195, *Att.* 3.15.5, *Lig.* 33, *Mur.* 86, *Scaur.* 49, *Rosc. Am.* 147.
33 In addition, those soliciting official support from the Senate and people of Rome also appeared in squalid clothing: the populace of Tusculum in 324 BCE (Livy 8.37.9) and Sicily in 201 BCE (Livy 26.29.3) came as suppliants to Rome *mutata veste*; Jugurtha in 111 BCE (Sall. *Iug.* 33.1). Heraclius of Syracuse and Epicrates of Bidis, who fled to Rome from Sicily and the machinations of Verres, stayed in *sordes* for two years as they petitioned the senate for help (Cic. *Verr.* 2.2.62; Hall 2014, 52).
34 And see Cic. *Font.* 33, in which he refers to Gallic provincials in a Roman courtroom lined up to give evidence for the prosecution dressed in cloaks and trousers (*sagatos bracatosque*) and "tries to interpret this garb as a sign of their arrogant disposition" (Hall 2014, 56).
35 Plut. *Ti. Gracch.* 10.7; also mentioned in Diod. Sic. 36.15, on Saturninus, and App. *BC* 1.67 (on Marius in 87 BCE).
36 Diod. Sic. 36.16; *BNP* Caecilius I 31; Hall 2014, 53 n. 47.
37 In addition to those mentioned here, see e.g., Cic. *ad Quir.* 8; *Dom.* 55; *Planc.* 21, 87.
38 Hall 2014, 45; Cic. *Sest.* 26; see Dio Cass. 37.43.3 for an earlier instance of the Senate dressing collectively in *sordes*. It is difficult to say whether, as Heskel (1994, 142) believes, the *vestem mutare* was in fact an "official protest" decreed by the Senate (and which could likewise only be reversed by consular edict) in which citizen males changed to *sordes*, or whether this is simply an interpretation based on Cic. *Sest.* 26. It is certainly implied in Livy 9.7.8 (*sine ulla publica auctoritate*: see below).
39 Lintott (1999, 11–21) has noted that this assumption of *sordes* as an assertive protest worked visually as a *quiritatio*: a crying out in protest publically (at an unjust action).
40 Thus at Cic. *Att.* 4.4.2 a man flings off his toga (*abiecta toga*) and throws himself on his knees when he is beseeching.
41 On the other hand, anthropologists see mourning customs as reversals of practice as a contribution to the state of chaos, that is, changes of direction aimed at confusing the departing ghost (Grainger 1998, 88). Thus clothing reversal and hair grown long (or cut short) are the opposite of normal custom (Grainger 1998, 85). Servius states at a Roman funeral everything was inverted (*A.* 11.93; and see e.g., Tac. *Ann.* 3.2.2).

4 Clothing and status

In this chapter I discuss how Roman male clothing and adornment could carry signs of status (high or low) for Roman men. 'Status' I define as one's informal prestige among peers or one's financial standing, 'rank' as one's actual juridical category (senator, equestrian, etc.). Obviously the two are intertwined in complex respects (in items such as gold rings, for example), but in this chapter however I try to restrict myself to ways in which a man's status and wealth could be worn on his body. Included here are fabric and color (purple, scarlet, white, gold, blues, and greens), patterned clothing (although the *toga picta* and *tunica palmata* are covered in Chapter 1), luxury footwear, the *synthesis/cenatoria*, and jewelry for men. I also examine lower-class colors, slave clothing and ornament, the concept of the male 'clotheshorse;' folds and cleanliness and how these indicated status, and finally sumptuary legislation and the morality of luxurious clothing.

Male clothing was less likely to show signs of status in Roman antiquity than female clothing, for a variety of reasons. The Roman upper classes "were obsessed with *existimatio* and *dignitas*" (D'Arms 1990, 318), and luxury was heavily implicated in the negotiation of status. Moralizing discourse on *luxuria* was aimed at the upper classes but with an eye on the parvenu. Julia Emberley writes that texts on sartorial abuse read the world of appearances as a "taxonomy of identifiable differences of social rank, class, and genders" (1997, 56, of seventeenth-century England), and argues these texts were even more important than sumptuary legislation in establishing ideological codes of symbolic status, as "they determined what acts of sartorial display were considered 'normal,' proper, legitimate, or transgressive in everyday practices."[1] By constructing an ideal of thrift and moderate use of luxury by the elite, a part of the dominant social group was trying to prevent usurpation of visual privileges which they had effectively lost anyway. In other words, reaction to increasing use of luxury and conspicuous consumption by the parvenus took the form of discourse on the virtues of Republican simplicity; the ideal of frugality indicated the elite, or a small section of them. "Codes of behavior were heavily implicated in marking the elite off from the rest of society... the discourses of morality in Rome were profoundly implicated in structures of power" (Edwards 1993, 4, 17). Perhaps a minority of Roman elites felt that by instituting a particular code of behavior the members of the dominant class would win back prestige lost through relentless appropriation of the trappings of status by inferiors. In the fierce competition for status amongst those in the top tiers of society, however, there is little evidence that thrift ever became fashionable. As was the case with the sumptuary legislation, ideals of frugality simply could not compete with the drive for status display: as for Tacitus' assertion that economy became fashionable under the Flavians, it "should be read with as much caution as his descriptions of earlier excesses" (Edwards 1993, 28).

According to this sector of society, *luxuria* was harmful: the house of P. Vedius Pollio was reportedly razed to the ground shortly after 15 BCE because its excessive grandeur was seen as injurious.[2] Men of wealth and rank were in exceptionally delicate positions: Cicero thought that "a transformation takes place in a nation's character when the habits and mode of living of its aristocracy is changed," and those who set bad examples by their behavior were dangerous to the state precisely because they had so many imitators.[3] Money spent in the proper way, however (a sumptuous house for a man of high standing, for example) was useful in maintaining distinctions of status, and as Edwards points out, "no one complains about freedmen ruining themselves through conspicuous consumption."[4] In relation to this, the meaning of "ostentation" obviously depended on which class the word was being used in reference to: overstepping the boundaries of what was appropriate to one's class was what earned social opprobrium. The acceptable use of wealth and *luxuria* varied by *ordo* and status.

Moral rectitude could be used as "symbolic capital" (Edwards 1993, 26), but there was a fine line between laudable thrift and miserliness. Horace jeered at the rich man who hid his money away instead of spending it, who dressed like a slave, and slept on his money-bags (Hor. *S.* 1.1.68–78, 95–7). Martial made fun of a man newly wealthy: having desired and received a million sesterces, Scaevola's lifestyle is shabbier than before he was made rich (Mart. 1.103). And because cloth and clothing was laden with connotations of status and so an important symbolic prize, "clothing becomes a field for rivalry in every society with some mobility" (Perrot 1994, 25). Rome was no exception. By Juvenal's day however, people reportedly only put their faith in orators who were obviously wealthy: "eloquence in rags is a rare phenomenon" (*rara in tenui facundia panno*; 7.145).

Extravagant dress "had always been a cause for concern in Roman culture" (Kuefler 2001, 57), for two reasons. Firstly, male status reflected in clothing seems to have been censured because of Republican ideals: the struggle against *luxuria* meant that upstanding moralistic Romans would disdain lavish garments.[5] Such signs may have been used by the *nouveaux riches* to parade their wealth and hence eschewed in some measure by men of the upper classes. Secondly, such color, fabric, and adornment seem to have indicated effeminacy to the Romans (a discussion taken up below, Chapter 5). In short, it was much rarer for men than for women to wear their status on their bodies. Men did have some choice however in the way of ornament and color.

Fabric

Although usually woven of undyed light wool, we do hear of togas of different textures and materials. The *toga rasa* or 'smooth toga' was a summer garment (Mart. 2.85.4; Juv. 2.97). The *OLD* defines *rasus* as "shorn of pile" (and so thin and fine; cit. Williams 2004, 259). The elder Pliny states that the *vestis undulata* (possibly the full Augustan toga, although *vestis* presumably can also refer to a tunic, female or male as well) was very popular at first; that the *vestis sororiculata* (? – this is an adjective of indeterminate meaning) fell from favor; that the *toga rasa* (the smooth toga) and the *toga Phryxiana* (made of Phryxian wool; Sen. *Ben.* 1.3.7) came into use in the latest times of Augustus (*Nat.* 8.195). Pliny also mentions [*togae*] *crebrae papaveratae*, togas of "poppy-cloth," perhaps wool woven with flax and poppy-stem fibre to give gloss (*Nat.* 8.195; see 19.21 for a substance being extracted from poppies to bleach linen). Since we do not know precisely what these descriptors signify, however, and because in most instances no exact dates are given, the passage is of little help; and merely informs us that there were different fashions and fabrics in togas. And although wool was the usual fabric for tunic and toga and other garments, we should note that not all wool was created equal: some types were finer and softer and whiter than others.[6]

Pliny also mentions a kind of fabric called *gausapa* or *gausapina*, coarse woolen cloth with a long shaggy nap on one side: he notes that weaving a broad-striped tunic "in the style of *gausapa* is coming in for the first time now."[7] This may in fact have been a pile-weave, perhaps for winter wear. The material was expensive and very hot.[8] In Lucilius 568 (598W) a table is wiped between courses with a piece of purple *gausapa* (*purpureo tersit tunc latas gausape mensas*; and see Hor. *S.* 2.8.11).[9] In Persius prisoners are given yellow *gausapa* garments, perhaps cloaks or tunics, to wear in a triumph after Caligula's military victory on the Rhine (*lutea gausapa*; 6.46). In Petronius we find a scarlet cloak(?) of *gausapa* on Trimalchio (*coccina gausapa*; 28.4), and a green or brown garment on a *cinaedus* (*gausapa myrtea*; 21.2).[10] In *Epp.* 53.3, Seneca is *gausapatus* on a sea-voyage. Martial mentions a gift of a pure white *gausapina paenula*, so beautiful the recipient would wish to wear it even in late summer (14.145); at 6.59.8 a man has several such cloaks (Leary 1996, 207–8).

Male clothing could also be made of silk. In the central period, "silk" was a material called *subserica*, in which the silk was interwoven with another material, such as linen[11] or cotton,[12] to keep the cost down. There appear to have been two types of silk available in Roman antiquity: wild silk (tusseh silk, *bombycina*, or Coan silk) and Chinese silk (*serica* or *metaza*),[13] and a distinction is made in the *Digest* between the two (34.2.23.1). The elder Pliny says, of Coan silk:

> Nor have even men been ashamed to make use of this clothing (*has vestes*), because of its lightness (*levitatem*) in summer: so far have our

habits departed from wearing a leather cuirass that even clothing is considered a burden. Nonetheless so far we leave the Assyrian [i.e., eastern/Chinese] silk-moth to women (*Assyria tamen bombyce adhuc feminis cedimus*).

(*Nat.* 11.78).

Varro mentions togas "transparent as glass" which showed the stripes of the tunic underneath, a material which might actually have been silk.[14]

Certain sectors of Roman society disapproved of silk garments for men, judging them unsuitable and effeminate: silk was often referred to in "morally coded and often gendered language" (Parker 2008, 170). Tiberius apparently even legislated against such clothing (Tac. *Ann.* 2.33; Dio 57.15.1; see below, Chapter 5). Parker has noted that silk clothing on men in the *Historia Augusta* "functions as an unambiguous marker of vice" (2008, 171). In Commodus' wardrobe were clothes of silk foundation shot through with gold (*HA* Pert. 8.2). Elagabalus gave garments of *serica* as gifts (29.6), and was the first Roman to wear garments wholly of silk (*holoserica*; *HA* Eleg. 26.1). Alexander Severus by contrast did neither (*HA* Alex. Sev. 40.1; *HA* Tac. 10.4). While a treacherous historical source, normative statements like these perhaps give us some idea of what types of clothing were considered overly-luxurious for men of the upper classes.

Besides wool and silk, other types of fabric were also in use for male clothing: Martial refers to very heavy tunics from Padua, triple-twilled (*[tunicae] Patavinae trilices*; 14.143).[15]

Aurelian gave to the people "fine linen tunics" from Africa (*HA* Aur. 48). Often, however, the type of luxury fabric from which clothing was made was referred to in vaguer terms. Ovid refers to a toga "of finest thread" (*toga... filo tenuissima*; *Ars* 3.445);[16] in Horace, the man who loves luxury will wear a fine toga (*tenuis toga*) and have shining locks (*nitidique capilli*; *Epp.* 1.14.32). Tertullian states a tunic was superior when it was woven "of fine thread" (*Pall.* 1.1.3). Writing in the late second century, Artemidorus thought that to dream one was wearing "a soft, costly garment is auspicious for both the rich and the poor. For the rich, it is a sign that their present prosperity will continue. For the poor, it signifies that their affairs will be brighter" (*Oneir.* 2.3).

Color

The code of normative male appearance at Rome dictated that the appearance of the Roman man was staid and plain (see below, Chapter 5). The *toga pura* referred to the natural undyed toga of the Roman citizen; color of any kind was frowned on by some as effeminate. On the other hand, there is plenty of literary, artistic, and archaeological evidence for color in male clothing.[17] Not all Romans wore somber colors, as we will see, and clearly "the Roman preference for dark colors [thought in keeping with Roman *gravitas*] was possibly a professed ideal rather than an actuality" (Leary 1996, 194).

Discussing color in antiquity has its difficulties, most notably the Latin terms employed for colors. This was a problem recognized by the ancients themselves. Gellius describes a discussion among a gathering of learned men at Fronto's house concerning how "shades of colors are manifold" (*multiplex colorum facies*), but the names for them are "few and indefinite" (*incertae et exiguae*; 2.26.2–3). The philosopher Favorinus comments that this poverty of language is more pronounced in Latin than in Greek (2.26.5). Because of this ancient imprecision, the modern study of abstract hues is "frustrating and confusing, although an investigation into the symbolism of the color of a particular item can be more rewarding and enlightening" (Llewellyn-Jones 2003, 225). The social perception of a color could change however according to "the need for meaning" (ibid.), and ancient color 'prototypes' were often at the "meeting points of several cognitive domains" such as color, light, movement, and mental states (Bradley 2009, 17).

Practically speaking, the array of colors achieved by dyes in antiquity was limited: "the Romans would not have possessed anything approaching our sophisticated range of colours which are produced by aniline dyes" (Clarke 2003, 4). As well, it is important to remember that the dyes used by the ancients were impure, their methods primitive and not properly controlled.[18] Thus dyed textiles could change color according to light or angle of viewing (there is 'color uncertainty' with some dyes even today; Clarke 2003, 112). Martial (14.133) speaks of an 'honest' *lacerna* not dyed by the vat; cloaks could be dyed any one of a number of colors.[19]

Purple[20]

Purple was the color which indicated rank most strongly, in the stripes on a senator's tunic and toga and on the equestrian tunic, for example. It was also a relatively safe status color that had connotations of power and masculinity unless worn exclusively. The most prized hue was sea-purple, which went by a variety of names in antiquity: *conchylium, dibapha, blatta, oxyblatta, amethystina, ianthina*; "there were also various concentrations, combinations or styles of these" (Bradley 2009, 208). Expensive and colorfast, the dye was extracted at great care and expense from the bodies of sea-mollusks, each of which only yielded a single drop of dye, and only when freshly caught.[21]

The very color of sea-purple was unstable, "underlying its functional complexity" (Bradley 2009, 195; Pliny *Nat.* 9.135). Pliny states that the colors of *murex* dye varied from blush (*color rubens*) to black (*nigrans/nigricans*), scarlet (*nitor cocci*), the color of amethyst (*amethysti colos*),[22] violet (*violacea*), the color of a gloomy and angry sea (*glaucum et irascens mari*) and congealed blood (*sanguis concretus*; Bradley 2009, 195–6).[23] Munro notes that

> by selecting various combinations of dyestuffs from these mollusks, by varying their exposure to sunlight, by using several additives (salt, honey, urine, orchil), dyers could achieve a wide range of colors: light to dark

purples, violets, heliotropes, deep red-blacks, reddish-browns, sanguine, crimson, rose-red, blues and even shades of green. Although such purples might vary considerably in price, because of their composition, even the cheapest was far more costly than any other dyestuffs.[24]

In addition, Tyrian had a special quality: sea-purple dye "was known to have had unique physical properties, sitting on the surface of garments rather than within the fabric and reflecting and manipulating sunlight in a similar fashion to oil floating on water" (Bradley 2009, 50). Seneca noted there were certain colors which showed their properties best at a distance, such as Tyrian purple: "the better and richer it is (*quo melior est saturiorque*), the higher you ought to hold it to exaggerate its gleam" (*altius oportet teneas, ut fulgorem suum intendat; NQ* 1.5.12). On Augustus claiming that a shade of Tyrian purple purchased for him was too dark (*obscuritas*), the salesman instructed him to "hold it up higher and look at it from below." Augustus replied, "What? In order that the Roman people think me suitably dressed (*bene cultus*) I have to walk about on my roof?" (Macrob. 2.4.14). There was clearly considerable social pressure for sea-purple to be seen and recognized (Bradley 2009, 201).

Intriguingly, the price one had paid for a purple-dyed garment often announced itself through smell.[25] Cicero claimed that the smell could cover body odour: one Decianus is able to be *lautus* (clean or washed) for a long time in one set of garments, since they are Tyrian purple (*Flac.* 70). Martial writes of country life: "nowhere will you see a crescent shoebuckle or a toga or clothes that smell of purple dye" (*lunata nusquam pellis et nusquam toga/ olidaeque vestes murice*; 1.49.31–2), and reported elsewhere that Tyrian purple was bad-smelling (4.4).

Purple was the quintessential symbol of wealth and success, employed legitimately by the elite and illegitimately by everyone else eager for a visual claim on that social group's status. The elder Pliny speaks of different fashions in purple, and quotes Cornelius Neops, who states that in his youth *violacea purpura*, violet-purple, was popular; later on the red-purple of Tarentum (*rubra Tarentina*; 100 denarii a pound); later double-dyed Tyrian purple (*Nat.* 9.137; 1,000 denarii a pound). Purple perhaps had to evolve new hues in order to remain a luxury color, "for as its tones were imitated by the non-elite, they lost their status properties."[26] Pliny in fact noted the glut of counterfeit dyes available to satisfy the demand for the color: scarlet-purple, Tyrian, amethyst, different violets, ianthine, murex, heliotrope; "at the present day," he reported, "nature and luxury are matched together and are fighting it out."[27] Evidence of 'intended for purple' clothing was brought to light by textile finds in the Bar Kochba caves in Israel (around 135 CE; Yadin 1963), and in the Roman *praesidium* at Didymoi, confirming that counterfeit purple was sought after and in use.[28] But archaeological evidence of true sea-purple clothing at both sites demonstrates that Tyrian dyes also trickled down to the lower classes, probably through the secondhand clothing market.[29]

The many references scattered throughout Latin literature to purple and its various shades as status colors in clothing are well-known to scholars, and I give just a few examples here.[30] In the Republic there was a tendency to associate purple garb in a derogatory manner with the insignia of Hellenistic kingship (Reinhold 1970, 42). Polybius mentions the use of purple to indicate rank and status in funeral processions in the early second century BCE (6.53). According to Cornelius Nepos, P. Lentulus Spinther was the first to use Tyrian *dibapha* on his *toga praetexta,* a show of luxury which met with disapproval in Rome (Pliny *Nat.* 9.137). Cicero mentions the arrogant Quinctius in a purple toga reaching to his heels (*ad talos de purpuram [togam] missam; Pro Cluent.* 111).

Some scorned the color, but in early Empire "the theme of the un-Roman tone of purple continued to be a contemporary rhetorical cliché" (Reinhold 1970, 44).[31] Augustus had Tyrian purple garments purchased for his use (ibid., 49), but only to keep abreast of the current mode of elegance (Macrob. 2.4.14, above). Aeneas' purple *laena* is shot through with gold (Virg. *A.* 4.262–4). Horace rejected the color purple for himself "as not consonant with his philosophy of simplicity and moderation" (Reinhold 1970, 48; *Carm.* 1.35.12, 2.18.8). Horace refers to purple clothes 'brighter than the stars' (*Carm.* 3.1.41–8) and clothes dyed with Gaetulian purple (*Epp.* 2.2.180–2). Silius Italicus wrote of a *laena* which "glows," likely purple or scarlet (15.421–2). Tiberius scorned the use of purple and wore a grey cloak in public (Dio 57.13.5). Purple as a status color is utilized throughout Petronius' *Satyricon* (e.g., 32, 38, 119). At Persius 1.32 a cloak is hyacinth-colored (*hyacinthina laena*; it is denounced as effeminate. See below, Chapter 5). Nero "interdicted the sale and general use of the two highest qualities of purple – *amethystina* and *Tyria* – so as to reserve it, no doubt, for the imperial court and other official purposes. He closed down the shops (presumably only in Rome) of all merchants selling these qualities of purple" (Reinhold 1970, 50; Suet. *Nero* 25.1 and 32.3). But after his death there was apparently a return to "complete freedom of manufacture, sale, and use of purple" (Reinhold 1970, 50). The younger Seneca railed against purple, the *color improbus*, but in fact the color was in use among all classes throughout the Empire for clothing and other articles of display.[32] Martial contrasted a greasy woolen *bardocucullus* with "city Tyrianthines;"[33] that is, purple cloaks worn by rich urban men (1.53). Richly-colored *lacernae* of purple and scarlet are also mentioned in Martial (2.29, 5.8, 8.10, 9.22.13; see also *HA Sev. Alex.* 42); and we glimpse a dandy's brilliant purple *abolla* or cloak at Mart. 8.48.1–4 (and see Suet. *Calig.* 35.2). In general, for Martial brightly colored and especially purple clothing on men was a token of extravagance (see Williams 2004, 115: Mart. 2.46, 2.57, 5.23).

Scarlet

The various forms of scarlet as well were symbols of status because of the difficulty and expense of dye extraction. As noted above, scarlets and purples were not strongly differentiated in antiquity: in Gellius 2.26.5, the various purples and reds are all subsumed under the term '*ruber.*' The elder Pliny states: "I note that [among] the principal colors are ... red, as of the kermes insect (*rubentem ut in cocco*), which, from the loveliness of the dark rose, shades, if you look up at it in a bright light (*qui a rosae nigrantis gratia nitido trahitur suspectu*), into Tyrian purple, double-dyed purple, and Laconian purple" (*purpuras tyrias dibaphasque ac Laconicas; Nat.* 21.45–6).

Scarlet went by various names in Roman antiquity. *Puniceus* (*phoeniceus, poeniceus*) was a shellfish dye, but distinguished from purple by being a bright vermillion.[34] Gellius wrote that *poenicus* is a "rich, gleaming shade of red" (*exuberantiam splendoremque significant ruboris*; 2.26.9). Virgil speaks of *cothurni* (actors' shoes) and fillets colored *poenicus* (*Ecl.* 7.32, Virg. *A.* 5.269); Tibullus (2.3.58) mentions it as a dye, and Propertius as the color of sacred fillets (4.9.27), or a priestess' *infula* (4.9.52). In the sixth century, Isidore spoke of *poenicus* as a military color. But most references to the color describe dawn, flowers, and fruit.[35]

Coccinus (*coccineus*) was an opulent scarlet hue, expensive, brilliant, colorfast, and once mixed able to be stored for long periods – something shellfish dye could not be. The dye was extracted from the eggs and embryos of the insect *kermococcus vermilio*: thousands of female insects were required to yield a single ounce of the precious dye (Pliny *Nat.* 9.140–1, although he believes it to be a type of seed; at 37.204 he names it as one of the most expensive substances on earth).[36] This adjective is more often used in literary sources to describe red or scarlet clothing. In the *Satyricon* Trimalchio is wrapped in *coccina gausapa* after his bath (a shaggy scarlet blanket or cloak; 28.4). At *Satyr.* 32 he appears in a crimson *pallium*; and has pillows filled with purple and scarlet stuffing (*conchyliatum aut coccineum tomentum; Satyr.* 38). Martial mentions a muleteer in a scarlet hood (10.76; *cocco mulio fulget Incitatus*), and a slave in expensive scarlet clothing (the man is *coccinatus* and pretending to be free and wealthy; 5.35). A *lacerna* of scarlet is found at Martial 14.131; at 2.29 a man's shoe is of soft scarlet leather. At 2.43.8 Martial speaks of his *coccinea lacerna* and declares it is not worth three sesterces (perhaps because it is old and worn out?). Juvenal wrote of a rich man in a scarlet *coccina laena* – he will not be beaten up by drunken bullies (because the cloak acts as a warning sign of his wealth and large slave retinue: *iubet vitari*; 3.283).

Hysignum, another luxury dye, was a reddish-purple; Pliny tells us the color is Tyrian purple over a cloth already dyed with scarlet.[37] Kermes was involved in the production of *hysignum*; however, it is not clear in what capacity (Forbes 1964, 106).

Greens and blues

Generally, the different shades and blends of scarlets and purples continued to be the most popular status colors during in the imperial period, but we do hear of a few other colors for male clothing in the literary sources. Green may have been a technologically challenging color. Sumner believes "green colours were most likely achieved by over-dyeing cloth dyed yellow with woad" and might have made the cloth more expensive (2009, 116). But if green were an expensive color one would expect it to receive mention as such in the classical authors. Unlike purple and scarlet, green is a problematic hue from which to tease ancient resonances. *Viridis* was employed in poetry to describe youth or sexuality (Cat. 17.14; see Grant 2004, 245); lushness or fertility (Cat. 63.30; Hor. *Carm.* 1.4.9), even inspiration or fulfilment (Prop. 3.3.27). But the color might also have conjured up visions of illness: Grant states that green bile "was a ubiquitous feature of ancient medical texts" (2004, 247),[38] and the color was also used to describe madmen and those looking unwell or disorientated.[39] More significantly, however, green seems to have been a marker of "bad taste and sexual deviance" when worn by men (Hopman 2003, 569; see below, Chapter 5).

Although there is some mention of it on soldiers, we hear almost nothing about shades of blue clothing on civilian men.[40] Martial writes of a colored hood (dyed a pale greenish-blue, *callainus*)[41] which runs in the rain and streaks the white *lacerna* it is attached to; the owner did not know enough to match the hood to the same color cloak (14.140). Some shades of green and blue may have marked the lower classes or the *nouveaux riches* (see below).

White

White was another significant colour, symbolizing purity (especially in the case of the Roman bride and the *flamen dialis*: see Sebesta 1994a, 48), and may have evolved into an important ritual color because of the difficulty and expense of rendering cloth white: some wool was naturally white, of course, but to get cloth a gleaming white cost time and money, and the results were not permanent (see below).

The majority of togas and tunics in Roman antiquity were not in fact pure white (*contra* Croom 2002, 33), but the color of undyed natural wool, and so cream, beige, or off-white. The descriptors *albus, candidus,* and *niveus* may have indicated different shades of white.[42] If whiteness was desired, laying linen out in the sun would have helped to bleach it (Croom 2011, 107) but for some clothes a purer white was required. In most cases white was an *applied* color: the method was to "impregnate the cloth with fine particles of white pigment to create a brilliant white. Chalk, kaolin, and lime all seem to have been used."[43] Theophrastus (*Lapid.* 62, 64, 67) speaks of sulphur[44] and special types of clay used to turn cloth white (and sulphur had the important effect of rendering garments softer; Pliny *Nat.* 35.175). The *toga candida* was one artificially whitened with chalk to proclaim that the wearer was seeking office.[45] Thus "whiteness as an expression of stainlessness could only be achieved by literally staining clothes white."[46]

White clothes were expensive to maintain and difficult to care for (see now Bradley 2002), and the color was not likely worn by the lower or working classes. Artemidorus states in his *Oneirocritica* that:

> [White clothes] signify disturbances, since those who go about in the midst of a crowd wear white clothes. For artisans... they signify unemployment and inactivity. The costlier the garments, the greater the inactivity. For workingmen, especially those engaged in the mechanical arts, do not wear white clothes.
>
> (Artem. *Oneir.* 2.3).

White articles of clothing were instead often a sign of wealth or foppishness. Thus Cicero says of Pompey "his *caligae* and chalked-white leggings were not pleasing to me" (*etinem mihi caligae eius et fasciae cretatae non placebant; Att.* 2.3.1). In Persius, the writer who gives a public performance will be dressed in a neatly combed white toga, wearing a ring of sardonyx (*pexusque togaque recenti/ et natalicia tandem cum sardonyche albus*; 1.15–16). At Petr. *Satyr.* 60.8 the slave boys wear white tunics, and Trimalchio will be buried in white (78.1). The (possibly wealthy?) stonemason Habinnas arrives dressed in white at *Satyr.* 65. At Mart. 14.145 a white cloak is a handsome gift (*paenula candor*; see also 14.139). Martial speaks of beautiful white togas at 9.49 and 2.29 (in which a freedman pretending to be a senator wears a toga whiter than snow). In one epigram Cinna has snow-white *calcei* and a toga dirtier than mud (*sordidior caeno cum sit toga*; 7.33), which he has foolishly allowed to droop down and soil his shoes. At 8.28 a threadbare cloak will be an amusing contrast to a brand-new white toga, the color of which is likened to lilies, privet, ivory, swans, doves, pearls, and snow. At 14.135 a white *lacerna* is designed to be worn over a toga in the amphitheatre.

Other colors

There were other colors, garish and ridiculous, which may have been considered vulgar, possibly associated by the elite with upstart *parvenus* struggling for status.[47] *Prasinus* (*prasinatus*) was a strong greenish-blue (Pliny *Nat.* 37.181; Mart. 3.82.11; André 1949, 192); *cerasinus*, a bright pinkish-red (André 1949, 118). *Galbinus* seems to have been a yellowish-green (see below, Chapter 5). Mention of these colors is made several times in Petronius' *Satyricon*: Trimalchio's porter is clad in *galbinus* and *cerasinus*, and even Trimalchio's ball is *prasinus*.[48] Other garish colors thought to be favored by the *nouveaux riches* were *russus* (*russeus, russatus*), a bright red (Trimalchio makes his first appearance in this color: *Satyr.* 27), and *venetus*, a dark blue (Juv. 3.170, on a hood).[49] It is questionable whether these colors were truly considered to be lower class, or whether modern historians of ancient clothing have labelled them as such merely because they occur in Petronius' *Satyricon* and on similar lower-class characters in Latin literature.[50] Sebesta however has noted that three of these colors (*prasinus, russeus,* and *venetus*) were also colors of the chariot factions in the Roman circus,[51] and this perhaps justifies their categorization as lower-class colors.

Clothing and status 115

Gold[52]

Both male and female clothes could be embroidered or woven with gold thread, which was a very thin strip of gold wire wound around a textile core.[53] This is why clothes are often said to be "stiff" or "heavy" with gold in literary sources (e.g., Virg. *A.* 1.648–9; Cic. *ND* 3.83). The *chlamys* or Greek military cloak, often a luxury garment,[54] is sometimes golden or shot through with gold, usually in epic (Virg. *A.* 5.250, 8.167, 11.775). Ovid mentions "pliant gold" worked in among the threads in a textile woven on a loom (*Met.* 6.68).[55] Pliny also refers to embroidering in gold (8.196, which he states originated in Asia; see also Val. Flacc. 3.11; Hor. *Carm.* 4.9.14). Suetonius reports that following his victories in Greece in the chariot races, Nero rode into Rome in Augustus' triumphal chariot wearing a Greek *chlamys* adorned with gold stars (*Nero* 25.1). At Juvenal 10.210–12 a *lacerna,* possibly a stage costume, is ornamented with gold; Paul ex Fest. defines *leria* as "gold ornaments for tunics" (*ornamenta tunicarum aurea*; 102L).[56] In *CIL* 6.9213 and 9214 we hear of an *auri vestrix*, a woman who wove or embroidered clothes with gold. And of course, the *tunica palmata* and the *toga picta* featured designs in gold thread. But many of our sources for gold-embroidered male clothes are outside the central period (e.g., Claud. *Stil.* 340). By the turn of the third century, "gold-embroidered, jewel-trimmed capes had become the emperors' state dress – at the same time as capes embroidered with precious metals had become the bodyguards' court dress" (Speidel 1997, 232; see Amm. 31.10.9 and 14).

The trabea[57]

As with so many articles of their clothing, the Romans liked to think the *trabea* had an Etruscan origin.[58] Casual references from the central period note the *trabea* was originally the garment of Roman kings or of persons of distinction, and that it was worn on ceremonial occasions.[59] Thus at Virg. *A.* 7.612 the consul opens the Janus temple in a *trabea*, tied with the *cinctus Gabinus*. But the garment was also associated with Roman equestrians, being worn at the *transvectio* or annual review of the *equites* long obsolete (revived by Augustus).[60]

Bonfante-Warren (1970, 60 n. 70) and Palmer (1998, 59) believe the *trabea* was a cloak, after Dionysius of Halicarnassus (2.70.2) who states the *trabea* was fastened with a brooch.[61] Other scholars (Wilson 1924, 36; Helbig 1904, and Gabelmann 1977) name it as a type of toga worn by *equites*, after Isidore (below) and Servius, who wrote that "the girt-up *trabea* [was] the toga of the augurs, of scarlet and purple."[62] Perhaps the name was given "at different periods to garments of varying shapes" (Wilson 1924, 38). In the absence of paint on existing works of art, visual sources for the *trabea* are difficult to identify, though scholars have achieved much in this area.[63]

Whatever its form, the *trabea* was a colorful garment. Wilson believed that the term *trabea* was derived from *trabs*, the beam of a building, and that "the name was applied to the garment because it was woven with stripes or bands which resembled *trabes*" (Wilson 1924, 38).[64] Dionysius states the *trabea* was "striped with scarlet and bordered with purple" (*periporphyrous phoinikopaphyrous*; 2.70), and was worn by the Salii, dancers and singers of praise to the Roman gods of war.[65] Servius tells us that "Suetonius in his book *de Genere Vestium* states that there are three kinds of *trabeae*: one consecrated to the gods which is wholly purple (*tantum de purpura*); another for kings which is purple, although it has some white (*purpureum, habet tamen album aliquid*); and one used by the augurs with purple and scarlet mixed" (*purpura et cocco; A.* 7.612). Isidore wrote:

> The *trabea* was a type of toga out of purple and scarlet cloth (*togae species ex purpura et cocco*). In the beginning, the kings of the Romans used to process dressed in these. People claim Romulus was the first to devise this garment to distinguish the king. The *trabea* is so named because it would elevate a person into greater glory (*maiori gloria hominem transbearet*); that is, it may make a person further blessed for the future with a greater rank of honor (*ampliori dignitate honoris beatum*).[66]
>
> (Isid. *Orig.* 19.24.8)

Isidore however is referring to the late antique *trabea*, a highly decorated and complex-tailored form of ceremonial dress for emperors and consuls (Croom 2002, 47–8), rather than the dress of the *equites* in the central period. Servius and Isidore do not seem to associate the *trabea* with the equestrian order, probably because by late antiquity the garment was a general indicator of nobility and wealth.

Footwear

Like clothing, male footwear could be the object of lavish ornamentation, and this sort of adornment when worn by men often (unsurprisingly) brought with it censure or ridicule for being effeminate. The *soccus* was a soft indoor slipper; perhaps even a true sock worn with boots and sandals,[67] an import from Greece (Goldman 1994b, 125).[68] Archaeological examples of *socci* or perhaps true socks have been found, made from sprang-work (Croom 2002, 59). Caligula comes in for censure for wearing "womanish *socci*" (*socco muliebri;* Suet. *Calig.* 52), and Seneca recounts the story of Caligula, who extends his foot, encased in a little gold *soccus* decorated with pearls, to be kissed by an aging senator (*socculum auratum, immo aureum, margaritis distinctum; Ben.* 2.12.1). Apuleius mentions golden or gilded *socci* at *Met.* 11.8, and Diocletian's *Edict* lists several varieties of decorated ones: Phoenician purple, Babylonian purple, white, or gilded (ranging from 50–80 denarii; *Edict* 9.18–23).

Greek shoes, perhaps slippers, called *phaecasia*,[69] often white in color, also had connotations of luxury, and Mark Antony wears them in Plutarch's *Life of Antony* (33.4). Fortunata wears white *phaecasia* embroidered in gold at

Petr. *Satyr.* 67.4, and later Encolpius tries to pass himself off as a Roman soldier but is betrayed by his Greek slippers (82). A philosopher buys a pair of these on credit at Sen. *Ben.* 7.21.1; at *Epp.* 113.1 they are mentioned as a Greek fashion. Another kind of luxury (and therefore un-Roman) footwear was *gallicae*, "Gallic shoes/slippers." Cicero when speaking of Antony's improper costume at *Phil.* 2.76 states that he ran about in Gallic slippers and a *lacerna*. At Juvenal 7.16, the *gallicae* of priests expose the marks of fetters, showing the men were former slaves. Aulus Gellius recalls how his teacher Titus Castricius rebuked several young men, his pupils then on holiday, for wearing Gallic slippers or sandals (*gallicae*) outside with tunic and *lacernae* (*NA* 13.22). From these passages, we may infer that *gallicae* were expensive footwear – and note that the very names *phaecasia* and *Gallicae* mark them as foreign and un-Roman.

There were other inappropriate shoes for noblemen. Cicero mentions with distaste the politician G. Sempronius Tuditanus' habit of dressing up as a tragic actor in public, wearing a woman's cloak and *cothurni*, the high platform-like shoes of actors (*Phil.* 3.16; *BNP* Sempronius I 22). Unlike heels in later Western culture, heels on male shoes were emphatically not a sign of status, as it was the footwear actors wore on stage. Suetonius complained that in his clothing, shoes, and general attire the emperor Caligula did not follow the usage of his country, his fellow-citizens, or even his sex: "he often appeared in public... now in *crepidae* (sandals) or *cothurni* (actors' shoes), again in *caligae* (military sandals), and at times in womanish *socci*" (*Calig* 52). Tertullian in his *de Pallio* complains of Venetian shoemakers fashioning effeminate boots: (*perones effeminatos*; 5.2.4).

Although wearing the *calceus* or shoe-boot normally marked one's rank as a senator or patrician, sometimes such footwear indicated status too, by colors other than black or red. At Martial 7.33 one Cinna has snow-white *calcei* and a toga dirtier than mud (*sordidior caeno cum sit toga*). White was a notoriously difficult and expensive color to care for, and this passage marks the man out as wealthy and stupidly careless of his clothing. In one of Phaedrus' fables the 'emperor' wears a snow-white tunic and shoes (5.7). Some *calcei* were inappropriately jeweled, in the emperor Elagabalus' case with engraved gems, the height of senseless luxury (*HA* Eleg. 23.4). This is similar to Roman moralizing stories concerning certain Eastern generals who required gold hobnails under their sandals (Val. Max. 9.1. ext. 4; Pliny *Nat.* 33.50).

Synthesis/Cenatoria[70]

The *synthesis* or *cenatoria* seems to have been a costume comprised of a tunic and a small wrap or *pallium*, the parts of which were designed to be worn together. The terms appear in the first century CE to designate an especially rich costume, garments for warm weather or for the Saturnalia (Mart. 6.24, 14.1.1, 14.142; Leary 1996, 3, 51, 205). It was also a dinner garment, replacing the more formal tunic and toga. It was not conventionally worn outside the dining room, and Suetonius reported scornfully that Nero often inappropriately appeared in public in a *synthesina* (*Nero* 51; perhaps it is only the tunic half).[71] Martial is our chief source for the *synthesis*, although it is mentioned in other authors,[72] and "according to him the garment formed a part of the rather expensive wardrobe that urban society demanded" (Brewster 1918, 131).

It is unclear what exactly the *synthesis* consisted of. "By etymology and analogy... a synthesis must be a garment which combines into a single robe various simple elements" (Brewster 1918, 139). She believes it comprised two attached though detachable parts, and the *palliola* might hang from one shoulder, or be draped from both (Brewster 1918, 142–3). McDaniel (1925) however denies that the two parts of the garment need any way be attached to each other; rather, it is a *synthesis* if the tunic and mantle are of the same cloth. This would also explain the phrases *laena cenatoria* and *abolla cenatoria*: they were the mantle pieces of the *synthesis* worn without the tunic, possibly for warmth (see *CIL* 8.4508; McDaniel 1925, 269–70). Wilson (1938, 171) postulates more simply that the tunic and *pallium* could be of any color and material; there was no prescribed manner of draping; and it could be as short as the wearer wished for comfort.

The *synthesis* was a colorful garment. The Arval brotherhood wore white *syntheses* at certain ritual feasts,[73] but we know of other hues. At *Satyr.* 30, Trimalchio's slave *dispensator* had been presented with a Tyrian purple *synthesis* by a client, which was then stolen in the baths.[74] Colored *syntheses* are mentioned at Mart. 2.46; and one Zoilus changes *syntheses* eleven times in the course of a dinner, pretending to be soaked with perspiration, but in truth wanting to show off his vast collection of expensive dinner garments (Mart. 5.79).

The *synthesis* was perhaps costlier than a separate tunic plus cloak (*Dig.* 34.2.38.1; Brewster 1918, 141), and in smaller Roman towns garments like the *synthesis* were worn infrequently and would last years (see Mart. 4.66.3; Brewster 1918). At Mart 10.87.12, multiple *cenatoria* given as Saturnalia gifts are a rich present.

The small *pallium* of the *synthesis* would have been worn about the shoulders when out-of-doors, but it seems to have had another role as well. In the *Historia Augusta* (Tyr. Trig. 23.5), a third-century Roman general ordered his soldiers to appear at dinner in a cape (*sagum*), heavy in the winter and light in the summer, so that they could cover their lower parts as they reclined. Although the story is fictitious, it is interesting to note that funeral banquet scenes on soldiers' gravestones usually show hips and legs covered by a cloak (Speidel 2012, 10), perhaps portraying the mantle and tunic of the *synthesis*.[75]

The *synthesis* was worn by both men and women (Brewster 1918, 133–4; Mart. 10.29.4), and the same style of garment may even have been in use by both sexes. In the mid-/late second century CE, the jurist Pomponius gave it as his opinion that:

There is no difference between men's clothing and men's garments (*inter vestem virilem et vestimenta virilia nihil interest*); but the intention of the testator makes for difficulty, if he himself had been in the habit of using certain clothing which is also suitable for women (*quae etiam mulieribus conveniens est*). And so, in the first place, it must be held that the clothing which the testator intended constitutes the legacy, not what is in fact female or male. For Quintus Titius also says that he knows that a certain senator was accustomed to use women's dinner-dress (*muliebribus cenatoriis uti solitum*), and if he were to leave 'women's clothing' (*muliebrem vestem*) would not be regarded as having expressed an intention in respect of what he himself used as if it were men's clothing (*quasi virili utebatur*).
(*Dig.* 34.2.33).[76]

It is hard to state categorically that this passage reflects actual Roman practice of a cross-dressing senator and is not just imaginative legal discussion.[77] 'Female' dinner dress however might have differed from male in that the tunic may have been longer or fuller,[78] or the costume may have had a wider range of colors.

The *synthesis*, like the *pallium* and the *chlamys*, may have been a Greek import to Rome, although there is no instance to my knowledge of the word *synthesis* used in ancient Greek to designate dinner-dress.[79] The fact that the costume had a Greek name however is interesting, as like the *pallium*, the *synthesis* attracted negative comment when worn out of context. The *synthesis* was situation-specific dress, and Nero at least garnered criticism for inappropriate dress when he wore it outside the dining room.

There are no securely identified artistic representations of the *synthesis*. Brewster has noted that in frescoes of *triclinia* the diners' costumes seem to be ungirt tunics but these could in fact be *syntheses*.[80] Tombstones of soldiers at banquets (see above) perhaps show the diners in the *synthesis*. A banquet scene from Pompeii now in the Naples Archaeological Museum shows a man in colored clothing with a mantle draped over his head in the upper right-hand corner, another possible representation of the *synthesis* (see Fig. 1.4).

Jewelry and status: rings

Even though rings were supposed to originally indicate rank, they soon came to indicate status. Signet rings were "part decorative, part amulet, and part personal seal" (Croom 2002, 73). Rings might have gems carved with apotropaic devices to protect against demons and bad luck, for example.[81] Pliny (*Nat.* 33.22) rails against the brilliance of male rings in his own day and of the fancy carving of the intaglios. Both male and female rings were used for sealing documents[82] (Augustus and his personal advisors used rings with a carving of the Sphinx, found by Augustus among his mother's jewelry; Pliny *Nat.* 37.10), and thus rings were often connected with crimes involving money such as fraud and forgery (Pliny *Nat.* 33.26). Sometimes however (as

Figure 4.1 Detail of toga, Roman funerary relief from the Via Statilia. Centrale Montremartini, Rome. 80–50 BCE
Photo: author.

Pliny points out in disgust) the gems were worn whole, so that the ring itself could not be used as a signet (*Nat.* 33.22–3). In the reign of Claudius, people apparently sealed with the gold of the ring itself instead of a gem (*Nat.* 33.23).

The number of and material of rings drew criticism from some. The elder Pliny complained of the number of rings worn at once, "loading the fingers with a wealthy revenue" (*censuque opimo digitos onerando; Nat.* 33.22); men wore rings on most of their fingers, and even additionally above the first joint.[83] The younger Seneca complained of this practice as well: "we adorn our fingers with rings: a gem is arranged on every joint" (*exornamus anulis digitos, in omni articulo gemma disponitur; NQ* 7.31.2; cf. Mart. 5.61.5). Martial wrote that one Stella had several expensive rings on a single finger-joint: sardonyxes,[84] emeralds, diamonds, and jaspers (*sardonychas, zmaragdos, adamantas, iaspidas*; 5.11; and see Pliny *Nat.* 37.6–7). Juvenal's Crispinus has weighted rings, for summer and winter use (1.27–30). Such a display would indicate wealth, and the obvious fact that the wearer was not a manual laborer, as such a number of rings would hinder banausic work.[85] For some, it also indicated effeminacy (see below, Chapter 5). Some men collected rings (Pliny *Nat.* 37.11), and stored or displayed them in special cases called *dactyliothecae* (Mart. 11.59, 14.123; *Dig.* 32.53).[86]

Rings often slipped off at the baths (Leary 1996, 188 with Mart. 11.59 and 14.123), and the gemstones fell out too (Leary 1996, 188).[87] Artemidorus wrote that for a man to dream of rings lost, broken, or falling apart was inauspicious, as it signifies the loss of those whom he relied on in his house, and also the dissolution of his property, "for these people have no further need of rings."[88]

Other types of jewelry on men are also known: Pliny detested the gold bracelets called *dardania* worn by men in his day, apparently the fashion (*Nat.* 33.39–40). Trimalchio sports a gold armband *(armilla aurea; Satyr.* 32.4). Artemidorus, writing later, states that necklaces on men are inappropriate (*Oneir.* 2.5).[89] Men also wore brooches to keep mantles and cloaks in place, the most common design from the first to the third centuries CE being a round disc with a central stone, glass, or even cameo setting.[90] An intriguing aspect of male jewelry, however, is that for some it indicated effeminacy (see below, Chapter 5).

Slaves and status

Roman emphasis on distinctions of dress meant that there was ideally a natural correlation between the clothing of the slave and his low social position. Dingy woolen clothing, unfashionable but practical and cheap, was the normal garment for a slave. For most slaves it was "the quality of what they wore, not the garments themselves, that allowed their appearance to be distinctive" (Bradley 1994, 97–8). In the late second/early third century CE, Ulpian specifically mentions tunics and hooded cloaks (*penulae*) in a list of slave clothing, along with *saga*, tunics, and bed linen (*Dig.* 34.2.23.2).

Columella recommended slaves wear garments of patchwork (*centonibus confectis;* R. 1.8.9). The dark wool of Pollentia was used for mourning clothing (Mart. 14.157), but Martial also thought it was a suitable material for second-rate serving slaves (14.158). Artemidorus thought that to dream of new clothes was inauspicious for the slave longing for freedom, "since [new clothes] are worn out with great difficulty and last a long time" (*Oneir.* 2.3). For some, *vernae* were ideally simple in dress and grooming (Juv. 11.145–9), but there was a golden mean: Cicero criticizes Piso for letting shabby slaves wait at table (*servi sordidati ministrant; Pis.* 67). Of course, some slaves worked naked (see Diod. Sicl. 34/35.2.38) or clad only in loincloths (Apul. *Met.* 9.12).

Some slaves however were dressed in expensive clothing and ornamented, a practice which called attention to the fact that their master or mistress was wealthy (Bradley 1994, 87–8); a large retinue of beautiful well-dressed slaves increased the status of the owner. Funerary inscriptions from the imperial households of Augustus and Tiberius indicate that included in the imperial household was an *ornator glabrorum* (*CIL* 6.8956, a male slave who served as a beautician to the smooth boys who distributed wine at table), as well as a *puerorum ornatrix* (a female beautician for the slave boys; *CIL* 6. 33099; see Williams 2010, 34, and 320 n. 116). Pliny (*Nat.* 16.77) speaks of purple used for slaves' clothing in Gaul, and gold-adorned *paedogogi* at the baths (33.40). Slaves who worked as porters (*ministratores, pedisequi*) had special liveries and uniforms; at the house of Trimalchio, even his *dispensator* (steward) supposedly owned purple clothing; his serving boys wear white, another status color.[91] Martial describes a Nubian slave in a cloak of expensive wool as a sign of wealth and status (Mart. 9.22.9). At Byrrhena's banquet, Lucius noticed that "several brilliantly robed waiters" (*splendide amicti*) elegantly served heaped platters, and that "curly-haired boys in beautiful clothes" (*pueri calamistrati pulchre indusiati*) offered vintage wine in cups cut from gems (Apul. *Met.* 2.19). As well, slaves might wear jewelry to display their owner's wealth: the slave Theagenes in Heliodorus' romance was given elaborate Persian apparel and jewelry to wear to serve as cupbearer.[92] Statius gives us a description of luxurious clothing on a favored *deliciae*, clothing the right size and appropriate for the boy's age (indicating perhaps that other, less preferred slaves were dressed in cast-offs that may not have fit very well), in various, sometimes luxury, colors: scarlet (*puniceus*), grass-green (*herbas imitante sinu*), and purple (*murex*). The boy's fingers are "afire" with vivid gems as well. He only lacks the *toga praetexta*, denied to him because of his servile status (*Silv.* 2.1.128–36).[93]

The clotheshorse

The man who owned an extensive wardrobe and who constantly appeared in new clothes is a feature of Martial's *Epigrams*. In 6.59, one Baccara prays for cold weather so that he may show off his numberless frieze cloaks (*sescentas... gausapinas*). In 2.57.5 a man who is gorgeous in violet (*amethystina*), has many mantles (*lacernae* and *paenulae*). A certain Cordus is called 'number one in *paenulae*' (*alpha paenulatorum*; 5.26, and 2.57); Publius has a collection of *lacernae* (2.57). A certain Naevolus also has an impressive wardrobe:

> As flowery Hybla is decked in various hues when the bees of Sicily plunder the short-lived spring, so your presses shine with the cloaks placed in them (*sic tua subpositis conlucent prela lacernis*), just as your wardrobe glitters (*micat*) with innumerable dinner-garments (*innumeris arcula synthesibus*), and your white garments (*tua candida*), that Apulia produced from flocks more than one, are sufficient to dress a whole tribe. But you gaze impassively at your freezing, girt-up friend (*hiemem succincti lentus amici*) – oh, it's abominable – and the threadbare chill of your escort (*lateris frigora trita tui*). Was it so much, you wretched fellow, to cheat of

a couple of rags (*pannis fraudare duobus*) – what are you afraid of? – not yourself, Naevolus, but the moths?

(2.46)[94]

Such passages perhaps show that certain men (at least in Martial's day) took a keen interest in their appearance. It is also noteworthy that the large wardrobes in these passages are not indicative of effeminacy or sexual passivity, but of wealth; further demonstrating, I believe, the presence of the dandy on Rome's urban scene (see below, Chapter 5).

Folds in clothing[95]

Granger-Taylor notes (1982, 17) that other marks on the Arringatore's toga, most visible above the left knee, which have been taken by other scholars as evidence of woven decoration (Wilson 1924, 36; Dohrn 1968, 8) are probably fold-lines. Clothing in antiquity was stored folded up, and even flattened in presses to create such lines. Similar lines have been found on Greek statues from the fourth century BCE onwards and have usually been identified as folds (Waywell 1978, 69; and Figs. 2.4 and 4.1).

Historians of ancient clothing have not traditionally examined the presence or meaning of fold-lines in material representations of clothing to any serious extent, with the notable exception of Granger-Taylor's excellent article (1987). The depiction of such fold-lines is sometimes thought to be exclusively a phenomenon of the Hellenistic Baroque (from about 220 BCE), but is found in Roman art as well. Such folds however required "some skill to depict and were probably much more common in real life than Roman art would suggest" (Croom 2011, 110; conversely, Granger-Taylor [1987, 118] asserts that in fact "less conspicuous fold lines are found quite commonly throughout classical art"). Even when they are present, such lines do not show up well in photographs and require a physical inspection of the statue to locate and identify.[96] In the bronze statue of Marcus Aurelius that Granger-Taylor examined (1987, 117), she found fold-lines all over the mantle and tunic, in pairs, 2–2.5 cm apart, frequently crossing one another at right-angles. On the bronze figure of a Roman boy wearing a *pallium* (Fig. 2.4), the garment has a series of parallel lines running across it: stripes or fold-lines?

"Neat fold marks in clothes would have emphasised the fact that they were either brand new or were just newly laundered" (Croom 2011, 110; Granger-Taylor 1987, 122), and for this reason fold lines came to be desired in their own right. Clothes-presses[97] and clothes-chests[98] may have thus been used to put creases and folds *into* clothes. In addition, wool garments required heat, time, and/or moisture to produce any kind of fold, and prior to pressing, the cloth would have been dampened (thus Sen. *NQ* 1.3.2). Clothes-presses seem "to have been heavily built but with a relatively small opening," so that the clothes would have to be folded many times before insertion; one textile fragment from Pompeii gives evidence of at least twenty neatly-aligned layers (Granger-Taylor

1987, 120; no. 84734, Naples Archaeological Museum). The younger Seneca states that "I do not like... a garment bright from a small chest (*ex arcula prolata uestis*), nor one pressed by weights and a thousand tortures to force it to be splendid (*non ponderibus ac mille tormentis splendere cogentibus expressa*), but a house-garment of little value (*domestica et uilis*), that has neither been watched over nor selected with care" (*Tranq.* 9.1.5). Granger-Taylor writes that "the picture created by the written sources is that flattening wool garments in the press was the last stage of the laundering process which began with washing... clothes were probably also treated in presses at times between washings" (1987, 120).

Creases could also be put into the toga by hot irons or tongs. Tertullian recommends that men wear the Greek cloak or *pallium* as it does not have to be subjected to pressing like the toga: "it is necessary to assign the folded cloth to the custody of *forcipes*," he notes (*Pall.* 5.1.4).[99] Fold-lines faded from prominence in late antiquity, a time when all-over figured decoration became popular in clothes and draped clothes start to disappear (Granger-Taylor 1987, 122).

Thus, fold lines in Roman clothing must be thought of as imparting status. As Granger-Taylor notes, "a common theme of the references to presses or pressing is that of extravagant display" (1987, 122). Fold lines showed the wearer could afford to have his clothes well-maintained, reinforcing status by emphasizing the "cleanliness, volume, and quality of the apparel" (ibid.). It is likely Romans looked a lot more crumpled than modern tastes would accept (Croom 2011, 111).

Clothing and cleanliness

As Mark Bradley has noted, it was important to the upper classes to look "well-washed," a way of marking themselves off from persons of lower social rank (both slave and free), who might be dirty and unkempt: "like all cultures, the Romans were obsessed with looking clean" (Bradley 2002, 23). Cleanliness in Roman antiquity was thus equated with distinction.[100] But as Bradley also points out, an outer appearance of cleanliness was more important than actually being clean: (2002, 23). Clothes "could be washed 'clean' in stale urine and clay, trampled by the bare feet of slaves, rubbed with chalk, and fumigated with sulphur," pointing to a system of cleansing very different from our own (Bradley 2002, 23).

Such methods however, while odd to us, conferred status on the garments' owners. Clothes when fulled or washed with urine continue to smell even after rinsing, but to the Romans, the scent may have been simply a sign of new or cleaned clothes (Croom 2011, 102; Bradley 2002, 36).[101] As noted, clothing dyed with Tyrian purple retained the stench of the dye (Bradley 2002, 36).[102] Treating cloth with sulphur left an odour as well: another example of a bad smell as status.

The rich may have demanded a steady supply of clean clothes, but fulling in fact damaged the cloth and faded the dye, and the number of times clothes had been washed helped identify their worth. In Petronius, a set of clothes is deemed not very valuable because it had been washed once already (clearly exaggeration: *Satyr.* 30; 42). Martial mentions a gift of a toga "washed only three or four times at most" (10.11.6), and later, a gift of strigils: "if you use these, the fuller will not so often wear out your linens" (*non tam saepe teret linea fullo tibi;* 14.51).[103] The emperor Elagabalus would never wear washed linen, saying this was fit only for beggars (*linteis lotis; HA* Eleg. 26.1). While perhaps an unreliable historical source, this perhaps gives some notion of the damaging effects washing had on clothes.

Despite the importance of looking clean, clothes cleaned regularly were incongruously less valuable, because fulling had this abrasive and destructive effect (Bradley 2002, 29). Thus at Mart. 7.86.8 *rudes lacernae* 'unworn/unfulled cloaks' are a rich present precisely because they have never been washed. And damaging nature of cleaning methods at the time may have meant that the same clothes "were worn for several weeks without being cleaned, rather than days" (Croom 2011, 95; Bradley 2002, 29 n. 76). This likely explains the necessity of the *tunica intima*, the tunic many Romans wore as an undergarment, underneath their regular tunic.[104] This garment, worn right next to the body, would have required the most regular washing, but since it was not normally visible, the injurious effect on the cloth would not have been noticeable or important. Interestingly, the *Edict* of Diocletian implies that tunics were not fulled very often, either due to the material from which they were made (linen, perhaps) or due to the fact that as the tunic was not the visual focus of an outfit, having such items 'finished' with a silky nap was a not a priority (Flohr 2013b, 63–4).[105]

Sumptuary legislation and the morality of clothing[106]

There were attempts at legislation aimed at curtailing the use of certain types of male clothing which indicated wealth and status, as distinct from the regulation of the usurpation of juridical symbols of rank in dress (such as the *latus clavus; ius anuli aurei*). Sumptuary legislation in relation to symbols of status in men's clothing is remarkable not only because it is infrequent,[107] but, infrequent as it is, it also because it stands in sharp contrast to the almost complete absence of such legislation directed at women.[108] There were notorious problems in enforcing any kind of sumptuary legislation in antiquity, most notably the lack of manpower and the general disinterest in frugality as a lifestyle. Still, some sumptuary laws on clothing remain for us.

Brutus is said to have advocated the abolition or modification of the wearing of purple (the royal insignia) at the founding of the Republic to certain festal occasions and triumphal robes (Dion. Hal. 4.74, 3.62). Caesar enacted a restrictive measure against wearing clothing of sea-purple (*conchyliatae vestis*): it could only be worn by certain persons "of a designated position and age" only on certain days (Suetonius specifies neither the days nor the persons, but likely men and women of the elite class and festal days are meant; *Iul.*

43). Reinhold points out that there were no other restrictions on other kinds of purple "of which there were many" (1970, 46). Antony appears to have granted a decree to the *Hieroneikai* at Ephesus, allowing the members of the association the exclusive right to wear purple during certain festivals.[109] According to Dio, Octavian as *triumvir* in 36 BCE enacted legislation which restricted garments of sea-purple to senators holding magistracies (49.16.1).[110] The emperor Tiberius legislated against the wearing of silk by men, citing its unsuitability.[111] The law did not, however, prevent Tiberius' successor Caligula from assuming silk garments (Suet. *Calig.* 52). There was also an attempt by the emperor Nero to restrict purple to official insignia and imperial garb (Suet. *Nero* 32). There may too have been other legislation, the details of which have not survived for us.

Whether aimed at symbols of rank or those of status, sumptuary legislation in most pre-modern societies had a broad social aim: to construct an ideal visual narrative of the social order (Emberley 1997, 45).[112] In Roman antiquity as well, clothing was a highly visible and extremely persuasive status marker, and the symbolism of certain garments was associated with the privileges and prestige of certain ranks and statuses. Although there does not seem to have been much Roman sumptuary legislation relating to clothing, and that which survives does not give us the finely graded categories present in for instance the Acts of Apparel ratified in Tudor England (1509–47), we may nonetheless posit that Roman clothing laws, and indeed even normative statements on male clothing constituted a form of social practice tied to the 'problem' of status and social mobility (Sponsler 1992, 267, 275, 279).[113] Roman legislation on private clothing therefore represents the tangible expression of a masculine and hierarchical ideal.[114]

Conclusions

In eighteenth-century England, "fashion became associated with women and the lower orders, and displaying wealth was no longer equated with displaying worth: gentlemen were called on to lead the nation by setting a moral example rather than by attempting to outspend their extravagant emulators" (Kuchta 1996, 60). For some ancient Romans, plain and uniform costume was an aristocratic ideal as well. Some felt that the war against the *nouveaux riches* could best be waged by eschewing rich fabrics and ornament, assuming instead a frugal appearance. Aristocratic men could therefore (oddly enough) claim moral leadership and status through inconspicuous consumption, and some no doubt embraced this.

But the call to frugality was never strong enough to override the demands of visual prestige,[115] and most upper-class Roman men dressed in keeping with their status: when Horace's father sends his son off to Rome to be educated, he sends with him the kind of clothing and a retinue of slaves that one would swear came from old money (*S.* 1.6.78–80). In addition, we know from epigraphical evidence that there existed in Rome purveyors of luxury and the appearance trades. The presence of the *crepidarius* (sandal-maker; *CIL* 6.9284), the *gaunacarius* (a furrier; *CIL* 6.9431), *gemmarius sculptor* (a gem-engraver; *CIL* 6.9436), *siricarius* (dealer in silk; *CIL* 14.3712), *plumarius* (the brocader in feathers; *CIL* 6.31898 and 6.9814), *vestiarius tenuiarius* (maker of fine clothing; *CIL* 6.9978 and 6.33923) in ancient inscriptions all attest to the importance of fine clothing and ornament for the upper classes, and surely not all these workers had a clientele composed exclusively of women. For some, in fact, fashioning an elegant and splendid appearance was not considered a betrayal of a masculine identity, but instead a means to realize it.[116]

But men had an uneasy relationship with fashion in antiquity. Cicero states that the deceitful man changes his opinions like his clothing: he has one set for indoor wear and other when he goes outside (*aut etiam, ut vestitum, sic sententiam habeas aliam domesticam, aliam forensem*; *Fin.* 2.77). He also derides the dishonest man whose clothes are showy: "outside, all show and pretense, but your genuine self-concealed within" (*ut in fronte ostentatio sit, intus veritas occultetur*; ibid.). Horace professed to believe that fine tunics only corrupt a man morally (*pulchris tunicis*; *Epp.* 1.18.33). In addition, fine clothing and ornament on a man was often considered effeminizing, a discussion taken up in the next chapter.

Notes

1 In late medieval and early modern society, it was taken for granted that a person's dress should reflect his rank. Given such a belief, two developments made sumptuary legislation desirable: the first the expansion in the number of different stations in life and the increasing mobility between them; the second the rise of fashion. "Social structure... was becoming increasingly complex" (Harte 1976, 139), giving rise to Henry VIII's Acts of Apparel (1509–47; on the Acts, see now Hayward 2009). Harte also states that complaints about people dressing above their station became a "characteristic of virtually every period" (141).
2 *BNP* Vedius II 4; Syme 1961. See also Ov. *Fast.* 6.639–48;
3 Cic. *Leg.* 3.32: *ego autem nobilium vita victuque mutato mores mutari civitatum puto.* See also 3.30–1.
4 Edwards 1993, 180. See Cic.*Mur.* 76: *odit populus Romanus privatam luxuriam, publicam magnificentiam diligit.*
5 Although, as Kuefler notes, condemnation also reveals "the greater availability of luxury items" (2001, 57).
6 Granger-Taylor 1987, 117. See also Granger-Taylor 2008, 7–8, in which she examines fragments of a Roman cloak of northern Mediterranean origin, probably imported to Nubia in the first century CE. The fragments are off-white, evenly and finely woven, with a brilliant purple border. The garment was clearly of extremely high quality and shows evidence of repair in antiquity. In Martial 4.28, a woman gives to her young man an expensive woolen toga from Galaesus (site of the famed Tarentine wool). The wool of Patavium was also celebrated (Strabo 5.1.12; Mart. 14.143); Mutina too had excellent wool (a pure white of the finest grade: Strabo 5.1.12).
7 *nam tunica lati clavi in modum gausapae texi nunc primum incipit*; *Nat.* 8.193; see also Strabo 5.1.12; Mart. 14.152.2 on a shaggy blanket. On pile-weave see Barber 1991, 150, 200–2.

8   Schmeling 2011, 62 misses the economic importance of *gausapa* here, merely stating it is a "rough" material while failing to note that it is also expensive.
9   In this passage Horace is perhaps commenting on Lucilius' slapdash writing: see Gowers 1993, 168 n. 198.
10 It is of course possible that the statements in Lucilius, Persius, and Petronius are all ironic and that they are speaking of expensive dye on a cheap material. Martial's allusions however (6.59, 14.145) would indicate otherwise.
11 On ancient linen, see Aldrete *et al.* 2013 (on linen body armour); Barber 1991, 11–15; Forbes 1964, 27–43; Gleba 2004. See also Baines 1989 for some excellent practical information.
12 On ancient cotton, see Barber 1991, 32–3; Forbes 1964, 43–9; Wild *et al.* 2008.
13 On ancient silk generally, see Barber 1991, 30–2; Forbes 1964, 50–8; Hildebrandt 2013; Humphrey *et al.* 1998, 350. On the differences between wild silk and Chinese silk, see Barber 1991, 31–2; Dalby 2000, 151–2; Forbes 1964, 50–4; Wild 2011. For *tusseh* silk manufacture and trade, see Pliny *Nat.* 11.75–8; Pers. 5.135, Day 1956; Forbes 1930 *passim*. Silk in the third century: see *HA* Eleg. 26.1, 29.6; *HA* Sev. 40.1; Harlow 2004, 54–5. While Roman writers do not seem to have been particularly curious about how silk was obtained, Pausanius correctly observed that silk was woven from the cocoons of the silk moth (6.26.6–7). Parker (2008, 156) notes that silk was predominantly imported from China in antiquity, although of course there is evidence that the island of Cos also supplied silk (Edwards 1993, 68–9; Griffin 1985, 10). But "the Coan variety was not spun by caterpillars, and was of a less fine texture" and in the imperial period was superseded by Asian silk (Parker 2008, 156; Pliny. *Nat.* 11.78). Because of the way it was woven, however, Chinese silk cloth does not seem to have been universally popular in the Mediterranean, and was sometimes taken apart and redone (Luc. *Phars.* 10.141–3; Forbes 1964, 54; *Edict* 22.13). Major issues beset the modern study of silk in the ancient world: price, for instance (see Raschke 1978, 624–5, 726 n. 315) and the existence of a 'Silk Road' (see Young 2001, 190–1). For possible archaeological examples of ancient silk, see Barber 1991, 32; Panagiotakopulu *et al.* 1997.
14 *quorum vitreae togae ostentant tunicae clavos; Modius* 8 (Non. 861L). Wilson 1924, 63 notes that there is no artistic evidence for these transparent togas.
15 See also Strabo 5.1.7; Morley 1996; Noé 1974.
16 Makers of fine clothes were called *vestiarii tenuiarii*; such shops were clustered around the Vicus Tuscus. See Liu 2009, 80 n. 101 for the relevant *CIL* VI inscriptions.
17 For evidence of dyed textiles in archaeology, see Bender-Jørgensen 2010; Cardon *et al.* 2011; De Ruyt 2001; Mannering 2000b; Taylor 1983. Commonly, the raw fibers or finished yarn were dyed, rather than completed fabric: piece-dyeing was rare in the ancient world (Halleux 1981, 44, 151; Wild 1992a, 97; Wild 2008, 476; *contra* Bradley 2002, 22, 28 n. 64).
18 Forbes 1964, 100–1; Munro 1983, 14–15.
19 At Mart 10.87.10 a *lacerna* is a rich Saturnalia present. At 4.61.4–5 a man has a *lacerna* costing 10,000 sesterces (although whether this is due to the fabric, dye, ornamentation, or all three, we are not told).
20 The color purple as a symbol of status and rank in antiquity has been admirably treated in English by Reinhold 1970. See now as well Bessone 1998; Goldman 2013, 27–31, 40–52; Napoli 2004. For hues of purple in antiquity, see Wilson 1938, frontispiece, pl. 1. Interestingly, on some clothing fragments from Didymoi in Roman Egypt, true purple was found to have been overdyed with kermes/ *coccineus* because, as chemical analysis showed, the purple in these cases had initially resulted in too strong a blue color (Cardon *et al.* 2011, 202). On the surprising use of *purpureus* in Latin literature to describe salt, the rainbow, swans, etc., see Bradley 2009, 49; Edgeworth 1979.

21 There is a solid bibliography on purple dye in antiquity: Alfaro Giner and Martinez 2013; Bessone 1998; Bradley 2009, 189; Bridgeman 1987; Cardon *et al.* 2011; Constandinidis and Karali 2011; Dixon 2001b; Edmonds 2000; Longo 1998b; Lowe 2004; Macheboeuf 2004 and 2008. On variability of the color see Giacometti 1998. On modern experimentation with ancient techniques of shellfish dyeing, see Kanold and Haubrichs 2008, with bibliography.
22 To achieve the "highly prized paleness" of this amethyst color, the dye was cut with urine (Pliny *Nat.* 9.138).
23 Pliny *Nat.* 9.133–5.
24 Munro 1983, 14. See also Bradley 2009, 189; Sen. *NQ* 1.3.12; Vitr. *Arch.* 7.13; Pliny *Nat.* 9.133–4.
25 For the smell of sea-purple see also Strabo 16.2.23; Pliny *Nat.* 9.127; Butrica 2005, 267–9.
26 Bourdieu (1984, 249–51) believes that dominant classes tend to withdraw from what is showy or vulgar, and also devalue objects and practices which have lost their status through lower class familiarity with them (however, see Bonanno 1988).
27 *Nat.* 21.45–7. On counterfeit purple dyes (various mixtures of sea-purple, the use of other animal dyes, and inexpensive mineral and vegetable dyes), see Theophr. *Hist. Plant.* 4.6.5; Strabo 13.4.14; Pliny *Nat.* 9.137, 16.77, 21.27, 22.4, 35.44–5. See also Sebesta 1994b, 70.
28 "Intended for purple" colors include greyish mauve all the way through to dark violet (Cardon *et al.* 2011, 198–9).
29 Cardon *et al.* (2011, 200) have discovered that at Didymoi, 17% of textiles recovered (11 garments out of 62) were dyed with true purple, and were spread throughout the entire chronological occupation of Didymoi (from the earliest to the latest layers of the heap).
30 See here Bessone 1998 and (in part) Reinhold 1970.
31 Reinhold (1970, 43) notes the tension between moralizing/nationalistic hostility towards the use of purple clothing in first-century BCE Rome and "the contemporaneous unfettered massive increases in its use" in this period.
32 Reinhold 1970, 50. See for example Sen. *Epp.* 16.8, 76.31, 94.70, *Ira* 1.21.1, *Vita Beata* 25.2; Pliny *Nat.* 9.137.
33 Clothing which is Tyrianthine was possibly clothing dyed Tyrian purple and then scarlet (André 1949, 197). See also Pliny *Nat.* 9.139 (*Tyriamethystus*).
34 Lucretius calls *poenicus* the "brightest colour of all" (*color clarissimus multo*; 2.830). Pliny states that the "shellfish supplying the purple dyes and scarlets – the material of these is the same but it is differently blended – are of two kinds" (*concharum ad purpuras et conchylia – eadem enim est materia, sed distat temperamento – duo sunt genera*; 9.130). Munro confuses *coccineus* and *puniceus*, stating they were both dyes obtained from insects (1983, 15; see also Isid. *Orig.* 19.28.1). On *puniceus*, see André 1949, 88–90.
35 See Lucr. 2.830–3 (on dyeing); *Elg. in Maecen.* 1.124; Stat. *Theb.* 4.218, *Silv.* 2.1.132; *TLL* s.v. '*puniceus*' 10.1.2047–8.
36 Pliny (*Nat.* 9.141) states the best cochineal comes from Lusitania (Spain), and part of Asia Minor (Galatia), the least desirable from Sardinia (16.32). Schmeling incorrectly states *coccineus* is "an effeminate color" (2011, 114; based on Petr. *Satyr.* 28.4 and Mart. 1.96). See below, Chapter 5. See André 1949, *coccineus* (116–17), and *coccinus* (116–17, 214, 218, 267, 270, 279, 286, 383, 393); Goldman 2013, 52–3; Forbes 1964, 102–7.
37 *Nat.* 9.140; see also Vitr. 7.14.1; *Dig.* 32.78.5; and above n. 33 on Tyrianthine. On *hysignum*, see André 1949, 116–17.
38 See Cael. Aur. *Acut.* 2.14.93; Ps-Gal. *Hum.* 19.488K; Gal. *Atr. Bil.* 2 = 5.110K.
39 Madmen: Pl. *Men.* 828. Unwell or disorientated: Pl. *Curc.* 232–3 (a sick pimp, although only his eyes are described as green); Virg. *Ciris* 225 (a lovesick

woman); Cels. *Med.* 2.4.7 (green vomit). On these resonances of green, see Bradley 2009, 8–9. On blue and green clothing, see Goldman 2013, 55–6.

40 For the color blue in military clothing, see Sumner 2009, 117.

41 The *callais/callaina/callaica* was a gemstone of "pale green" (*viridi pallens*; possibly green turquoise; Pliny *Nat.* 37.110). See also *Nat.* 37.112, 37.151; Isid. *Orig.* 14.4.4, 16.7.10.

42 See Bradley 2009, 76; Clarke 2003, 4; Goldman 2013, 62–3.

43 Croom 2011, 108. And see Bradley 2002, 29; Flohr 2013b, 60–2.

44 It is thought by scholars that the process of sulphuring clothes also helped to bleach them white. Done by professional fullers, the method was to "drape the clothes over a semi-circular wickerwork frame and fumigate them by burning sulphur underneath" (Croom 2011, 107). The clothes naturally smelt of sulphur at the end of the treatment and had a tendency to turn yellowish in time (ibid.). See the wall painting of *fullones* in a fullery at Pompeii (VI 8, 20–21.2); Apul. *Met.* 9.24. Flohr (2013b, 117–18) however believes that this was not the whole purpose of treating clothes with sulphur: colored clothes were also handled this way (and substances applied to them afterwards to help counteract the effects).

45 On the *toga candida*, see Titin. *Com.* 167; Livy 27.34.12, 39.39.2;, Val. Max. 4.5.3; Pliny *Nat.* 7.120; Pers. 5.177; Mart. 8.65.5; Isid. *Etym.* 19.24.6; Denaiux 2003. Religious processions: Tib. 2.1.6; Ov. *Fast.* 2.654, 4.906.

46 Bradley 2002, 29 (see also 40). On the differences between fulling and dyeing establishments, see Bradley 2002; Flohr 2003, Flohr 2013b, 81–3; Wilson 2003. Flohr (2013b, 61) denies that the purpose of fulleries was to keep Rome "white." Using fresco evidence from Pompeii he believes most clothing dealt with by fullers was colored. On fullers and fulling generally see now Flohr 2013b.

47 The wearing of bright colors by *parvenus* in ancien régime France led to a kind of "semantic twisting" (Perrot 1994, 133): trying to construct a status, such people simultaneously dismantled it, and color at once denoted their social position and social aspirations (ibid., 128–35).

48 *Satyr.* 27, 28, 64, 70 (*prasinus*); 67 (*galbinus*); 28, 67 (*cerasinus*). Smith (1975, 54 and 58) asserts that "there is a notable frequency of red and green in the description of Trimalchio and his surroundings," but believes these colors were chosen merely for their sharp contrast. He does not point out they might be indicative of social status. Grant (2004, 244 n. 2) believes that in the ancient world there was a "gross lack of taste associated with the combination of red and green." See Beran 1973, 232–3 (which I have been unable to obtain).

49 *Russus*: André 1949, 83–4; *venetus*: André 1949, 181–2.

50 On color in Petronius, see Beran 1973; Currie 1989; Goldman 2013, 81–93; Grant 2004; Schmeling 2011, 114–16, 277.

51 Sebesta 1994, 70–1. Colors of racing factions: *prasinus*: CIL 6.10053; Petr. *Satyr.* 70; Mart. 10.48.23, 11.33.1; 14.131; Suet. *Calig.* 55.2,*Nero* 22.1. *Venetus*: CIL 6.10047.a.3, 6.37835; Mart. 6.46, 14.131; Suet. *Vitell.*7.1, 14.3. *Russatus*: CIL 6.10048.1, 14.2884; Juv. 7.114. See also Goldman 2013, 85–97; Leary 1996, 195–6.

52 On the use of gold in ancient textiles, see now Bedini *et al.* 2004; Benazeth 1989; Chioffi 2004; Alfaro Giner 2001 and 2005; Gleba 2008a. Speidel (1997, 232) believes the Roman custom of wearing clothing "stiff with bullion" was Eastern in origin.

53 Alfaro Giner (2001, 77) examines certain textile fragments out of the tomb of a noble adolescent girl from Gadir (Cádiz), the threads on which were composed of 23.4 carat gold. Both samples "are made from spirally spun gold strip (gold filé). The strip is 0.2 mm wide, and 3.6 microns thick, twisted around a fibre core… according to literature on gold textiles, the core thread was normally made from silk, linen, or even from very finely spun wool. The final result is a thread of 0.1 mm diameter" (in other words, a gold spiral around a textile core;

Alfaro Giner 2001, 78). For an examination of how gold threads was constructed and woven by hand in Fez in the first third of the twentieth century, see Vicaire and Le Tourneau 1937. For a bracelet from Roman Dorchester with a braided textile core originally wrapped with silver metallic wire, see Batcheller 1995.
54 For the *chlamys* as a luxury item, see Varro (*L.* 5.133, *Vita Pop. Rom.* in Non. 862L); Virg. *A.* 8.588 (Pallas wears it into battle), 9.582 (a *chlamys* embroidered by the needle); Horace (*Epp.* 1.17.31) a *chlamys* woven at Miletus is a luxury item and will not be worn by a philosopher, who prefers his 'doubled rags' (*duplici panno*; 1.17.25); Val. Max. 9.2. ext. 5 (cloak of an Egyptian prince); Pers. 6.46; Juv. 8.101; Tert. *Pall.* 4.8.2.
55 Sometimes the gold thread was part of the weft (see Alfaro Giner 2001, fig. 9.5; Wace 1948. On tapestry weaving see Barber 1991, 372–83). For gold thread 'interwoven' among other threads on a loom, see Virg. *A.* 3.483, 4.264, 8.167, 10.818; Ov. *Ars* 3.131. See also Virg. *Georg.* 2.464; Suet. *Nero* 50.
56 This is a Greek loan-word, and the definition does not specify whether male or female tunics are meant.
57 On the *trabea*, see Bonfante-Warren 1970, 60; 1973, 613–14; Dewar 2008; Gabelmann 1977; Goette 1990, 6; Helbig 1904; Palmer 1998, 59–60; Veyne 1960; Wilson 1924, 36–9; Wrede 1988. For the late antique *trabea*, see Croom 2002, 47–8.
58 Bonfante-Warren (1973, 613–14) believes the *trabea* and a shorter version, the toga, were the direct descendent of the Etruscan *tebenna*. On the Greek origin of the *trabea*, see Artem. *Oneir.* 2.3.
59 Virg. *A.* 7.187; Ov. *Fast.* 2.503, 6.796; Pliny *Nat.* 8.195. See Palmer 1998, 60, n. 280.
60 On the *trabea* as a sign of the equestrian order, see Dion. Hal. 6.13.4; Val. Max. 2.2.9; Pers. 3.29; Dio 56.31.2–3, 63.13.3; Tac. *Ann.* 3.2; Mart. 5.41; *CIL* 11.3204 ([*qui*] *equo publico transvectus est*). Wrede (1988) believes the *trabea* was kingly garb first and then was transferred to the cavalry (399–400). On the *transvectio*, see Gabelmann 1977; Rebecchi 1999; Wrede 1988; Suet. *Aug.* 38.3. Gabelmann (1977) and Rebbechi (1999) believe some of the visual depictions of the *transvectio* actually depict men of the senatorial class.
61 But as Wilson states (1924, 48–9) it is probable that the toga too was attached to itself at some point by a brooch or pin. The *trabea* must have differed in some way from the *lacerna* (see above, Chapter 2) – surely the point of Mart. 5.23 (*contra* Wrede 1988, 398).
62 *succinctus trabea: toga est augurum de cocco et purpura*; Serv. *A.* 7.188. By the fourth century, the *trabea* was synonymous with the *toga picta* (Dewar 2008, 220, 233). Dion. 6.1.3.4 describes a *transvectio* in the time of Augustus and names the garment of the *eques* as a 'purple *tebenna*' which might be the *trabea* or a special form of the toga (Dewar 2008). Helbig (1904, 174) believed the *trabea* was the predecessor of the *toga praetexta*.
63 Gabelmann 1977 (for criticism of this article, see Linderski 2002, 357 n. 75); Granger-Taylor 1982, 17; Rebecchi 1999.
64 Although one might expect the decoration to take a naturalistic form such as plants or human figures (Granger-Taylor 1982, 19), Wilson here relies on etymology (1924, 39).
65 The cloak was practical "since it was short, and pinned securely at the shoulder" (Bonfante-Warren 1970, 60 n. 70).
66 Dewar (2008, 219) states that by the late fourth century CE, the *trabea* was associated with the consulship.
67 Croom (2002, 63) notes that "some scholars are reluctant to believe that the Romans commonly wore socks in their shoes or sandals"; see Mart. 14.140.
68 Croom correctly notes that it is difficult to tell the difference in literature between socks and what may have been a true cloth shoe, an impractical material for footwear – although their impracticality underscores their use as a luxury item (2002: 63).

69 On *phaecasia*, see Baroin and Valette-Cagnac 2007, 538 n. 89, with references.
70 On the *synthesis*, see Brewster 1918; Croom 2002, 40; McDaniel 1925; Pausch 2008, 194–7 (the *tunicopallium*); Wilson 1938, 167–72. Synthesis had other meanings besides 'dinner costume:' a set of pottery, for example (Stat. *Silv.* 4.9.44; Mart. 4.46.15). See Wilson 1938, 169–70.
71 Dio 63.13 describes Nero in a short flowered tunic (*kitonion*) and a neck-cloth (*sidonion*), perhaps a *synthesis*. Walsh (1970, 38) sees a correlation between Trimalchio's napkin with its broad stripe (*laticlavum; Satyr.* 32) and Nero appearing in public with a neckerchief (*sudarium*; Suet. *Nero* 51).
72 Thus at Petr. *Satyr.* 56, one of the *apophoreta* at Trimalchio's *cena* is "dinner-dress and dress for the forum" (*cenatoria et forensia*, this last presumably a toga; cf. Mart. 14.136; Suet. *Aug.* 73).
73 See Henzen 1874, XII. 27, cciii and ccxxv; Brewster 1918, 132.
74 The *dispensator* dismisses the loss by saying, "Tyrian purple, of course, but it had been washed once already" (*Tyria sine dubio, sed iam semel lota*), and that the clothing "had scarcely been worth 10,000 sesterces," a considerable amount of money for any household but Trimalchio's; see Schmeling 2011, 107; Smith 1975, 64.
75 Brewster (1918, 142–3) also noted that in some material representations of the *palliolum*, the small mantle has been stretched over the wearer's knees. And see Speidel 1994, 5. In the first three centuries CE, equestrian officers had a special dinner tunic: the *tunica cenatoria* (e.g., *HA* Max. 30.5). Suetonius (*Calig.* 45.2) ridicules Caligula for ordering his officers to dine with him, clad as they were in armor. Thus it seems "to have been normal, or generally required, to have the appropriate dinner dress even when on campaign" (Speidel 2012, 10). Common soldiers also had some sort of tunic for dinner, probably not the same one they wore everyday (Speidel 2012, 10).
76 Wilson (1938, 172) postulates that *cenatoria* was an earlier word for male dinner-dress. On terminology, see Tuori 2009, 195–7.
77 As Tuori 2009 states. See here for a summary of earlier scholarly arguments on the passage.
78 On the female *tunicopallium*, see Olson 2008, 51.
79 Tertullian (*Pall.* 4.4.1) uses the term to describe the effeminate costume of the Greek boxer Cleomachus.
80 Brewster 1918, 142–3. For further artistic sources, see this article, p. 142.
81 See Johns 1982, 113. At Petr. *Satyr.* 74.2 Trimalchio transfers a ring to his right hand to ward off evil; see also see Pliny *Nat.* 28.57, in which this is done in response to hiccups or sneezes (often taken as ominous; see Deonna and Renard 1961, 9ff; Grondona 1980, 68–9; Schmeling 2011, 310; Wolters 1935, 61–7). Some rings had a more gruesome function: the hollow stone could contain a poison: see Pliny *Nat.* 33.15; 33.25; Artem. *Oneir.* 2.5.
82 See Ov. *Pont.* 2.9.69–70, *Am.* 2.15.16, *Tr.* 5.4.5–6; Juv. 1.68, 13.138; *Dig.* 34.2.25.10.
83 Characteristically, Pliny also takes aim at ostentatious wearers of rings: some wear a ring only on their little finger, and use it to indicate the presence of a costlier signet ring kept locked away safely. Or some people put all their rings on the little finger. Some "show off the weight of their rings;" others count it hard work to wear more than one; some have hollow gold rings filled with a lighter material, in case of their dropping, to ease their anxiety about their gems (*Nat.* 33.25).
84 Male sardonyx rings: Pliny *Nat.* 37.86–90; Mart. 2.29; Pers. 1.16; *Dig.* 48.20.6. For the sardonyx as an emblem of wealth and luxury, see Mart. 4.28, 4.61.6, 5.11.1, 9.59.19, 10.87.14, 11.27.10, 11.37.2. See also Williams 2004, 114–15.
85 Although counterfeit gems of glass were also available: see Pliny *Nat.* 37.197–200; Olson 2008, 46.

Clothing and status   133

86 For possible archaeological evidence of a gem collection, see Spier 1992, 75 (Pompeii), with references.
87 For personal ostentation at the baths, and finds of jewelry in the drains, see Fagan 1999, 215–16 and 216 n. 82, with references.
88 It may also mean the man is going to go blind: because of the brilliance of the stones there is a "certain relationship between eyes and rings" (*Oneir.* 2.5).
89 See however Rowe (2002, 73), who names a gold necklace as a status symbol for an *eques*. On jewelry as a reward for military valor, see Linderski 2001.
90 Croom 2002, 73; Parani 2008, 500–1; Stout 1994, 80, 83.
91 Petr. *Satyr.* 30 and 60.8; *Dig.* 15.1.25.
92 *Ethiop.* 7.27; Bradley 1994, 87–8. See also Amm. Marc. 22.4.9–10. On slaves wearing jewelry, see Bradley 1994, 87; Sen. *Tran.* 1.8. Clarke (1998, 156 and pl. 6) has determined that the *cubicularius* in the fresco from the House of Caecilius Iucundus (V, 1 26) at time of excavation in Pompeii was wearing a gold hairnet and armlet in applied gold.
93 Although some slave dealers tried to avoid paying duty on young male slaves by disguising them in the *toga praetexta* of the freeborn: see Suet. *Rhet.* 1.
94 i.e., Naevolus has so many clothes he cannot wear them all, and thus the moths get at them.
95 What follows is a summary of Granger-Taylor's excellent article (1987).
96 These are normally identified as fold-marks, although some scholars believe they are decoration (Granger-Taylor 1987, 118).
97 On clothes-presses, see now Flohr 2013b, 145–8, 162–3, with references; Maiuri 1965, fig. 172 (a wooden clothes-press from Herculaneum).
98 On clothes-chests see for example Cat. 25, in which a well-stocked chest exhibits gaping cracks and thus Catullus has his *pallium* stolen by one Thallus (an effeminate).
99 On one existing piece of cloth from a fourth-century dalmatic, tiny kinks by the main fold line could indicate that tongs were used (Granger-Taylor 1987, 121 and fig. 8).
100 As it was in pre-modern France: see Vigarello 1988, 79–80. See also the younger Seneca, who wrote: "the choice of neat/elegant clothing (*mundae vestis electio*) is a fitting object of a man's efforts, for man is by nature a neat and well-groomed animal" (*mundum et elegans; Epp.* 92.12–13). Artemidorus was of the opinion that in dreams it was always better "to wear bright, clean, well-washed clothes than filthy, unwashed clothes, except for those who earn their living from occupations that involve filth and dirt" (*Oneir.* 2.3).
101 See Bradley 2002, 31–2 on urine as both cleansing and polluting.
102 Although recent excavations in Barcelona suggests Roman fulleries used lavender and possibly other perfumes in the rinsing process: Juan-Tresseras 2000.
103 Linen was probably not often fulled in antiquity (or not fulled completely), as it will not produce a nap when fulled due to the nature of the linen fibres. See Flohr 2013b, 63.
104 On this tunic, see Olson 2003, 209.
105 Fulling woolen garments imparted a shining finish or 'nap' to cloth, "a thin layer of interlaced and matted fibres which had a smooth surface and obliterated the weaving patterns so that the textile shared some of the characteristics of silk" (Flohr 2013b, 62).
106 On sumptuary legislation in Roman antiquity, see Dauster 2003; Déry 1993; Marshall 2008; Zanda 2011, especially 1–71.
107 Unlike that of much of Western culture, most of Rome's sumptuary legislation was not aimed at clothing but at *cenae,* a fact which has been noted by scholars: e.g., Zanda 2011, 18–24, 52, 55–8, 128. For ancient Roman attitudes to luxury and consumption of luxury goods, see Holleran 2012, 232–41; Casinos Mora

2013b; Parker 2008, 165–71; Wild 2013; Zanda 2011, 7–26. Parker (2002, 55) writes of the difficulties "involved in isolating ancient economic practices from the language in which they are frequently expressed in the sources."

108 On the *Lex Oppia* and its implementation as a war measure, not as sumptuary legislation, see Olson 2008, 101–4, with references.
109 On this decree, see Bradley 2009, 200 n 25; Brandis 1897; Kenyon 1893, 476; Reinhold 1970, 46–7.
110 This is a "troublesome passage," as Reinhold 1970, 46 points out, because private persons had been using sea-purple in their garments unrestrictedly since the end of the second Punic War. Perhaps Dio meant all-purple garments, or purple-bordered ones; surely it was not a blanket interdiction on purple for everyone.
111 *ne vestis serica viros foedaret*; Tac. *Ann.* 2.33. Legislation on male clothing: Casinos Mora 2013a; Dalla 1987, 18–23.
112 Sumptuary legislation "might generally be taken as an identifying characteristic of that period that economic and social historians have come to call 'pre-industrial'" (Harte 1976, 134). See also Hayward 2009; Paulicelli 2014: 5; Shively 1964–5; Sponsler 1992.
113 "By the end of the 14th century [in England], status had come to be based less on the traditional standard of birth than on visible and acquirable markers of social identity, such as civic offices, land holdings, houses, household furnishings, coats of arms, seals, and apparel." Because social mobility was easier, there was corresponding concern in this time period over clothing distinctions (Sponsler 1992, 266–7).
114 After Harte 1976, 139.
115 See Kuefler 2001, 56; Edwards 1993, 80.
116 This is true in other cultures as well. Treherne (1995, 105, 110) notes that the *Kriegergrab* or 'warrior grave' is found across Europe from the late Bronze Age through the early historic period, and although it centres on the male warrior and his weaponry, "the full suite" also includes articles of toilet and bodily ornamentation, and textiles. Articles of adornment in graves thus need not be limited to female burials: "central to both life and death was a specific form of masculine *beauty* unique to the warrior" (ibid., 106). See also Kilian-Dirlmeier 1988.

5 Class and sexuality[1]

In addition to rank and status, Roman clothing also articulated concerns of gender and sexuality: clothing and self-presentation could reflect and strengthen a man's sense of his masculine self. In this chapter I will examine the nexus of effeminacy and masculinity in Roman antiquity by first setting out the conventional signs of *mollitia* and their (often implied) connection both with pathic homoeroticism and the *cinaedus*,[2] but then go on to detail the instances in which an appearance conventionally held to be effeminate was also linked with youth, urbanity, and heteroeroticism, finally arguing for the existence of a male figure on Rome's urban scene seldom acknowledged by scholars: the dandy, or urban young man of fashion.

Sexuality

There have been a host of recent excellent studies on gender and sexuality in antiquity.[3] It is important to note at the outset that the Romans operated on a different sexual blueprint from ours, in which the labels 'homosexual,' 'heterosexual,' 'bisexual,' and 'queer' did not apply. The Romans operated on a system of *gender identity* (i.e., taking one's primary identity from one's sense of self as male or female, adhering to the behaviors inherent in a socially-constructed gender category) rather than *sexual orientation* (i.e., taking one's identity from the sex of one's preferred sexual partner). Clearly the two can be related, but Roman ideas of masculinity and manhood included the penetration of other males, something which was not derided or censured but admired, as long as the males were non-citizens; that is, slaves or foreigners, and young. In addition, we should note that enjoying homoerotic intercourse with a young man did not make one (as it might today) "gay," or "a homosexual;" it was, as far as we can tell, normal behavior for a citizen male. It is imperative to distinguish between homoerotic *acts* (which frequently occurred in Roman antiquity) and homosexual *identity* (which the Romans seem to have had no concept of, not even in the figure of the *cinaedus*; see below). To feel desire for a woman or a boy was perfectly natural and normal (within particular boundaries: see e.g., Mart. 11.43, 12.96).

It is also perhaps worthwhile to spend some time laying out Latin sexual terminology and labels.[4] *Effeminatus* and *mollis* refer to a man who does not embody traditional masculine looks (although as Williams points out, a boy who was effeminate or soft was charming, whereas a grown man often was not).[5] Such men could also display a penchant for being the receptive partner in homoerotic intercourse, but not necessarily. *Pathicus* was "a blunt term," referring to a man who had been or who continued to be anally penetrated.[6] *Delicatus/deliciae* often allude to slave-boys kept for visual and sexual pleasure.[7] Lastly, the *cinaedus* was a man who wore loose colorful clothing, perfume and curled hair, who walked along with a mincing gait, and who was apt to be anally penetrated and enjoy it.[8] Although the *cinaedus* looks to us like a proto-homosexual identity, he was also often an enthusiastic practitioner of heteroerotic sex.[9] Scholars have thus suggested that what made a *cinaedus* was his general lack of self-control and the abrogation of sartorial masculinity, both forms of gender deviance, rather than being anchored in any specific sexual practice or preference (Edwards 1997, 81–4; Williams 2010, 193). But words in the slippery vocabulary of effeminacy (*effeminatus, pathicus, mollis,* even *cinaedus*) were often used interchangeably by Roman authors, and it is often difficult to assign any specific term to one practice or appearance. Lastly, it is also important to note that when such words occur in Latin texts, they are used in invective – never in neutral or merely lexical contexts. In addition, we have no first-person statements from a dandy or a *cinaedus* in Roman antiquity; these are always words the Roman authors use to hurl at another person. The voices of the passive, as the Romans would have called them, are absent from our sources.

The male sartorial code

It is true that normal appearance for an elite Roman man was staid, even plain. Ovid writes:

> But take no pleasure in curling your hair with the iron (*ferro*),
> or in scraping your legs with biting pumice-stone (*mordaci pumice*).
> Bid them do that by whom mother Cybele
> is sung in howling chorus of Phrygian measures.
> An un-cared for beauty is becoming to men… (*forma viros neglecta decet*)

> Let your person please by *munditia*,[10] and be made sun-tanned by the Campus (*fuscentur corpora Campo*);

> let your toga fit and be spotless (*bene conveniens et sine labe toga*);

> let the tongue[11] of your belt not be too tight (*lingula ne rigeat*); let your teeth be free of rust (*careant rubigine dentes*),

> and let your feet not float about in shoes too loose (*nec vagus in laxa pes tibi pelle natet*).
> Nor let your stubborn locks be spoilt by a bad cutting;

> let hair and beard be dressed by a practiced hand.[12]

Do not let your nails grow long,[13] and let them be free of dirt (*sine sordibus*);

nor let any hair be in the hollow of your nostrils.
Let not your breath be sour and unpleasing (*nec male odorati sit tristis anhelitus oris*),
nor let the lord and master of the herd offend the nose.
All else lascivious girls do (*lascivae*)

and any man who wishes to have another man (*et siquis male vir quaerit habere virum*).[14]

(*Ars* 1.505–24)

The sartorial code of everyday appearance for men was in part dictated by conservative Roman tastes, and male flamboyance or other vestimentary departure from the norm was often censured. As in many other time periods in Western culture, "aristocratic masculinity was to be expressed by independence from the servitude of fashion."[15] Adornment for men in ancient Rome was to be kept to a minimum.[16] Roman ethicists saw aesthetics and morality as being (with some exceptions) inextricably linked, and thus deviation from the male vestimentary code at Rome could bring social censure.[17] Cicero wrote that the eyes judge beauty, color, and shape, and more important things, "for they also recognize virtues and vices" (*atque etiam alia maiora, nam et virtutes et vitia cognoscunt; ND* 2.145). Maud Gleason has noted that "Dio called effeminate mannerisms *symbola* because masculine deportment and grooming habits constituted a system of social communication" (1995, 68). Too little concern with personal appearance brought ridicule: Horace at least speaks slightingly of one such man, the object of derision for a bad haircut, a tattered undertunic, and a toga sitting badly and askew; he is dressed little better than a slave (*Epp.* 1.1.94–7). Elsewhere a man is scorned for having a country haircut, a toga that is ill-fitting, and a loose *calceus* (*S.* 1.3.31–2). At 2.58, Zoilus laughs at Martial's worn-out clothes: *mea [toga] trita*.

Conversely, too much attention to one's appearance casts aspersions on one's masculinity, since adornment was conventionally associated with women.[18] Thus the jurist Paul stated in the third century CE, of men's clothing: "when a legacy is left of men's clothing (*veste virili*), only those are included which are appropriate for a man's use without shaming his masculinity" (*salvo pudore virilitatis attinent; Sent.* 3.6.80; cf. Sen. *Contr.* 9.2.17). There are several statements concerning the "golden mean" of male grooming in the literary sources.[19] Cicero wrote, "we must besides present an appearance of neatness (*munditia*) – not too punctilious or exquisite (*non odiosa neque exquisita nimis*), but just enough to avoid boorish and ill-bred slovenliness (*agrestem et inhumanam neglegentiam*). We must follow the same principle in regard to dress."[20] The younger Seneca wrote "as far as I am concerned, both [types of men] are equally at fault. One grooms himself more than he ought (*se plus iusto colit*), the other less; one plucks the hair from his legs, the other neglects even his armpits" (*ille et crura, hic ne alas quidem vellit; Epp.* 114.4). Martial wants his lover Pannychus to neither curl his hair nor have it be unkempt; he doesn't want his skin to glisten nor have it be dirty (*splendida sit nolo, sordida nolo cutis*); he does not want him to be clean-shaven or have a long unkempt beard. "I don't want too much of a man and I don't want too little," he says (*nolo virum nimium... nolo parum*; 2.36). Quintilian also commented that "toga, shoes, and hair invite criticism both for too much care and for not enough" (*Inst.* 11.3.137). Thus, interestingly, an ideal Roman masculinity did not equal deliberate untidiness – a certain amount, a degree, of refinement was in order (Gleason 1995, 75). Too little personal grooming, and a man was branded miserly, rustic, or unsophisticated; but too much, and he drew social censure for a suspicious sexual identity: he was labeled effeminate.

Scholars have recognized that the concept of effeminacy is founded in misogyny. Certain manners and behaviors are stigmatized by associating them with 'the feminine,' – perceived as weak, ineffectual, and unsuited for the world of affairs. The main idea is that a man is falling into the laxity and weakness "conventionally attributed to women... the function of effeminacy, as a concept, is to police sexual categories, keeping them pure" (Sinfield 1994, 26; cf. Arist. *Nich. Ethics* 7.7). And indeed "sexual ambivalence is often attributed to those seen as a threat to the speaker's power."[21] The signs of *mollitia*[22] or softness were well-known in Roman antiquity, both those of appearance[23] and gesture.[24]

The signs of effeminacy

Cosmetics, hair, perfume, jewelry

There are very few literary references to men wearing cosmetics.[25] A Plautine character states that among the audience thieves are hiding themselves under a respectable façade of clothes and chalk (*qui vestitu et creta occultant sese; Aul.* 717), perhaps implying that men were using cosmetics.[26] Cicero describes the effeminate Aulus Gabinius as having cheeks "bright with rouge" (*Pis.* 25). In Petronius, Encolpius disguised as a slave is made-up (*facies medicamine attrite*), with nicely-combed hair (*flexae pectine comae; Satyr.* 126.3).[27] Seneca the Younger complained of slave boys with made-up faces (*Epp.* 123.7). Quintilian condemned the use of womanish cosmetics on men indirectly, in his censure of over-embellished oratory.[28] The effeminate (or cross-dresser, or *gallus*) in Juvenal lengthens his eyebrows with soot (*fuligo*) on the edge of a hairpin, and paints his eyes.[29] Clearly cosmetics were bound up with constructions of sexuality and power in Roman antiquity: persons who used cosmetics – boy-slaves used for sexual pleasure, women, male whores – were located outside traditional legal power structures.

Face patches made of thin soft leather (*splenia* or *alutae*) were also used by men.[30] Pliny mentions a superstitious advocate who wore a white *splenium* on one side of his forehead or the other depending on whether he was counsel for the plaintiff or the prosecution (and also drew a line around his eye, right if he appeared for the plaintiff and left for the defendant: *Epp.* 6.2.2).[31] In Martial 2.29 a former slave uses such patches to cover branding-marks on the face;[32] at 8.33.22 they are crescent-shaped, with no sex given as to the wearer.

Long hair or long curly hair was a sign of desirability and sexual availability[33] and is mentioned most often in reference to *delicati,* slave-boys kept for visual and sexual pleasure.[34] These are termed *capillati* in ancient authors,[35] or otherwise described with long or curly hair.[36] *Capillatus* is often translated as 'curly-haired,' but it actually means literally 'haired,' or possibly 'long-haired.' And, despite the many examples of the term, we cannot discount the possibility that *capillatus* is merely metonymy for "sexually attractive/available boy," no matter what kind of hair the boy actually had, because, as we have seen, the Romans often employed sartorial or visual terms to stand in for rank or sexual status.[37]

Mature freeborn men are also derogatorily described with long and/or curly hair in Plautus and Catullus.[38] Cicero accuses Gabinius of using a curling iron.[39] Plutarch relates how Caesar used to arrange his hair with nicety (*Caes.* 4.9). Maecenas' hair was described as "ringlets dripping with perfume."[40] Suetonius states that Nero had curly hair and let it grow long when he went to Greece (*Nero* 51). In a lost work, the elder Pliny forbade orators to arrange their hair.[41] An effeminate man/cross-dresser has 'enormous' hair put up in a gold hairnet at Juv. 2.96 (*comis... ingentibus*; see Courtney 1980, 138; Herter 1959, 631).

Depilation was also held to be a conventional sign of the pathic.[42] Such men removed the hair from their legs,[43] chest,[44] buttocks,[45] even genitals,[46] by means of plucking, pitch, or other depilatory,[47] and were said to be hairless or 'smooth.'[48] Gleason has observed that a man's natural hair was thought to be the product of the same abundance of inner heat that concocted his sperm;[49] "depilation therefore could be considered a particularly dangerous practice. Those who depilated themselves "were rightly suspected of undermining the symbolic language in which male privilege was written."[50] Suetonius wrote of Caesar that "he was somewhat overnice in the care of his person (*circa corporis curam morosior*), being not only carefully trimmed and shaved (*tonderetur diligenter ac raderetur*), but even having superfluous hair plucked out (*uelleretur*), as some have charged" (*Iul.* 45.2). The elder Pliny and Quintilian condemn the use of depilatories by men.[51] Seneca (*Epp.* 47.7) describes the slave who serves wine as plucked and adorned like a woman even though he is past the age of boyhood. Like the social censure directed at long hair, that directed against men who indulged in depilation is connected with the confusion of gender boundaries (i.e., such practices are womanish) but also with dissonance of rank: such men deliberately, and to some inexplicably, positioned themselves as sexually available slave boys.

Much of the ancient vitriol against male use of perfume comes from Cicero: effeminate men reek of unguents, or have cheeks "moist with unguent;" Catiline's insurgents glisten in perfumed oils.[52] Dio reports that Q.

Fufius Calenus accused Cicero of perfuming his hair.[53] But other authors also tell us that to over-scent was un-manly: Pliny, Seneca, and Macrobius complain of men drenched in scent.[54] In addition, to use a certain type of perfume could also be a sign of effeminacy, such as the expensive concoctions normally used by women.[55] Juvenal writes of *opobalsamum* on a hairy yet effeminate man.[56] Perfume may also have been seen as un-Roman.[57]

Wearing more than one ring was also a conventional sign of softness or *mollitia*. "We adorn our fingers with rings; a gem is displayed on every joint," complained the younger Seneca (*NQ* 7.31.2–3). Isidore quotes a speech of Gaius Gracchus: "Examine his left hand, citizens – do you see? This man whose authority you follow, has, on account of his desire for women, adorned himself like a woman."[58] Quintilian recommended that the hand of an orator should not be loaded with rings, and that the orator should especially eschew any which do not go over the middle finger joint – presumably because wearing rings in this fashion meant one was able to display more of them.[59] A sarcastic reference concerning the boxwood rings of Ascyltos is made at Petr. *Satyr.* 58.11: they are gilded or painted wood (*anulos buxeos*), "stolen from your mistress." Necklaces on effeminate men are mentioned by Juvenal (2.85; cf. Ov. *Her.* 9.57). Even shoes could betray effeminacy. Caligula was censured for wearing "womanish *socci*" (Suet. *Calig.* 52; see above, Chapter 4).

Clothing

But the ancients thought that it was by his clothing that a man most clearly indicated his sexual proclivities, and there are several general statements in the literature to this effect.[60] Women and men were to be clearly distinguished by clothing; the sartorial blurring of gender boundaries was ridiculed and censured by many. "Let all finery not suitable to a man's dignity (*viro non dignus ornatus*) be kept off his person" wrote Cicero (*de Off.* 1.130). Seneca stated that "what used to be called *mundus muliebris* is now a man's baggage" (*NQ* 1.17.10; on *mundus muliebris,* see Olson 2008, 7–9). Quintilian observed that "a tasteful and magnificent dress [*cultus*]... lends added dignity to its wearer (*auctoritas*); but effeminate and luxurious apparel fails to adorn the body and merely reveals the foulness of the mind" (*muliebris et luxuriosus non corpus exornat, sed detegit mentem; Inst.* 8. pref. 19–20).[61] Clothing could specifically indicate effeminacy in various ways: by fabric, color, sleeves, and cincture.

Lighter fabrics for the tunic and toga than wool were known and often denounced as effeminate, despite the fact that they also demonstrated the wearer's wealth. The emperor Tiberius legislated against the wearing of silk by men, citing the fabric's inherent effeminacy as his reason.[62] The younger Seneca (*Epp.* 90.15) complained of silk vestments on men. The elder Pliny wrote of the very thin (possibly even transparent) Coan silk: "nor have even men been ashamed to make use of this fabric, because of its lightness in summer."[63] Quintilian believed womanish attire (*vestem muliebrem*) was an indication of an effeminate and unmanly character (*mollis et parum viri signa;* *Inst.* 5.9.14). Juvenal tells us that the advocate Creticus used to plead his cases in a light toga;[64] he is "clothed in transparency" (*perluces*; 2.78). This sartorial trend is a *contagio* (2.78), which will lead to effeminacy and cross-dressing.[65]

Color in clothing, although often expensive and luxurious, could also be suspect. An effeminate poet in one of Persius' *Satires* wears a lavender *laena* around his shoulders (*hyacinthina laena*, a cloak: 1.32). The younger Seneca complained "we men have taken over the colors of whores, which would not indeed be worn by *matronae*" (*colores meretricios; NQ* 7.31.2–3). Martial writes that Maternus is "a lover of sad-colored cloaks (*lacernae*),[66] clad in Baetic wool and in gray (*et baeticatus atque leucophaeatus*),[67] one who thinks that men in scarlet (*coccinatos*) are not men at all, and calls violet clothing womanish (*amethystinasque mulierum uocat uestes*); but although he praises native colors (*natiua*) and always affects dusky hues (*fuscos colores*),[68] his morals are *galbinus*" (1.96.4–9). It seems that this color, a bright yellowish-green, was metonymy for passive homoeroticism: elsewhere in Martial, the rich *fellator* Zoilus is clothed in *galbinus* and wears Cosmus' scent.[69] At Juvenal 2.97, men who are effeminates or *galli* wear clothing of blue *scutulatus* (see below) or smooth yellowish-green,[70] colors and patterns associated with woman and pathics. He also mentions purple clothing "fit for a delicate Maecenas;"[71] in describing a purple cloak (*Tyria … abolla*), Martial sneers that it suits "only elegants" (*deliciis*; 8.48.6).

There is some indication that green generally was considered an unfit color for a man (Hopman 2003, 568–9). in Petronius' *Satyricon* a *cinaedus* appears wearing a cloak(?) of this color (*myrtea … gausapa;* 21.2).[72] At Mart. 3.82.5, 11 a slave fans with a green fan (*prasinus*) a *fellator* who is dressed in *galbinus* (but some scholars believe *prasinus* indicates *parvenu* status: see above, Chapter 4). In 5.23, one Bassus wears clothes the color of grass in the theatre (*Herbarum fueras indutus, Basse, colores*) until the seating rules began to be enforced; then he tries to illegally sit in the rows reserved for *equites* by donning expensive purple and scarlet clothing (*cocco madida uel murice tincta/ueste…*). At Juv. 9.50 the *viridis umbella* is just one of a number of items that denote effeminacy (balls of amber, a *cathedra*) offered by one Naevolus to his *cinaedus* patron. The *viridis thorax* of Juv. 5.143 may well carry the same connotations (Hopman 2003, 569). Yellow was a woman's color, and men who assumed this hue were labeled social and sexual deviants.[73]

It is normally too women's clothing in the literary sources which is spoken of as patterned; when men wear patterned clothing it is often because they are effeminate or wearing female garments (as in Apul. *Met.* 8.27). Quintilian in fact disapproves of men in decorated tunics, saying that while "a stripe or purple in the right place adds a touch of splendor, a garment (*vestis*) with a number of different marks in the weave would suit no one."[74]

A pattern called *scutulatus*[75] does appear on men's clothing in the literary sources. A *scutula* was a diamond or lozenge shape (Vitr. 7.1) or a square (Pliny *Nat.* 8.196), and Juvenal's effeminate man wears blue clothing of this pattern at

Sat. 2.97 (*caerulea indutus scutulata*). A papyrus from second-century CE Hermopolis lists among the contents of a wardrobe a scarlet checked *synthesis* (*sunthesidion kokkinon skoutoula[ton*; whether this is male or female clothing is not specified; Wessely 1921, no. 41.5). Effeminate men appear in clothing which is *scutulatus* in late antique literature (Prud. *Hamar.* 287–91), as do women (Hier. *Epp.* 65.20.6). *Scutulatus* might refer to the weave, a colored checked or tartan pattern, or a combination of both;[76] however, *scutulatus* may have had barbarian connotations as well. Pliny states checked patterns on clothing were introduced by Gaul (*Nat.* 8.196; see also 8.191), and Wild is of the opinion that perhaps "the weaving of checks was an original contribution of the Celtic and Germanic peoples to the textile technology of the Roman world" (1964, 264–5; 266). Most archaeological examples of this type of patterning come from Roman Gaul and Germania (Granger-Taylor 1987, 118). The *Edict* of Diocletian refers to a female worker who works in silk *skoutlāton* (20.11); her maximum daily wage of 60 denarii is higher than a worker in plain silk (25 denarii; 20.10).

Style of clothing could also indicate one's effeminacy, such as tunics with long sleeves.[77] Gellius tells us that

> for a man to wear tunics coming below the arms and as far as the wrists, and almost to the fingers, was considered unbecoming in Rome and in all Latium. Such tunics our countrymen called by the Greek name *chiridotae* [long-sleeved], and they thought that for women only, a long and full flowing garment was not unbecoming, to hide their arms and legs from sight.
> (6.12.2–4 = *ORF* 21.17)

Cicero described some of Catiline's followers as having "tunics that reach to the ankles and the wrists, clad in veils, not in togas" (*Cat.* 2.22). At Virg. *A.* 9.614–20, Aeneas and his band of men are accused of wearing effeminate long-sleeved tunics embroidered in yellow and gleaming purple, and they wear *mitrae*, foreign turbans, with ribbons attached.[78] Caesar wore a broad-striped tunic "with fringed sleeves reaching to the wrist" (*usum enim lato clauo ad manus fimbriato*; Suet. *Iul.* 45).[79] Suetonius complains that in his clothing, shoes, and general attire Caligula did not follow the usage of his country, his fellow-citizens, or even his sex: "he often appeared in public in cloaks covered with precious stones, in a long-sleeved tunic and bracelets, sometimes in silk and in a *cyclas*."[80] The younger Seneca (*Epp.* 33.2) contrasted 'bravery' with 'wearing long sleeves' (*manuleatus*).

In addition to sleeve length, a tunic which was girded too short was also cause for censure.[81] Horace speaks of "a whimsical man, with garments tucked up as far as his indecent groin" (*inguen ad obscenum subductis usque facetus*; by contrast, another walks with his tunics trailing low, *tunicis demissis*; *S.* 1.2.25–6;). A tunic in which too much of the material was pulled up and bloused over the belt resulted in a short hemline. This is likely in part a reflection of the fact that high-belted tunics recalled a servile appearance and the sexual penetration associated with that status:[82] Seneca complained of the importance people placed on trivial cares, among which was to carefully "gird up the tunics of their *exoleti* (*quam diligenter exoletorum suorum tunicas succingant; Brev.* 10.12.5)."[83] Artemidorus thought that to dream one was wearing a "short, indecent costume" signified losses and unemployment (*Oneir.* 2.3).

For a nobleman, to wear a tunic loosely-girt or one without a belt altogether, also indicated an effeminate nature. Caesar wore a tunic with "a girdle overtop (*super eum cingeretur*), though rather a loose one (*et quidem fluxiore cinctura*), and this, they say, was the occasion of Sulla's *mot*, when he often warned the optimates to beware the ill-girt boy" (*male praecinctum puerum; Iul.* 45.3; see also Dio 43.43.1–4). Servius tells us that a man's unbelted tunic hung down to the ankles (*discinctos: vel habitum eorum ostendit, qui usque in talos fluebat; A.* 8.724) – like a woman's.[84] Such practices carried negative moral implications and were often used as metonymy for ethical failings. Cicero paints a derogatory picture of Verres in an effeminate ankle-length tunic, and of Catiline's followers in similar dress.[85] Persius uses the phrase *discinctus Natta*, 'ungirded Natta,' to mean that Natta is dissolute and paralyzed with vice (3.31). Maecenas is also charged by the younger Seneca with failing to gird his tunic: "does not the looseness of his speech match his ungirt attire?" Seneca asks (114.4).[86] (For a perfectly belted tunic, see Fig. 5.1).

Figure 5.1 Detail, south frieze, Ara Pacis Augustae, Rome. 13–9 BCE
Source: Bestand-Microfiche-D-DAI-ROM-0926_G02.jpg

144 *Class and sexuality*

Graver has noted that the state of 'unbeltedness' was near to being the exact opposite of ideal masculinity in antiquity. "As a point of dress, the absence of cincture indicates defiance of convention and also unreadiness for action, in the particular, the inability to wear a weapon."[87] Kraus postulates that "picturing someone without a belt... is a way of showing them to be imperfectly controlled" (2005, 109). Thus Caesar is belted and wears his *calcei* even while he is with the pirates (Vell. 2.41.3).

The foregoing makes a statement of Quintilian's all the more puzzling, an assertion which has hitherto gone unremarked by dress scholars. In *Inst.* 11.3.138 he implies that if one wears the tunic with the *latus clavus*, a belt is not worn with it, stating, "among those who wear the broad stripe, it is the fashion to wear it somewhat lower than garments that are retained by the belt" (*latum habentium clavum modus est, ut sit paulum cinctis summissior*). Perhaps he simply means "[worn belted] somewhat lower than [the aforementioned] garments that are retained by the girdle;" this is in fact what Wilson assumes (1938, 59). Otherwise, Quintilian is implying that senators by the late first century CE are no longer wearing the girdle, with all the moral laxity that that implies. Possibly if it were not the fashion after 88 CE for upper-class men to gird their tunics, there would be no point in Suetonius saying this of Caesar's tunic. On the other hand, Suetonius might be referring to a fashion which passed out of circulation. It is undoubtedly true that post-Quintilian references in which a senator's unbelted tunic is cause for comment are rarer than before this time, and most such references are metaphorical in nature.[88] Thus in Sidonius '*cinctus*' and '*discinctus*' are used metonymically to mean 'in office' and 'out of office' (*Epp.* 1.7.3, 1.9.4, 5.7.3); certain races too are characterized as 'ungirded' or perform certain activities ungirded (*Sil.* 2.56 [Libyans], 3.26 [the Carthaginians]). Servius tells us "we call sloppy men 'ungirded'" (*sicut econtra neclegentes discinctos vocamus; A.* 1.210). At *CT* 8.7.20 an official is deprived of his "official cincture" by condemnation for wrongdoing or negligence.[89]

Certain toga drapes could be unmasculine as well. Macrobius states that Cicero thought Caesar's style of toga drape was effeminate: Caesar used to belt his toga (*toga praecingebatur*) in such a way that "an edge dragged and his walk looked effeminate."[90] Quintilian states that while orating, throwing back the fold of the toga from its bottom onto the right shoulder is "lax and effeminate" (*solutum et delicatum*; 11.3.146).[91]

Publius Scipio Africanus summed up the signs of effeminacy and their associations with pathic homoeroticism when he reproached Publius Sulpicius Gallus for his *mollitia*:

> For if someone, drenched daily in perfumes (*cotidie unguentatus*), adorns himself before a mirror (*adversum speculum ornetur*), shaves his eyebrows (*supercilia radantur*), walks about with his beard plucked and thigh hairs pulled out (*qui barba vulsa feminibusque ... subvulsis ambulet*), who, as a young boy with his lover, wearing a long-sleeved tunic (*cum chiridota*

tunica), was accustomed to lie in the low spot at banquets, who is not only fond of wine, but fond of men also, then would anyone doubt that he has done the same thing that *cinaedi* usually do?

(Gell. 6.12.5 = *ORF* 21.17).[92]

"Daily we invent ways whereby an indignity may be done to manliness, to ridicule it, because it cannot be cast off," complained the younger Seneca (*NQ* 7.31.2–3; cf. Dio Chrys. 33.63–4). Such behavior was read as culturally feminine, "richly subversive of normative gender and sexual roles" (McNeil 1999, 419, and 2000, 383 on the macaroni).

Youth, urbanity, heterosexuality

"Traditionally… scholars have used references to men behaving in an effeminate manner to determine, firstly, how widespread homosexual practices were in ancient Rome."[93] But allegations of effeminacy, in which the accuser implies that the effeminate is like a woman and thus inferior to other men, tell us much more about how Romans conceived of the differences between men and women than they do of how common male–male relations in ancient Rome were (Edwards 1993, 76). Although some descriptions of effeminacy connect this appearance with pathic homoeroticism, as we have seen, there is also an intriguing cluster of references which associates 'effeminate' visuals with a) youth, b) urbanity, and c) heterosexuality.[94]

First, youth. Gellius tells us "habituated to this older fashion" (*hac antiquitate indutus*) of wearing a short-sleeved tunic, Publius Africanus reproved Sulpicius Gallus for wearing long-sleeved tunics, implying perhaps it was trendily youthful (6.12.4). Diodorus wrote that after 146 BCE the younger generation in Rome wore garments in the marketplace which were exceptionally soft, so sheer as to be transparent, quite like women's attire (*Frag.* 37.3.4). In 56 BCE the prosecution used his unconventional fashion sense against Caelius, to which Cicero replies: "if his shade of purple (*purpurae genus*) gives offense, well his youthful spirits soon will be cooled" (*Cael.* 77). The elder Seneca complained that

> the model for our youths is in curling the hair (*capillum frangere*), lightening the voice to the caressing sounds of a woman, competing with women in physical delicacy (*mollitia corporis cum feminis*), and adorning themselves with filthy elegance (*immundissimis se excolere munditiis*) – this is the pattern our young men set themselves… Go on, look for orators among those [who are] depilated and smooth (*vulsis atque expolitis*), in no way men except in lust.
>
> (*Contr.* 1 pr. 8–10).[95]

Elsewhere, he brings up the possibility that a son may buy luxurious clothing (*luxuriantem habitum; Contr.* 2.1.6). Quintilian was of the opinion that "purple and deep red garments do not suit old men; in the young, however, we can endure a rich and even perhaps a risky style."[96] Martial (11.39) speaking in the voice of a young man, complains that his old chaperone/tutor polices his activities and dress (including Tyrian purple garments and pomaded hair), and that he protests "your father never did that," indicating these are a young man's fashion. Despite the range of authors and genres, we may note some tension between the generations as to what was acceptable in the way of clothing.[97]

Secondly, in addition to its associations with youth, attention paid to personal appearance was also related to male urbanity and sophistication. In Plautus, dandified city-boys are described as *mundulos urbanos* (*Truc.* 658–9). Plutarch reports that fashionable shades in men's clothing changed: thus, "when [Cato the Younger] saw a purple which was excessively red and much in vogue, he himself would wear a dark shade" (Plut. *Cato Min.* 6.3), implying the refined man kept up with changes in clothing colors. Caelius used unguents, and Cicero states that a little sip of this kind of life does no harm, as opposed to immersing oneself in it (*Cael.* 27, 28). Elsewhere, he describes Piso as unsophisticated and unfashionable when he states that he was "clad in our common purple (*purpura plebeia*), almost in brown (*fuscus*), with hair so dreadful (*capillo ita horrido*), that at Capua… he looked as though he meant to carry off the Seplasia with him."[98] Horace stated that the man who loves luxury will wear a fine toga and have shining locks (*tenues togae… nitidique capilli; Epp.* 1.14.32); elsewhere, the poet is teased for assuming a "style beyond his means" (*cultum maiorem censu; S.* 2.3.323; *Epp.* 1.18.31–6), implying male *cultus* is desirable, within reason. The younger Seneca wrote that urbane men put on perfume two to three times daily to keep the scent from evaporating entirely off the body, and noted that when luxury spreads men first begin by paying more attention to their personal appearance (*Epp.* 86.13, 114.9). The elder Pliny held that "unguents are among the most elegant and honorable pleasures in life" (*lautissima atque etiam honestissima vitae bona; Nat.* 13.3). The urbane man wore hair-unguent, and certain types were a sign of wealth and status – some, wrote Martial, could be smelt all over the theatre (2.29). Martial painted Truth in one of his epigrams as "rustic and dry-haired" (*siccis rustica Veritas capillis;* 10.72.11); one Charmenion elsewhere is scornfully described as "smart" with his curled hair (*flexa nitidus coma;* 10.65). In describing a purple cloak (*Tyria… abolla*), Martial sneers that it suits "only elegants" (*deliciis;* 8.48.6). Juvenal described one Naevolus, who used to pass for a home-bred knight (*verna eques*), but who now has skin no longer smooth and brilliant from depilatories; instead, his legs are dirty and hairy (9.13–15). The sophisticated urbanite thus paid some attention to his appearance. This has not gone unnoticed by scholars: Gleason has noted that "some men aspired to the sort of chic that might attend the successful 'carrying off' of elegant grooming habits that invited accusations of effeminacy" (1990, 406); Edwards that "urbane did not have to be a pejorative term" (1993, 96); Williams (2004, 115–16) that "perfume and depilation in themselves were not necessarily markers of excessive effeminacy."

Thirdly, many of the conventional characteristics of effeminacy were attached to men who were active, even overly-active, heterosexually. A fragment of Lucilius uses the term *barbati moechocinaedi*, "bearded *cinaedi*-adulterers."[99] In the speech of Gaius Gracchus preserved in Isidore (*Orig*. 19.32.4, above), Gracchus impugns a fellow-politician who has "on account of his desire for women, adorned himself like a woman." Verres cavorts with married women wearing a purple *pallium* and an ankle-length long tunic (*cum pallio purpureo talarique tunica;* Cic. *Verr.* 2.5.31, 81, 86). Elsewhere, Cicero commented he had seen not only Roman citizens but high-born young men and even some senators of eminent family wearing dark tunics (the *tunica pulla*) in the populous town of Naples, "for the sake of love affairs and pleasure."[100] One man, the witty Egilius, looked "rather soft" but was not so in fact (*qui videretur mollior nec esset; de Orat.* 2.277). Tibullus states richly dressed men are attractive to women: "whoever dresses his hair with art, and whose voluminous toga falls with a roomy *sinus*" (*quisquis colit arte capillos,/ et fluit effuso cui toga laxa sinu;* 1.6.39–40).[101] Tibullus 1.8 is a subtle and clever poem, the subject of which is the love of a *puer delicatus* for a girl who does not return his affections, despite the attention paid by the boy to his hair, cosmetics, nails, clothes, and shoes (1.8.9–14; Murgatroyd 1977). Unguents in the hair were also appealing to the opposite sex (Prop. 2.4.5; Ov. *Ars* 3.433–48). Horace described Priscus, a *moechus* or adulterer, as one who adorned: he "often attracted notice by wearing three rings, but once in a while by wearing none" (*S.* 2.7.8). Maecenas was characterized as an effeminate adulterer (Macr. *Sat.* 2.4.12; cf. Mart. 2.47). Ovid also suggests the connection between fashionable male appearance and adultery with the term *cultus adulter* ('well-groomed adulterer;' *Tr.* 2.499). In the *Satyricon*, Encolpius as an adorned slave has a soft fondness in his glance and an arranged walk "with never a footstep out of place" (*quo incessus arte compositus et ne vestigia quidem pedum extra mensuram aberrantia; Satyr.* 126.3); an *ancilla* approaches him to come and make love to her mistress, who burns for lower-class men. Martial has many examples of the *bellus homo*. In one, he portrays a man with curly hair (*crispulus*), be-ringed fingers and smooth thighs who chatters into a married lady's ear and presses her chair; although claiming to be the woman's 'businessman,' his appearance and behavior, says Martial, obviously indicates that he is her lover (5.61). As we have seen, at Martial 2.62 Labienus depilates his chest, shins, arms, and genitals "for his mistress."[102] Martial 3.63.3–10 contains the fullest description of a *bellus homo*:

> A beautiful man (*bellus homo*) curls his hair and arranges it carefully (*flexos qui digerit ordine crines*), always smells of balsam or cinnamon (*balsama qui semper, cinnama semper olet*), hums tunes from the Nile and from Gades, moves his plucked arms (*bracchia vulsa*) in time with changing measures, lounges all day among ladies' chairs and is forever murmuring into some ear; reads billets sent from this quarter and that, and writes them, and shrinks from the cloak on a neighbor's elbow (*pallia uicini qui refugit cubiti*).[103]

148 *Class and sexuality*

At 12.38, however, the man so described is a pathic. In Juvenal *Satire* 6 we find that the effeminate man "enhances his eyes with soot (*oculos fuligine pascit*), his saffron tunic unbelted (*discinctus croceis*), a hair-netted adulterer (*reticulatus adulter*)![104] The more sensuous his voice, the more often his right hand lingers in his smooth crotch, the more suspicious you should be. In bed he'll be supremely virile (*fortissimus*)... keep that masquerade [*mimum*; i.e., of being a pathic] for other people."[105] Arrian claims a smooth man has depilated himself to be attractive to women.[106]

It is true that some men who presented a fashionable appearance were active with both sexes: Ovid wrote:

Avoid men who profess *cultus*[107] and good looks (*formamque*),

and who arrange their hair in its proper place (*quique suas ponunt in statione comas*).[108]

What they tell you they have told a thousand women;
their fancy wanders, and has no fixed abode.
What can a woman do when her lover is smoother than herself (*cum sit vir levior ipsa*),
and may perhaps have more [male] lovers than she?...
Some make their assault under a false appearance of love (*mendaci specie ...amoris*),
and by such approaches seek shameful gains.
Don't let their hair, sleek with liquid nard, deceive you (*nec coma vos fallat liquid nitidissima nardo*)

nor the tongue [of the belt] tucked tightly into its own creases (*nec brevis in rugas lingula pressa suas*),

nor the toga of finest texture play you false (*toga decipiat filo tenuissima*), nor if there is one ring and yet another on their fingers (*anulus in digitis alter et alter erit*).
Perhaps out of their number the most elegant
will prove a thief, and be inflamed by longing for your clothing...(*vestis*)
(*Ars* 3.433–48)[109]

All these men may be examples of *cinaedi*, who it should be noted could be active heterosexually: the sophist Polemo claimed that men will sometimes assume items of personal adornment and clothing "to please other men and women."[110] Nonetheless, I would like to offer an alternative label.

To a modern reader the ancient association between an effeminate appearance and an interest in women comes as a bit of a surprise, but Pollini has correctly observed that to assume that an effeminate individual was in fact a homosexual "is to force on antiquity a modern stereotypical preconception of what constitutes a homosexual" (1999, 25). Gibson (2003, 276) has ingeniously noted that the stereotype of effeminate men in Roman antiquity "need not wholly overlap with that of the pathic male." Edwards remarks that in the ancient sources the same men were often accused of effeminacy and adultery (Antony);[111] or effeminacy and uxoriousness (Maecenas).[112] Effeminate appearance was not, then, simply equated with pathic homoeroticism in Roman antiquity, but could be a mode of self-presentation associated with youth, urban sophistication, and hyper-heterosexuality. Gleason (1990, 405) believes that such practices were designed to translate the ideal of beardless ephebic beauty, via depilation and ingratiating mannerisms, into adult life. Women, boys, and at least some men found the results attractive.[113] In one of Lucian's dialogues, Eros tells Zeus if he wants reciprocal enamorment, he must adopt an effeminate manner, as his tough-guy looks are unattractive to women.[114] Women's erotic desires were apparently directed at the softer sort of male.[115]

Finally, Graver has noted that "effeminate behavior is not so much behavior of one kind or orientation as it is behavior which calls attention to itself. Masculinity appears in purely negative terms" (1998, 616). Thus the younger Seneca complained of men who like to be looked at:

> You note this tendency in those who pluck out or thin out their beards (*aut vellunt barbam aut intervellunt*), or who closely shear and shave the upper lip while preserving the rest of the hair and allowing it to grow (*qui labra pressius tondent et adradunt servata et summissa cetera parte*), or in those who wear cloaks of outlandish colors (*lacernas coloris inprobi*), who wear transparent togas (*perlucentem togam*), and who never deign to do anything which will escape general notice; they endeavor to excite and attract people's eyes, and they even put up with censure, provided that they can advertise themselves. That is the style of Maecenas (*talis est oratio Maecenatis*) and all the others who stray from the path, not by chance, but consciously and voluntarily.
>
> (*Epp.* 114.21)[116]

At Martial 2.57, a man in violet (*amethystinus*) saunters aimlessly around town (*gressibus vagis lentum*), a man who owns many *lacernae* and *paenulae*, clearly "trying to be seen by as many people as possible" (Williams 2004, 193).

Thus, we have a description of a man who is young, sophisticated, heterosexual (or perhaps not), and likes to draw attention to himself by means of personal appearance as social spectacle. Were such men necessarily always pathics? Can we locate men in other historical societies to provide us with an alternative hypothesis?

Pre-modern effeminacy and dandies[117]

Before so doing we need to examine some comparative evidence on effeminacy. Scholars of pre-modern social history have observed that effeminacy was not wholly associated with same-sex passion before the late nineteenth century. Gleason notes that the ancients thought excessive sexual indulgence with either sex was thought to cool the body down too much; since proper masculine warmth could not be maintained, effeminacy was the result (1999, 73, 76). Catullus threatens his detractors with sexual punishments when they impugn his masculinity, implying that his "many thousands of kisses" to Lesbia indicate that he is less than a man (16). Much later, in Shakespeare, effeminacy came about through excessive love for women (Sinfield 1994, 27–30). Trumbach locates two meanings of 'effeminacy' in the seventeeth century: first the smooth-cheeked transvestite (the younger male partners of sodomitical rakes), but also, and more importantly for our purposes, the adult male obsessed with women, aggressive, masculine, and generally disreputable – indolent, extravagant, and debauched (1991, 134). "Mostly, [effeminacy] meant being emotional and spending too much time with women. Often it involved excessive cross-sexual [i.e., heterosexual] attachment" (Sinfield 1994, 27).

In the early eighteenth century the pattern changed, and a new figure emerged: the effeminate molly, a lower to lower-middle class man, who wanted sex exclusively with men, who was passive and perhaps transvestite. Despite this partial 'relocation' of effeminacy, one scholar argues that we still need to bear class in mind when examining homoerotic relations: in aristocratic circles the pattern seems to have been unchanged, and males could address women and boys.[118] And, in the early years of the eighteenth century "the foppish paraphernalia of court dress was held to attract women and enhance heterosexual allure," although by the 1760s such extravagance was read, claims one scholar, "as evidence of a lack of interest in women" (McNeil 1999, 412, 417).

Thus, it may look to a modern eye highly debatable, but effeminacy has not always been thought to be an outward manifestation of male homosexuality.[119] Up to the time of the Wilde trials, "it is unsafe to interpret effeminacy as defining, or as a signal of, same-sex passion" exclusively, especially when an upper-class man was involved.[120] At the time of the trials in 1892, effeminacy was still flexible, "with the potential to refute homosexuality, as well as to imply it" (Sinfield 1994, 93). Thus Oscar Wilde's 'effeminate' manner and interests had excited comment and hostility, but they "had not led either his friends or strangers to regard him as obviously, even probably, queer;" rather as an aristocrat and aesthete (Sinfield 1994, 2–3, 71; Breward 1999, 247). The thesis of Sinfield and others is that the trials produced a major shift in perception of the signs of same-sex passion.[121] Thus, it was only after the Wilde trials that the public began to associate aestheticism/ effeminacy with homosexuality.[122]

Eighteenth- and nineteenth-century England is a time and place not particularly relevant to Rome, perhaps, but contemporary evidence is best for this era, and the secondary literature tends to focus here, making it the best option for generating new hypotheses about Roman antiquity. Young men in eighteenth- and nineteenth-century England who paid close attention to their appearance, fostering self-love and "an infatuation with the possibilities of ultra-fashionable living" (Breward 2004, 26) were known by various names.

The macaroni persona, for instance, popular in England from 1765 to 1780,[123] "was activated as much through a mannered and performative behavior as through expensive garments, with an emphasis upon Francophile artifice in posture, gesture, speech, cosmetics, and hairdressing."[124] The macaronis thus overturned preconceptions of gender and of sexuality (McNeil 1999, 412).

'Dandy' is the word applied in the late eighteenth and early nineteenth centuries to men who adopted "the more extreme features of the contemporary wardrobe... that symbolized irresponsibility and excess... [utilizing] the effete and exquisite associations of continental tastes to signify a subversive attitude towards... a variety of social and economic concerns" such as "acceptable gender roles."[125] One important characteristic of both macaronis and dandies was that their sexual preferences were often unclear: such men had a "sexually ambiguous social polish," and a "rerouted sexuality;" that is, they were sometimes seen as asexual (Garelick 1998, 3; Kelly 2005, 311–12, 472). Or, conversely, the dandy could commute "without explicit commitment, between diverse sexualities" (Sinfield 1994, 73; Delbourg-Delphis 1985, 140–65). Beau Brummel's name was linked sexually both with young men and female courtesans of the day (Kelly 2005, 309–15, 318–20); Count D'Orsay scandalized London society by marrying his mistress' sixteen-year-old stepdaughter, and was the lover of the bride's father as well (Kelly 2005, 471). The dandy's virility thus remained "indecipherable to an audience, concealed by artful arrangements of manner and dress" (Garelick 1998, 30). In addition, the pre-modern dandy functioned as a social spectacle, with an appearance purposely geared to that end: the dandy engaged in "self-conscious, highly theatrical gender play" (ibid., 3).

Dandies prove that the male could function as the object of the gaze, an area of scholarly inquiry which has not been well-defined.[126] McNeil and Karaminas note that male dress was as gaudy and flamboyant as female dress from 1350–1850, after which men began to eschew bright color and ornament in clothing in favor of dark and somber hues (the "great masculine sartorial renunciation").[127] Silverman has thus theorized that before the mid-nineteenth century extravagant fashion was a prerogative not of gender but of class. Therefore, "the history of Western fashion poses a serious challenge both to the automatic equation of spectacular display with female subjectivity and to the assumption that exhibitionism always implies woman's subjugation to a controlling male gaze" (1986, 139). If men's bodies can be sites of consumption, spectacle, and performativity,[128] this contradicts the basic premise of traditional heterosexuality – that only women are looked at and only men do the looking, and poses a serious threat to Berger's (1972, 47) and Mulvey's (1975)[129] theories concerning the eternally 'male viewer' and the eternally 'female viewed.' The phallocentric idea that women are passive spectacle and men active viewers is however one that has strangely persisted within the world of classical studies.[130]

So a dandy is an urban young man of fashion who seeks to create social spectacle through his appearance, and whose sexuality may be ambiguous.[131]

152 *Class and sexuality*

We have located 'fashionable' or effeminate men in Roman antiquity who were associated with display, youth, and urbanity, as well as sexual ambiguity. Can we term them dandies?

Ancient dandies

In fact, a derogatory term for a young man of fashion did exist in Latin: *trossulus* or *comptulus*, which modern translators render as 'dandy.' The elder Pliny reported that under Romulus and the kings *equites* were known as *trossuli* because they had taken a town of that name in Tuscany without any assistance from the infantry; he goes onto quote Junius Gracchanus, who states that:

> so far as concerns the equestrian order (*equestrem ordinem*) they were previously called the *trossuli*, but are now simply designated the Cavalry, because many people do not understand what the word *trossuli* means and many of them are ashamed to be called by that name (*multosque pudet eo nomine appellari*). But in Gracchanus' time they were still called *trossuli* though they did not wish to be.
>
> (*Nat.* 33.35–6).[132]

Fuller descriptions of Roman dandies exist, although the term is admittedly not a common one, and is usually found in Roman prose of the mid first-century CE. Varro associated *trossuli* with personal adornment and with paying outrageous sums for horses.[133] Persius (the only poet to use the word *trossulus*) wonders, "need you ask the origin of this outrageous [poetry] that puts your young dandy into an ecstatic frenzy along the benches?" (*trossulus exultat tibi per subsellia levis?*; 1.81–2). The younger Seneca (*Epp.* 87.9) described the *trossulus* as refined and well-attended (*cultior comitatiorque*) in comparison to Cato the Censor (who used to ride a donkey); the dandy in the midst of all his luxurious paraphernalia (*inter illos apparatus delicatos*) is chiefly concerned "whether he should turn his hand to the *gladius* or the toilet-knife" (*utrum se ad gladium locet an ad cultrum*) and who has many fine horses: plump ponies, Spanish cobs, and trotters (*obesis mannis et asturconibus et tolutariis*; 87.10). Elsewhere, he writes:

> You are familiar with the young dandies (*comptulos iuvenes*), brilliant in beard and hair (*barba et coma nitidos*), complete from the book-box (*de capsula totos*); you can never expect from them any strength or any soundness. *Cultus* (self-presentation) is the speech of the soul: if it is trimmed, or made-up, or fashioned by hand (*si circumtonsa est et fucata et manu facta*), it shows that there are defects and a certain amount of flaws in the mind. Excessive refinement is not manly ornament (*non est ornamentum virile concinnitas*).
>
> (*Epp.* 115.2–3).[134]

In referring to the hearing of philosophy lectures, he asks "shall I do the same thing as the dandies and young men do?"[135]

Dandies, effeminacy and class

There is one last, and essential, component to understanding ancient dandies. Why would a Roman man sport the kinds of effeminate characteristics which might lead to social censure and the label of *cinaedus*? The answer must lie in part that such effete self-presentation must have indicated some pretensions to upper-class status, at least in certain circles.[136]

Again, comparative evidence may help us here. Besides being associated with youth, urbanity, and ambiguous sexuality, there is also some indication that the pre-modern dandy had his roots in class and wealth. Thus Sinfield (1994, 40–1) states that in eighteenth-century England, effeminacy came to function as a general sign of the aristocracy: noblemen were decorative and otiose in comparison to the hard-working vigorous middle class. Because effeminacy was expected of the aristocrat, "same-sex passion was not foregrounded by his manner," although it could not definitely be ruled out: aristocratic dissipation of all sorts was associated with dandyism.[137] But while effeminacy figured upper-class uselessness and debauchery, it also embodied aspirations toward refinement, sensitivity, and taste: "for some members of the aristocratic oligarchy fine dress [was significant as] a mark of personal and social distinction" (Steele 1985, 99; Sinfield 1994, 52; and 'dandy' was often used as a commonplace word describing aristocratic foppishness; Gelder 2007, 123). And of course elite fashions were also imitated by less favored individuals.[138] Effeminacy was thus partially coded up to the time of the Wilde trials as a signifier of class, or of excessive heterosexuality, rather than necessarily of homoerotic dissidence.

We do have some slight indications that in antiquity as well the dandy was more exactly an embodiment of leisure-class dress and mannerisms, and this is because as we have seen perfume, and jewelry, and expensive, excess, or colorful fabrics could indicate status, rather than merely indicate effeminacy. Thus in Martial plucked arms (otherwise a conventional sign of the pathic) are mentioned in and amongst all the other signs of the patrician man: Tyrian purple, a white toga, sardonyx rings, the patrician's red *calceus* with the *luna* (2.29).[139] See also Martial 5.41, in which an effeminate man (*spado*) is perhaps an equestrian: status symbols mentioned here include the *trabea* and the *fibula*, and he points with a smoothed hand (*pumicata... manu*). I would argue there existed both a correlation and a confusion between the signs of wealth and status and signs of 'effeminacy:' was a violet silk tunic an indication of some or all of effeminacy, wealth, or dandyism, for instance? Edwards (1993, 67–8) proposes that "the apparent ambiguity of some forms of behavior suggests the difficulty members of Rome's educated upper classes seem to have felt" in distinguishing between sophistication, elegance and urbanity and effeminacy.[140]

The connection of the dandy or fashionable man with the aristocratic lifestyle in antiquity is perhaps also evident from the association of the *trossulus* with intellectualism: poetry recitations and philosophy lectures thrill them (above), and Seneca describes them as being "complete from the book-box." While not an exclusive characteristic of the upper-classes, some pretensions to learning also surely indicated similar pretensions to a noble status.

Conclusions

I have argued in this chapter that dandies also existed in Roman antiquity. Fashionable male appearance could indicate dandyism rather than pathic homoeroticism necessarily, although certain Roman authors equate or confuse urbanity and dandyism with sexual passivity. Ridicule of pre-modern dandies and their sexuality is also noticeable in literature of the period. I would further argue that dandyism and effeminacy were not exclusive indications of sexual passivity, but of membership in or aspirations towards the upper class. While not equating the two specifically, Gleason has previously noted the ambiguous elisions between the *cinaedus* and the sophisticated urbanite: "*were* all dandies pathics? We must ask why any man, given that depilation, dainty grooming, and sing-song speech would be interpreted by many of his peers as a sign of sexual passivity, would court censure by adopting these practices" (Gleason 1990, 405). The answer must be, in part, that some signs of 'passivity' might be nothing more than "aspirations to elegance" (Gleason 1995, 74), a possibility I have tried to explore in detail here.

Of course, to some Romans, especially the moralists, there was no difference between dandies and *cinaedi*, and indeed even from a modern standpoint it is hard to distinguish them. Both were figures which functioned as loci for Roman social anxieties concerning wealth, class, masculinity, and political authority, and the two intersected inasmuch as they both embodied sexually and socially disruptive modes of dressing and behavior.

Why weren't more *cinaedi* designated as what they perhaps were – *trossuli*? To call someone a *cinaedus* (rather than a *comptulus*) might have been a deliberate put-down, a result of intergenerational tension or discomfort with the confusion of sexual categories. Both words occur in invective and generalizing contexts, as well – texts accuse men of being *cinaedi* and mention what appears to be a subculture of *cinaedi*, but what the real-life referents called themselves we are ignorant of. We can note however that there were derogatory overtones even in the words for 'dandy;' thus the *equites* in the passage from the elder Pliny are ashamed of being called by that name (*multosque pudet eo nomine appellari*) "because many people do not understand what the word *trossuli* means." There was more than a whiff of sexual ambiguity about the dandy even in Roman antiquity,[141] which only serves to highlight the diverse and dynamic character of gender performance and identities in the Roman world.

Notes

1 A shorter version of this chapter has appeared in *The Journal of the History of Sexuality* (Olson 2014a).
2 On *kinaidoi* in ancient Athens, see Corbeill 1996, 160 n. 80. Winkler 1990, 48; Davidson 2007, 55–60, 445–6; Fox 1998, 7–13. Paris had a reputation as "a dandified fop," famous for his excessive attention to his looks (*Il.* 3.39, 44ff, 391ff; Eur. *Iphigenia* 71–7; Virg. *A.* 4.215–17). Sapsford (2015, 117) has noted the discrepancy between *kinaidos/cinaedus* as a sexually loaded term in Roman literary sources and as a sexually neutral term in documentary sources from Hellenistic and Roman Egypt, in which a *kinaedos* is a performer. On the *cinaedus* in ancient Rome, see Butrica 2002 and 2005, 221–3; Clarke 2005; Corbeill 1996, 131–73; Dyck 2001; Edwards 1993; Gleason 1990 and 1995; Kuefler 2001, 217; McDonnell 2006; Richlin 1993; Taylor 1997; Williams 2010, 177–245. On the semantic development of the term *cinaedus*, see Adams 1982, 194; Corbeill 1996, 137; Gleason 1990, 396–9; and especially Williams 2014. And see Cic. *de Orat.* 2.256; Petr. *Satyr.* 21.2; Sen. *NQ* 1.16; Juv. 2.50.
3 There are far too many excellent works to list here, but see Clarke 2001; Masterson et al. 2014; Skinner 2005.
4 See Adams 1982; Williams 2010, 177–245.
5 Williams 2010, 203; Walters 1993, 29. For a linguistic examination of *mollitia*, see Williams 2013 and 2014, esp. 465, 470–8. For artistic examples of young males with soft, pre-pubescent physiques in Roman sculpture, often placed in Roman baths and villas, see Bartman 2002.
6 Adams 1982, 123, 133, 228; Williams 2010, 193, with references; Williams 2014, 461, 465–6.
7 On *delicati*, see Olson 2014a, 185 n. 16, with references; Bartman 2002 for visual evidence.
8 Taylor records a graffito with the *cinaedus* in an active role (*CIL* 4.2319b; 1997, 353).
9 On *kinaidoi* in ancient Athens, see Olson 2014a, 185 n. 17, with references.
10 For the word applied to men see Sen. *Con.* 1. praef. 8; Cic. *de Off.* 1.130, Nepos *Att.* 13.5. But the term is more often used in relation to women: see Olson 2008, 7–8. On *munditia* and *immunditia*, see now Blonski 2014, 69–76.
11 *Lingula* may refer to a tongue-shaped projection or flap on a shoe: see Mart. 2.29.7; Juv. 5.20 (loose *lingulae*); Paul. exc. Fest. 103L; Larg. 208. Hollis 1977, 120 (at 515) notes that the text reads: +*lingua ne rigeat*+. Various emendations have been proposed, including Kenney's *gingiuae niteant* (1965) and Palmer's *lingua* to *lingue*. Goold 1965 preferred *ne rigeat* rather than Palmer's *rigeat*, although "it will then be necessary to refer '*dentes*' to the 'teeth' of a shoe-buckle" (Hollis 1977); he admits we have no supporting evidence for this. The Oxford Latin Dictionary seems to prefer *lingua*, stating that *robigus* here refers to the mouth or teeth (and see Ov. *Met.* 2.776). *TLL* s.v. '*lingula*,' 1453–4. Quintilian does warn the orator about excessive attention to shoes (*Inst.* 11.1.137; and see Tib. 1.8.14). On the other hand, see *Ars* 3.433–48, below, in which *lingula* appears to refer to the end of a belt, with which the tunic was girded, tucked into itself, a more likely solution.
12 *nec male deformet rigidos tonsura capillos:/ sit coma, sit trita barba resecta manu.* On beards in Roman antiquity, see Cic. *pro Cael.* 33; Mart. 2.36; Bonanno 1988; Croom 2002, 64–8; Hollis 1977, at 518; Kaster 2005, 161; Williams 2004, 135–6. Mart. 8.47 describes several different styles of facial hair all on one man. On the *depositio barbae* ceremony, see Suet. *Nero* 12.4 and 34.5; Stat. *Silv.* 3.4; Juv. 3.186–9; Courtney 1980, 179–80; Richlin 1993, 547. The *locus classicus* is Petr. *Satyr.* 29.8 (the sexual implications of which are ignored by Smith 1975, 60–1).

156   *Class and sexuality*

On the length and precise nature of Trimalchio's career as a *delicatus*: see Bodel 1989a and 1989b; Pomeroy 1992; Richardson 1986. Puberty for boys occurred roughly four years later in the ancient world than it does today; on which see Davidson 2007, 80–3.

13 Hollis (1977, at 519) notes nails were kept trimmed and cleaned; the Roman barber did this (Hor. *Epp.* 1.7.50–1). Barbers shops were found throughout the city (Pl. *As.* 394; Vitr. 9.8.2, Apul. *Met.* 3.16), although there may have been clusters in the vicinity of the Temple of Flora and the Circus Maximus (*CIL* 15.7172 and *CIL* 6.31900). Such establishments were recognizable by the scissors or mirrors displayed outside the premises (Holleran 2012, 126; Lucian *Ind.* 29; Alciphr. 3.30; Pl. *Curc.* 577–8; Boon 1991; MacMahon 2003, 114). Barbers shaved and trimmed hair in the streets before their shop as well (Mart. 7.61.7 [Domitian forbade this], *Dig.* 9.2.11). Some barbers were itinerant: *CIL* 2.5181. Excavation of a barber's shop: Nilson *et al.* 2008, 56.

14 On Greek precedents for this passage, see Hollis 1977, 118; Labate 1984. There were male beauty ideals at Rome: Cicero talks of Caelius' beauty, his tall figure, his looks and eyes (*candor huius te et proceritas, vultus oculique pepulerunt; Cael.* 36; see also *de Off.* 1.130). Lucius' physical appearance is praised by his aunt at Apul. *Met.* 2.2: he is tall and slim, with a good complexion, hair worn without affectation, and flashing blue eyes. Quintilian advocates good looks brought about by manly exercise: "healthy bodies, enjoying a good circulation and strengthened by exercise (*exercitatione fermata*), acquire grace from the same source that gives them strength (*vires*), for they have a healthy complexion, firm flesh and shapely thighs" (*colorata et adstricta et lacertis expressa sunt; Inst.* 8. pr.19).

15 Kuchta 1996, 63. Breward (1999, 246) has noted that in many Western societies, normative male characteristics are those which have an aversion to surface, decoration, and looking.

16 As it was in ancient Athens: men who were driven by their appetites and wants and who spent lavishly to support them violated the masculine ideal of self-restraint, more closely resembling the Athenian stereotype of women as consumers (Roisman 2005, 89; see also Davidson 1997, 174; Foucault 1985, 63–77). Unmanly, luxurious clothing appears at Dem. 21.133, 36.45 and Aes. 1.131; ethical interpretations of a man's appearance and gait at Arist. *EN* 4.3.1125a13–17; Lys. 16.18, Dem. 45.68–9, 77, 54.34; Is. 5.11; Aes. 1.25–6, 131; and Theophr. *Characters* 24.8, 26.4. See also Roisman 2005, 103 n. 40. On the other hand, the Old Oligarch (1.10), complained that Athenian citizens dressed no better than their slaves and metics. See Geddes 1987.

17 "In Republican Rome, the reading of morality becomes an aesthetic practice" (Corbeill 2002, 183; Corbeill 1996, 151, 156, 169); see also Bourdieu 1984, 44–50.

18 Livy 34.7.9; Ov. *Med.* 27–8, *Ars* 3.133, *Am.* 2.4.37–8; Tib. 1.9.67–74. See Olson 2008.

19 On the ancient theme of the golden mean, see Edwards 1993, 96; Siedschlag 1977, 59–62; Williams 2004, 134.

20 *de Off.* 1.130. See McNeil and Karaminas 2009a, 7 for early modern English parallels to Cicero's 'golden mean' in male appearance.

21 Gibson 2003, 276. Edwards (1993, 74–5) discusses how "accusations of effeminacy may be seen as diluted threats of rape."

22 *Mollitia* ('softness') has been meticulously defined by modern historians of ancient sexuality: it is a failure to discipline oneself; excess; or a heightened susceptibility to emotion. It might be a failure to perform unpleasant duties, or an inability to put up with pain or inconvenience (see Graver 1998, 611 nn. 10–11 with refs).

23 In this chapter I look at effeminate clothing (men wearing 'womanish' clothing), not cross-dressing or transvestism (men wearing women's clothing), often though

Class and sexuality 157

not always associated with disguise (Sen. *Contr.* 5.6; Apul. *Met.* 7.8, 11.8; Kuefler 2001, 57–9). The most famous incident of cross-dressing in Roman antiquity is probably that of Clodius infiltrating the Bona Dea ceremonies in 62 BCE (Cic. *Dom.* 139, *Har. Resp.* 44, *Orat. Frag.* 14.22 and 23 with Geffcken 1973, 82; see also Varro Men. 313; Gell. 6.12.4–5; Corbeill 2002, 205; Leach 2001; Williams 2010, 159–60). On transvestism generally in Roman antiquity, see *Dig.* 34.2.33; Kuefler 2001, 57–8; Manfredini 1985. For some interesting artistic evidence, see Birk 2011.

24 Williams 2010, 141. On effeminate gesture, see Var. *Men.* 301; *CIL* 4.1825; Cic. *Orat.* 59, *Off.* 1.128, 131, *Clod.* 22, *Fin.* 5.35; Phaedr. 5.1.12–18; Sen. *Contr.* 2.1.6; Sen. *Epp.* 52.12 and 114.3, *NQ* 7.31.2–3, Petr. *Satyr.* 119; Juv. 2.15–22; André 1981, 102, 124; Barton 1993, 116–18; Bremmer 1992, 21–4; Fögen 2009; Cèbe 1987, 1324–5; Corbeill 2002 and 1996, 166; Gleason 1995, 32, 64; O'Sullivan 2011, 16–22; Parker 1997; Richlin 1993, 542 n. 46. See also ps-Arist. *Physiog.* 808a, 810a. Voice quality was also a sign of effeminacy (Cic. *de Orat.* 3.216; Gleason 1995, 82–121; Barton 1993, 116–18). There was also the suggestive "finger to the head" gesture, in which the effeminate man scratches his head with one finger, perhaps to avoid disarranging his hair. See Val. Max. 4.6.4; Plut. *Pomp.* 48 and 53, *Caes.* 4.9, *Mor.* 89e, 800e; Sen. *Epp.* 52.12; Juv. 9.133; Suet. *Aug.* 68; Luc. *Rhet. Praec.* 11; Corbeill 1996, 164; Courtney 1980, 441–2; Edwards 1993, 63; Herter 1959, 632; See also the Calvus fragment in Buechner 1982, 122. Courtesans in ancient Greece walked wiggling their hips (Anacreon *fr.* 458) – and interestingly, so did the rich (Aristoph. *Wasps* 1169, 1171–3).

25 The modern bibliography on ancient Roman cosmetics is growing, although work to date has naturally focused on women: see Johnson 2016; Olson 2008, 58–79, with references, and in addition Stewart's excellent work of 2007, (which includes information on cosmetic and perfume use by men: see 19–21, 82, 96–7). At Mart. 4.42, the ideal catamite will be from Egypt but with skin whiter than snow; at 1.77 a *cunnilinctor* paints his face to avoid looking pale (*tinguit cutem Charinus et tamen pallet;* Bradley [2009, 155–6] comments that "even his shameful sexual habits cannot produce a blush)".

26 On chalk as an ingredient in women's cosmetics, see Olson 2008, 61, 66. Alternatively, *vestitu et creta* may mean the men's clothes were treated with chalk: so the thieves here are politicians and wear the *toga candida*. Or the thieves may be women.

27 Schmeling (2011, 472–3) focuses on what he sees as an appearance indicative of homosexuality.

28 *fucata muliebriter comat; Inst.* 8. pr. 19–20; and see 8.3.6–11; Sen. *Epp.* 115.2.

29 2.93–5; see Courtney 1980, 137–8; Herter 1959, 634. A *gallus* was a self-castrated eunuch priest of Cybele On *fuligo* in antiquity, see Olson 2008, 62 and 133 n. 37 (with references); Saiko 2005, 135–6. On effeminate male grooming, see also Tert. *Cult. Fem.* 2.8.2; Dio 62.6.3.

30 On *splenia,* see Olson 2008, 65 and 135 n. 63 (with references).

31 Richlin 1995, 205 characterizes Marcus Regulus as "an orator in makeup." The story has not been satisfactorily explained to my mind; perhaps it represents an instance of personal superstition.

32 Cic. *Red. Sen.* 16; see also Mart. 2.29. Williams (2004, 118) gives a long list of references to slaves being branded on the face, noting that such slaves could be known as *inscripti* (Pliny *Nat.* 18.21; Mart. 8.75.9; Macr. *Sat.* 1.11.19), *notati* (Mart. 3.21.1), or "with cruel irony," *literati* (Plaut. *Cas.* 401; Apul. *Met.* 9.12). The tattoo probably consisted of a single letter, "F," for *fugitivus,* but for other suggestions see Williams 2004, 118.

33 On long male hair see Butrica 2002; Pollini 2003. But such hair could oddly also be a sign of a hardened generation of times past: see Sen. *NQ* 1.17.7. Juvenal talks of a wine bottled "in the days when consuls wore long hair" (*ipse capillato diffusum consule potat*; 5.30).

34 On *delicati* see Bodel 1989a and 1989b; Butrica 2005, 223–4 (with references), 231–8; Fless 1995, 95 and *passim*; Laes 2003 and 2010; Lilja 1983, 20–33; Murgatroyd 1977; Pomeroy 1992; Pollini 2003; Richardson 1986; Richlin 1992, 32–56, 221, 223. Augustus collected small boys loveable for beauty and prattling (Suet. *Aug.* 83; see also Pliny *Nat.* 7.56; Cassius Dio 48.44, 67.15.3; Plut. *Antony* 59; Herodian 1.17.3). Such boys were also called *glabri* (smooth-skinned: Cat. 61.135, Phaed. 4.5.22, Sen. *Epp.* 47.7, *Dial.* 10.12.5; and see Butrica 2005, 234; *TLL* s.v 'glaber,' col. 1998–9), *effeminati* (Cic. *Mil.* 89; Sen. *Epp.* 99.17; Tac. *Ann.* 15.67; *TLL* s.v. 'effeminatus,' col. 136), *concubini* (Cat. 61.126; Mart. 5.41; Tac. *Ann.* 13.21; *TLL* s.v. 'concubinus,' col. 99), or *exoleti* (see below, n. 83; *TLL* s.v. 'exolesco,' col. 1542–4).

35 *Capillati*: Sen. *Epp.* 95.24; Petr. *Satyr.* 27.1, 29, 57, 58, 110; Mart. 2.57.5, 3.58.31, 10.62, 11.78. On *capillati* see Fless 1995, 58; Pollini 2003; *TLL* s.v. '*capillatus*,' col. 313. Long hair: Mart. 1.131, 7.29, 11.78, 12.18, 12.49, 12.70, 12.84, 12.97; Juv. 8.128. See also Hor. *Carm.* 1.29.8, 2.5.23, 3.20.14, 4.10.3, *Epod.* 11.28.

36 Sen. *Epp.* 95.24. Pollini (2003, 157) claims that the younger Seneca distinguishes between curly-headed slave boys and straight-haired freeborn boys, but the distinction here seems to be between curly- and straight-haired slave boys. Of course we may also make a distinction between naturally and artificially-curled hair and between long and short curly hair. Pers. 1.29 speaks of 100 curly-headed schoolboys (*cirratorum*), who may be freeborn; in Mart. 9.29 the schoolboys/ schoolchildren are curly-haired (*cirrata... caterva*). See also Obermayer 1998, 94–144. Henriksen (2012, 54–5 and 132) believes freeborn boys wore their hair long until their adoption of the *toga virilis*.

37 Martial (4.42.5) does not like curls on his boy. In Petronius' *Satyricon* Hermeros boasts that although once a *capillatus*, he now walks around bare-headed: *capite aperto ambulo* (57; see Smith [1975, 156] who glosses this as "undisguised and unashamed," as in Pl. *Capt.* 475). The speaker here used to be a long-haired slave (*capillatos*).

38 *Truc.* 609; Cat. 37 (and see Martial below). In Cat. 37, Egnatius is Lesbia's lover, from Celtiberia, a *capillatus*. Quinn 1970, 205 does not speculate on the man's status, merely stating here that "smart young men wore their hair long." See Ellis who takes *capillatus* as a reference to Egnatius' Celtiberian identity adducing, wrongly, Mart. 10.65.6–7 (Ellis 1889, 135, at line 17). Effeminacy was thought to be a characteristic of the Gauls: Caes. *BG* 1.1; Diod. 5.32.7. On the looks and habits of barbarians, see Balsdon 1979, 214–22, 225–30.

39 *Red. Sen.* 12, 13, 16, *Pis.* 25, *Pro Sest.* 18. See also Pl. *Asin.* 627 (*cinaede calamistrate*); Sen. *Epp.* 114.5; Mart. 10.65. On the *calamistrum*, see Olson 2008, 73, 140 n. 132, with references.

40 *myrobrechis... cincinnos* (Suet. *Aug.* 86); which may not be a reference to literal hair, but to literary style. On Maecenas' effeminacy, see Graver 1998; Kennedy 1992, 39; Sen. *Epp.* 114.4; Tac. *Ann.* 1.54 (in which he is violently in love with an actor called Bathyllus); Dio 54.17.5, 19.3, 30.4, Vell. Pat. 2.88.2; *Elegiae in Maecenatem* 1.21–6, 59, with Schoonhoven 1980, 40–2, 106–9, 129. Williams (2010, 176) notes the fact "that [Maecenas'] behavior is something intrinsically *needing* indulgence is never questioned."

41 *componi*: Quint. *Inst.* 11.3.148; see also 8. *pr.* 22. The advocate's hair was to be cut, and not arranged in tiers and ringlets (Quint. *Inst.* 12.10.47). More so than the average Roman, the orator had to pay heed to his dress, since "his is noticed more" (*sed magis in oratore conspicitur*; Quint. *Inst.* 11.3.137). He thus must especially embody the golden mean, looking neither untidy and lower-class, nor be so dandified that aspersions were cast on his masculinity. In addition to the importance of personal appearance, many Roman authors were firm that an

Class and sexuality 159

orator's or writer's character could be read from his literary style (Cic. *de Orat.* 142; Sen. *Epp.* 114.607; Tac. *Dial.* 26; Quint. Inst. 12.10.47; Bramble 1974, 38–45; Kraus 2005, 104 nn. 24–6).
42 Sen. *Epp.* 47.7; Athen. *Deipn.* 13.564–5f; Fless 1995, 61, nn. 440–1; Richlin 1992, 35–9.
43 Mart. 2.36, 9.27, 10.65, 12.38; Dio Chrys. 33.63; Gell. 6.12.5.
44 Mart. 12.38, 2.62. Williams notes that hairy chests operated as a symbol of masculinity, and thus references to men who depilated their chests are "hard to find" (2004, 207), but see Mart. 2.36.
45 Mart. 6.56, 9.27 (with Obermayer 1998, 117–19); Juv. 2.11–13.
46 Pers. 4.39; Mart. 2.62, 9.27; Dio Chrys. 33.63; Juv. 8.16.
47 Plucking: Sen. *Epp.* 56.2 (hair-pluckers hawking their services in the bathhouses); see also Mart. 10.90. and *CIL* 6.9141. Domitian reportedly depilated his concubines himself: Suet. *Dom.* 22. Pumice: Ov. *Ars* 1.506; Pliny *Nat.* 36.154 (used as a depilatory for women and men). Resin: see Juv 8.114–15, where he states that the Greeks are smooth-bodied with resin (*resinata*), and Pliny *Nat.* 29.26 in which the use of resin itself produces effeminacy (*pilorum eviratio instituta resinis eorum*; see also *Nat.* 14.123; Mart. 3.74, 12.32.21–2; Tert. *Pall.* 4.1.3). *Dropax*, a kind of depilatory ointment, is mentioned by Martial at 3.74 and 10.65.8; Pliny mentions other depilatory creams (*Nat.* 30.132–4, 29.26) including *psilothrum* (*Nat.* 24.79, 23.3, 21). Martial also mentions this product (3.74.1; used by a man) and 6.93.9 (where it is green in color, used by a woman).
48 For *glaber*, see above, n. 34. Among other reports of effeminacy, it was rumored Augustus used to singe his legs with red-hot nutshells to make the hair grow soft (*mollior pilus surgeret*; Suet. *Aug.* 68).
49 Gleason 1995, 69: Arist. *Gen. An.* 765b, 783b; *Problems* 10.24. See also *AP* 11.190 and 11.368; Williams 2010, 141–5.
50 Gleason 1990: 401. Otho's effeminacy: Plut. *Galba* 25.1, *Otho* 4.3 and 9.2; Suet. *Otho* 6.3, 12.1; Juv. 2.99–109.
51 Pliny *Nat.* 14.123; Quint. *Inst.* 8. pr. 19. Of course, hairiness could be just a smokescreen for effeminacy (Mart. 1.24, 6.56, 7.58, 9.47, and 9.27.6–9, in which a depilated man swaggers and tries to act manly; Juv. 2.9–19; Lucian *Igno. Book Coll.* 23). See also Gleason 1990, 405–11; Richlin 1992, 138–9, 201–2.
52 Cic. *Red. Sen.* 16, *Pro Rosc.* 135, *Phil.* 3.12, *Pis.* 25; *Pro Sest.* 18, *Cat.* 2.5, 2.22. Holleran has noted that perfumes and unguents were imported into Rome but were also mixed on-site at *tabernae unguentariae* (2012, 128; Var. *LL.* 8.55, Sen. *Epp.* 108.4, Suet. *Aug.* 4.2; Pl. *St.* 383; Juv. 2.42), and distributed in flasks or alabaster boxes (Mart. 11.8, 14.110). Perfume, like meat, was sold by weight (Holleran 2012, 129; Petr. *Satyr.* 39). See also Colin 1955; Holmes 1992.
53 46.18.1–3, *BNP* Fufius I 4. Spikenard is mentioned as a hair oil at Mart. 3.65.8 (Olson 2008, 76; Dalby 2000, 196–7, with references). Myrrh was also used as to perfume the hair: Hor. *Carm.* 3.14.21–2; Colin 1955; Frank 1940, 225; Holmes 1992; Miller 1969. See also Ov. *Ars* 3.443; Mart. 5.64, 11.39. Hair surviving from a grave in Roman Britain still had oil or fat in it (Croom 2002, 68). Williams 2004, 116 notes that the adjective *pinguis* "can be used to describe cheese (Virg. *Ecl.* 1.34), meat (Cels. 4.9.3), and hair-unguent (Mart. 11.15 and 11.98)." He also states the adjective *madidus* is more usual, as *pinguis* is "hardly flattering" (see Ov. *Met.* 3.55, *Her.* 14.30; Mart. 14.50). At Mart. 6.57, a man fabricates hair on his bald pate with ointment.
54 Pliny *Nat.* 13.25; Sen. *Epp.* 51.10, 86.13, 108.16; Macr. *Sat.* 3.16.15. "Masculinity was associated with a certain uncultivated roughness" (Williams 2010, 142). Thus Vespasian rebuked a young officer for reeking of perfume (*adulescentulum fragrantem unguento*; Suet. *Vesp.* 8.3). See Stewart 2007, 96–7.

55 Mart. 3.82.26. See Olson 2008, 78, 141 n. 162, 82, 88.
56 2.40–42 (with Courtney 1980, 129); Mart. 14.59; Herter 1959, 634.
57 Sen. *Contr.* 2.1.6: *madentem unguentis externis,* "dripping with foreign perfume;" Aeneas' enemies describe him with effeminate, oil-sleeked hair (Virg. *A.* 4.215–17, 12.97–100).
58 Isid. *Orig.* 19.32.4 = *ORF* 48.58; trans. Corbeill 1996, 164. Corbeill does not comment on what to modern readers is an internal contradiction.
59 *Inst.* 11.3.142; see also Petr. *Satyr.* 32.3; Pliny *Nat.* 33.24. According to the *HA,* Alexander Severus maintained jewels were for women and should not be worn by men (*HA* Sev. 51).
60 "The mockery of effeminate dress at Rome has a heritage dating back to our earliest extant texts" (Corbeill 1996, 159). For possible visual evidence of *cinaedi,* especially in the case of the Leiden gemstone, see Clarke 2005 and Butrica 2005.
61 Prudentius, although a fourth-century author, states that ageing men (*vetulos*) will turn effeminate and wear silk clothing (*Hamar.* 287–8), embroidered garments (288–99), and soft clothes (294–5). One man chases after extravagant tunics (*lascivas… tunicas*; 293–4).
62 *ne vestis serica viros foedaret*; Tac. *Ann.* 2.33. In a letter to the Senate, Tiberius complained of (luxurious) dress, equally enjoyed by male and female (*promiscas viris et feminas vestis; Ann.* 3.53).
63 *nec puduit has vestes usurpare etiam viros levitatem propter aestivam; Nat.* 11.78.
64 *multicia*; 2.66; this word also occurs at 11.188, on a woman; and see Courtney 1980, 132. *TLL* s.v. '*multicius,*' col. 1582, defined as *multicia: vestes molliori textas subtemine, quibus solent uti puelle* ("softer clothing of thread loosely/ openly woven, which girls are accustomed to wear"). For further instances of the word see Tert. *Pall.* 4.4.3; Petr. *Satyr.* 30.1.
65 Juv. 2.84–7; Courtney 1980, 133–4.
66 On *lacernae,* see Wilson 1938, 117–25.
67 For Baetic wool see Pliny *Nat.* 8.191; Mart 9.61.3–4 (with Henriksen 2012, 262), 8.28.6, 12.98.2, 14.133; Juv. 12.40–2; Tert. *Pall.* 3.6.1. On *leucophaeatus* see André 1949, 74, 211, 294.
68 *Nativus*: see André 1949, 72, 281, 294. *Fuscus*: see ibid., 123–5, 209, 274, 279, 289, 294, 297, 299, 364, 365, 369, 394. For *fuscatus,* see ibid., 229.
69 The scent was that of a woman; 3.82.26; see Olson 2008, 78. On *galbinus,* see André 1949, 148–50, 295; *galbinatus* ibid., 149, 211, 295; Goldman 2013, 77. Fortunata appears in this color in the *Satyricon:* 67.4. See also *HA* Aurel. 34.2 in which a barbarian captive wears a luxurious scarlet cloak and a yellowish-green tunic (*chlamyde coccea, tunica galbina*).
70 *caerulea indutus scutulata aut galbinus rasa.* On *caeruleus,* see André 1949, 162–71; *caeruleatus* ibid., 210, 343.
71 12.38–9. Mart. 10.73 praises an Ausonian toga which Maecenas would have loved. Juvenal mentions other fine fabrics here as well; see Courtney 1980, 522.
72 Schmeling however believes that myrtle is used here because it is sacred to Venus (2011, 62).
73 For instance, at Virg. *A.* 11.775–7: Chloreus, a former priest of Cybele, wears a cloak of yellow and other bright garments and is described as a fop rather than a true warrior. See also Cic. *Hars.* 44; see also Var. *L.* 7.53; Juv. 6 O22; Apul. *Met.* 8.27. On yellow as the province of women, see Pliny *Nat.* 21.46. On yellow in Roman times, see Dana 1919; André 1949, 128–61. On the connection between saffron (which yields a yellow dye) and the female menstrual cycle, see Sebesta 1997, 540 n. 33, with references.
74 *Porro, ut adferunt lumen clavus et purpurae loco insertae, ita certe neminem deceat intertexta pluribus notis vestis; Inst.* 8.5.28. The analogy is utilized for rhetorical purposes: Quintilian is discoursing on the need for few but brilliant

sententiae in a speech (see also Hor. *Ars* 15–16; Petr. *Satyr.* 118.5). Tertullian writes that men of old wore tunics 'harmonious of hue' or 'unified by color' (*luminis concilio; Pall.* 1.1.3) with a four-sided mantle overtop. For colored tunics, see Pausch 2008, 100–3.

75 On *scutulatus*, see Courtney 1980, 138–9; Granger-Taylor 1987; Wild 1964. The pattern is also found in Etruscan art: see Bonfante-Warren 1973, 611–12. And see Isid. *Orig.* 12.1.48.

76 Wild 1964, 263. But perhaps a *scutulatus* weave would have been somewhat obscured by the fulling of the garment, which would have blurred the weaving pattern to produce a shiny nap (see Flohr 2013b, 62).

77 Long sleeves as a sign of effeminacy: Corbeill 1996, 159–65, Richlin 1992, 92–3; Pausch 2008, 86–9, 172–80.

78 On the *mitra*, see Olson 2008, 53, 129 n. 148. The reference to *mitrae* in Mart. 2.36 is taken by some scholars to mean the headdresses of *galli* (Williams 2004, 135).

79 On Caesar's effeminacy, see Plut. *Caes.* 1; Dio Cassius 43.20.2; Corbeill 1996, 189–215 and 2002; Kraus 2005; Leeman 2001. Plutarch states that Cicero was the first to notice the contrast between Caesar's "feminine" care and his "masculine" ambition (*Caes.* 4; Leeman 2001, 99).

80 *Calig.* 52. For the *cyclas*, see Olson 2008, 51, 128 n. 141. Similarly, Commodus drew criticism according to Cassius Dio (73.17) because before he entered the theatre he put on a long-sleeved white silk *chiridota* embroidered in gold. On the *chiridota* or *dalmatica* see Croom 2002, 34–5; Harlow 2004, 54–9.

81 On the girding of the tunic, see Pausch 2008, 89–96.

82 Or a lower-class one. Edwards 1993, 70–3. See Petr. *Satyr.* 60.8.

83 On *exoleti*, see Butrica 2005, 223–31, 236–8. He also makes a strong case that *pulchri* (a term from early Latin) and *exoleti* (a term from later Latin) were expressions that referred to such boyish pleasure-objects, now grown, some of whom continued to have sex with their master (Butrica 2002). He rejects *exoletus* as meaning "male prostitute" (2005, 226–7). See also Butrica 2002; Taylor 1997, 358–62; Williams 2010, 90–3.

84 See Pausch 2008, 168–72 on the *tunica talaris*.

85 *Ver.* 2.5.86; *Cat.* 2.22. See also Cic. *Clu.*111, who states that even Quinctius' clothes were cause to hate him, "such as the purple robe he used to wear, right down to his heels" (*amictum atque illam usque ad talos demissam purpuram*). Dio reports that Q. Fufius Calenus accused Cicero of wearing a long tunic (46.18.1–3). At Pl. *Poen.* 1298, 'tavern-boys,' possibly male prostitutes, are described as wearing long tunics (*quis hic homo est cum tunicis longis quasi puer cauponius*).

86 He is *solutis tunicis* and *a discincto*; 114.6–7. While Seneca is probably referring to oratorical style, it is interesting to note that McNeil states the macaronis in eighteenth-century England adopted a particular speech pattern – peculiar pronunciations and unusual words – "perhaps projecting an alternative identity through speech as well as dress" (1999, 427; see also McNeil 2000, 382).

87 Graver 1998, 620. See also Corbeill 1996, 160 n. 82; Edwards 1993, 90; Richlin 1992, 92. For Greek notions of un-girt see Bremmer 1992, 19 and n. 11.

88 Although Tertullian complains of a tunic shortened by means of a belt, a tunic so long that "it were better to have woven of more moderate length in the first place" (*quam praestabat moderatiorem texuisse; Pall.* 5.1.4).

89 See also 10.20.14, in which a lower-class man assumes the forbidden insignia of high office and "cinctures of office that are absolutely denied to him."

90 *ut trahendo laciniam velut mollis incederet*, 2.3.9; Cic. *Facet.* 2. The connection of 'toga' with 'belting' is puzzling, inasmuch as it is the tunic, the under garment, not the toga, that is belted. Perhaps Macrobius, writing in the early fifth century CE, is referring to the *umbo* of the toga, in which the drapery is knotted on one

162   Class and sexuality

side; however, that feature of the toga did not evolve until the Augustan era. See Stone 1994, 17; Wilson 1924, 49, 67.

91   And see Cicero on Caesar, above. Gellius reports that Quintus Hortensius, the most renowned orator of his time with the exception of Marcus Tullius, was accused of effeminacy because he dressed with extreme foppishness (*multa munditia*) and arranged the folds of his toga with great care and exactness (*circumspecte compositeque indutus et amictus esset*; 1.5.2–3). Clodius described Pompey as a man who pulls up his toga and shakes it (Plut. *Pomp.* 48.7, an effeminate gesture; and see Varr. *Men.* 313).

92   *BNP* Cornelius I 70; Sulpicius I 14. On obsessively pulling out hair on the chin, see Tert. *Pall.* 4.1.3.

93   Edwards 1993, 76, with notes. Tracy 1976 treats as one category lesbians, dandies, *pathici*, and male and female transvestites.

94   In eighteenth-century England, color and pattern were part of macaroni fashion, and represented both youth and luxury (McNeil 2000, 375–8).

95   Trans. Corbeill 1996, 154.

96   *Sicut vestibus quoque non purpura coccoque fulgentibus illa aetas satis apta sit: in iuvenibus etiam uberiora paulo et paene periclitantia feruntur; Inst.* 11.1.31–2. For comparative evidence from eighteenth-century England, see McNeil and Karaminas 2009a, 7.

97   In 1880s England, one trade publication observed that "the younger class of customers are as a rule more changeable and erratic in their [sartorial] ideas" (*The Tailor and Cutter*, 28 January 1886, 113; cit. Breward 1999, 35).

98   *Sest.* 19. *RE* Calpurnius 63. The Seplasia was the street in Capua where perfumes and unguents were sold (Val. Max. 9.1.ext.1; Pliny. *Nat.* 33.164, 34.108). On *fuscus*, see above. And see Cicero's description of the tribune Rullus at Cic. *de Leg. Agr.* 2.13 (*BNP* Servilius I 26).

99   1058, on which see below. Taylor (1997, 347 n. 91) speculates Lucilius' term *barbati moechocinaedi* might imply that the men are philosophers (beards were "rarely grown" by men of the late Republic).

100   *deliciarum causa et voluptatis; pro C. Rab. Post.* 26. The text is corrupt here; as noted above, Chapter 3. Black may have been assumed as a fashionable color here – or it may have been dark tunics assumed for the purpose of disguise.

101   Murgatroyd states: "the point here is that this care over the appearance is to attract girls" (1980, 197; see also Tib. 1.8.2.3.78). The clothing here is not, as Murgatroyd believes (ibid), a reference to an unbelted tunic, for which he adduces as comparandum Cic. *Cat.* 2.22, but to a voluminous toga.

102   That Labienus depilates himself in order to please his girlfriend "gives us an interesting glimpse into women's possible tastes or, rather, into men's ideas about women's tastes" (Williams 2004, 207). Even if Labienus had no girlfriend, "he expected to be able to convince others that he had an *amica* for whom he depilated" (ibid., 208). See also Mart. 2.47.

103   In case it should soil or disarrange his own dress?

104   The *reticulum* was a female hairnet, and thus *reticulatus adulter* is an oxymoron. Hairnets: see Jenkins and Williams 1985; Mottahedeh 1984; Olson 2008, 21, 76.

105   O. 21–5, 27. See Courtney 1980, 307–9. Effeminacy can be adopted, not inherent (Weeks 1989, 205–6). Phaedrus tells the fable of the *cinaedus*-soldier who robs his commander's baggage-train but escapes punishment for his crime because Pompey believes him incapable of it (*Fab.* app. 8); Gleason (1995, 134) believes this may be "effeminacy assumed for self-protection."

106   *Discourses* 3.1.32–5. See further Dover 1978, 71–2 on effeminacy in Attic red-figure vases. Lucian *Am.* 9 states that a young man will use cosmetics to be attractive to women (*exonta ti kai kommōtikês, askêseōs hate oimai qunaiois evōraizomenon*).

Class and sexuality 163

107 Gibson 2003, 277: *cultus* is used of men only in a perjorative sense (see Cic. *Amic.* 49; Ov. *Ars* 3.447, 3.681; Sen. *Benef.* 1.10.2), and "any recommendation of *cultus* to men had to be qualified" (ibid.; e.g., Quint. *Inst.* 8. pr. 20).

108 *In statione* at lines 433–4 suggests "feminine attention to the hair" (Gibson 2003, 277; see Pl. *Asin.* 627; Plut. *Caes.* 4). Quintilian stated eloquence is not supposed to polish her nails and take care over her hair (*Inst.* 8. pr. 22).

109 Ovid recommends that women avoid effeminates, as such men seek only shameful sexual gains, or by suggesting, somewhat fantastically, that they are really after the clothing of the *puellae* (Gibson 2003, 275, 282; on the importance of Cic. *de Off.* in the *Ars* see Gibson 2003, 22 n. 57). Clothes could be valuable: see Cic. *Verr.* 2.2.20; Pliny *Epp.* 2.20.10; Sebesta 1994b, 70. Or perhaps the effeminate wants the clothing for his own use.

110 *Phys.* 49, 1.256–58F; cit. Gleason 1995, 79. Scholars are divided as to whether or not heteroeroticism was a significant part of the *cinaedus*' sexual activity. Richlin states (1993, 549) that the involvement of a *cinaedus* with a woman is "usually set up as a surprise; overwhelmingly and explicitly, *cinaedi* are said to be passive homosexuals" (see also Butrica 2005, 221–3; Corbeill 1996, 150, 157–8 ["effeminacy connotes a specific sexuality"] and nn. 57–9; Taylor 1997, 338–40, 345). But men labeled *pathicus, cinaedus, exoletus,* and *catamitus* could be active heterosexually (Pollini 1999, 2.6; Clarke 2005). Being penetrated was not the only practice that could brand a man as effeminate: being overly-active with women could also be seen as such, as self-control was seen as a masculine province (Edwards 1993, 78; Williams 2010, 156–70). This may be the explanation of *cinaedior* applied to a woman at Cat. 10.24; the force of the word is not merely 'shameless' (Adams 1982, 132), but 'lacking in self-control.' "The various manifestations of effeminacy are symptoms of an underlying failure to live up to the central imperative of masculinity: control and dominion, both of others and of oneself" (Williams 2010, 139). In addition, "effeminates... were often implied to be more open to sexual experiences of any kind (with either sex) than other men" (Gibson 2003, 276; cf. Philo. *AP* 11.318; Sen. *Contr.* 1 pr. 8ff; Juv. 6.365). Or perhaps an effeminate man was someone who aimed to please anyone, male or female, in his erotic encounters (Gleason 1995, 65). Gellius (3.5.1–2) recounts the following story: "Plutarch relates that the philosopher Arcesilaus used strong language concerning a rich man [who was] exceedingly effeminate, but was said to be uncorrupted and free from *stuprum* (*qui incorruptus tamen et a stupro integer dicebatur*). For when [Arcesilaus] perceived his broken speech and artfully arranged hair and playful eyes filled with charm and desire, he said, "it doesn't matter with what parts you're a *cinaedus*, those in back or those in front" (*"nihil interest," inquit "quibus membris cinaedi sitis, posterioribus an prioribus"*). But see Taylor (1997, 355–6 and n. 124) who elaborates on the figurative meaning of the maxim ("up front or in secret").

111 Antony: see Cic. *Phil.* 2.77–8; Edwards 1993, 64–5; Griffin 1985, 32–47. *Cinaedi* have been identified by some scholars as a subculture in Roman antiquity, (Richlin 1993; Taylor 1997), and modern subcultural theorists also look at the relation between affect and style. See Muggleton 2000, 91; see also Horn 2009, 134.

112 Maecenas: Hor. *Epod.* 14; Sen. *Epp.* 114.4; Graver 1998, 610. Corbeill (1996, 160 n. 82) does state Maecenas' tunics were effeminate but fails to mentions M.'s excessive attention to his wife. See also Plut. *Pomp.* 48.7, in which Pompey is both effeminate and uxorious.

113 Even today, a particular masculine style may be admired in quite different ways by older or younger men or by women (Cornwall and Lindisfarne 1994, 38).

114 *Dialogues of the Gods* 6; Konstan 2002, 354–5.

115 Konstan (2002, 361) writes of "the sexual bivalence of a Paris or a Dionysus, in which the contrast between masculine and feminine identities is subdued."

Class and sexuality

116 See also Cic. *Brut*. 224: L. Appuleius Saturninus (a popular tribune) "took the fancy of the public by externals, such as by his action or even his dress" rather than by eloquence (*et motu atque ipso amictu capiebat homines*). One scholar has posulated that "dandyism is itself a performance, the performance of a highly stylized, painstakingly constructed self, a solipsistic social icon" (Garelick 1998, 3).

117 The modern literature on dandies has become much more sophisticated, and is re-examining the figure with a view to the male gaze, men as consumers, affect and sexuality, subculture, gender and performance, effeminacy, style and patriotism. See for example Delbourg-Delphis 1985; Garelick 1998; McNeil 1999; Moers 1960; Sinfield 1994; Spooner 2004, 86–107.

118 Sinfield 1994, 40. Scholars have noted that "the early modern period was as much interested in the difference between men and boys as women and men; their mindset often used a triangulated gender system" (McNeil and Karaminas 2009a, 5).

119 Interestingly, there is a twentieth-century example as well. In the 1960s UK there sprang up the so-called 'Peacock movement' of flamboyant male dress. As Peacocks wanted to be – and generally were – admired by women, they were not afraid of fashion, and in fact the "overwhelming percentage of Peacock men wearing the new, colourful finery were unquestionably heterosexual... this extravagance was a way of signalling presence and availability to the opposite sex" (Ross 2011, 72).

120 Cole 2000, 23; Sinfield 1994, 27; Spooner 1994, 94–5. Of course, scholars differ regarding affect and sexuality: Cole for instance states that "apparel and adornment had provided an indication of homosexuality or of a tendency toward same-sex sexual activity since the seventeenth century" (2000, 2, 31).

121 Boscagli 1996, 31; Cole 2000, 31; Kosofsky-Sedgwick 1985, 173; Sinfield 1994.

122 Because aestheticism was predominantly an ideology of the upper classes in the late nineteenth century, as there was a more clearly defined homosexual identity among those men, twentieth-century gay identity was a "*bricolage* of effeminacy, aestheticism, and class" (Cole 2000, 17, 19).

123 On the macaroni, see McNeil 1999 and 2000; Steele 1985.

124 In Roman antiquity, "an effeminate appearance and excessive preoccupation with one's toilet could be presented as typical of a Greek" (Edwards 1993, 93): Romans often referred to homoerotic acts using Greek terms; there were many words for 'sexually passive' in Greek (Edwards 1993, 94; MacMullen 1982). Perhaps some fashionable Romans equated homoerotic relations with Greek sophistication (Edwards 1993, 94). On Greek dress, see Wallace-Hadrill 2008, 38–70; Olson 2014b; Pausch 2008, 41–3.

125 Breward 2004, 35. The most enduring examples of the dandy were Beau Brummel (1778–1840) and the Count D'Orsay (1801–1852). On Beau Brummel see Chancellor 1927, 24–31; Barbey d'Aurevilly 1845; Garelick 1998, 6–10; Kelly 2005; Moers 1960, 17–38. On Count D'Orsay see Chancellor 1927, 32–5; Foulkes 2003; Moers 1960, 147–63.

126 Sartre believed that "what recovers the myth of dandyism is not homosexuality, it is exhibitionism" (1947, 178).

127 McNeil and Karaminas 2009b, 7. Bell (1976, 141) believed sartorial sobriety for males was associated with the rise of the middle class in the nineteenth century and the premium it placed upon industry. But scholars differ here. Breward writes that Brummel's "highly sophisticated switch to minimal decoration and fine tailoring" in the early nineteenth century has been erroneously characterized as 'the great masculine renunciation' of fashion – but in fact it "set a new template for modern sartorial beauty" (2011, 11–13). Silverman (1986, 139) puts the great masculine sartorial renunciation towards the middle or end of the *eighteenth* century.

128 Karaminas 2009, 147. Vainshtein (2009, 85) writes of the bay-window where Brummel used to sit and pass judgment on passers-by, "… where the distinction between subject and object of contemplation, the observer and the observed, was instantly erased. There arose a completely unique visual tension, in which two impulses successfully interacted, voyeurism and exhibitionism." Silverman (1986, 141, 145) believes that men become associated with voyeurism in the nineteenth century because they could at that point no longer be spectacle the themselves.

129 Although Mulvey re-formulated her position ([1977] 1989b; [1981] 1989a), admitting that her initial focus "closed off avenues of inquiry that should be followed up" ([1981] 1989a, 30), she still defends her original thesis, claiming that "in-built patterns of pleasure and identification impose masculinity as 'point of view,'" and that even a woman spectator watching a female heroine has a masculine perspective (ibid.). Many theorists have gone on to question or modify Mulvey's male-spectator theory: Cowie 1993; Gledhill 1987; Rich 1990; Rose 2001, 123; Silverman 1992, 125–56; Snow 1989. Chaudhuri (2006, 31–44) gives a good overview not only of Mulvey but also of the challenges to her position.

130 Like much other scholarship, two recent books on gaze in the Roman world, for instance, do not seem to discuss the possibility that men are spectacle or that women look: see Fredrick 2002, 2, 24 and 1995 (although oddly Fredrick 1995, 269–70, n. 13 is a bibliography of critiques of Mulvey's theory within film studies). For other modern authors in the field of Classical studies who apply Mulvey's 1975 theory, see Fredrick 2002, 29. n. 50; Koloski-Ostrow 1997; Salzman-Mitchell 2005, 7–8; Wallace-Hadrill 1996, 114. Bartman (2002, 270) refreshingly acknowledges the female gaze.

131 We still have dandies in the modern world, but we now call them metrosexuals, a word coined by queer critic Mark Simpson in 1994 but which did not make it into common parlance until around a decade later (Simpson 2002). Such men have all the sexual ambiguity and love of self-display as their pre-modern counterparts. "The typical metrosexual is a young man with money to spend, living in or within easy reach of a metropolis… He might be officially gay, straight or bisexual, but this is utterly immaterial because he has clearly taken himself as his own love object and pleasure as his sexual preference" (Simpson 2002). "Metrosexual man might prefer women, he might prefer men, but when all's said and done nothing comes between him and his reflection" (Simpson 1996, 227).

132 See also Paul ex. Fest. 505L. M. Junius Congus (called 'Gracchanus,' because of his friendship with G. Gracchus), was an antiquarian, fl. 130 BCE (*BNP* Junius I 20). The fact that the meaning of the term *trossuli* shifted so dramatically from a proper name to a derogatory name for a young man of fashion is not easily explained but not without parallels: we might similarly examine the twentieth-century evolution of the word "gay," for example.

133 "The *trossuli*, brilliant with nard, commonly purchase a horse for an Attic talent" (*nunc emunt trossuli nardo nitidi vulgo Attico talento ecum; Varro Sesqueulixe 480;* Non. 69L).

134 See also Pliny *Epp.* 2.11.23, in which a *legatus* of a shady lawyer had been paid 10,000 HS illegally "under the heading of cosmetics," *nomine unguentarii,* and is described as a man who is *comptus et pumicatus,* 'adorned and smoothed.'

135 *idem faciam, quod trossuli et iuvenes? Epp.* 76.2. A much later source, St Jerome, writing in the fifth century CE, warns Christian women that playful young dandies (*lascivi et comptuli iuvenes*) will often bribe attendants and nurses for access to the young girls of the family (*Epp.* 128.4).

136 One scholar holds that depilation "like most things, was acceptable in moderation" for Roman men (Kraus 2005, 112 n. 54). And see MacMullen 1982, who believes that there was considerable variety in Roman attitudes to effeminacy and depilation, and that some segments of upper-class society were more accepting of

these practices than others. And see Veyne (1985, 30) who correctly states that "the passive individual's effeminacy was not the result of his perversion, far from it; it was simply one of the results of his lack of virility, and this was still a vice, even where no homosexuality was present."

137 Sinfield 1994, 41. "Artifice and performativity" were eighteenth-century aristocratic ideals, and "some macaronis may have utilized aspects of high fashion in order to effect new class identities" (McNeil 1999, 441–2); perhaps many viewers associated macaronis with nobility in general (McNeil 2000, 391).

138 See McNeil (1999, 432–3 and 2000, 391) on macaroni fashion in the lower classes; Adams (1995, 23) on how dandyism in nineteenth-century England reflected middle-class social aspirations; Cole (2000, 23) on the dandy as an embodiment of leisure-class dress and mannerisms.

139 Williams states this is an epigram of a man "ostentatiously living the life of one wealthy enough to achieve equestrian status, and of patrician descent at that" (2004, 112). Sardonyx ring: Pers. 1.16; Pliny *Nat.* 37.85; Juv. 6.382 (with Courtney 1980, 311); 7.144.

140 "It also suggests the implication of ideas of *mollitia* in a whole range of other discourses we might not immediately associate with sexual behavior" (ibid.). Edwards argues that concepts of *mollitia* "have a much broader frame of reference than the specifically sexual" (1993, 68; see also Sinfield 1994, 109).

141 "Being masculine need not be an exclusive identity. It can involve self-presentations which include behavior conventionally associated with *both* masculinity and femininity" (Cornwall and Lindisfarne 1994, 15).

Conclusion

Why should we care about men's clothing in Roman antiquity? Quite simply, because the Romans did. Clothing resonance and symbolism were deeply embedded in the Roman cultural discourse, and certain types of garments carried much more emblematic weight for them than (I would argue) clothing does in modern Western culture. Male garments signified, even helped determine, juridical rank, seen in the way in which the Romans conceptualized legal category in part as the right to wear certain articles of clothing. Thus, often naming the article of dress (*anulus aureus, latus clavus*) was equivalent to naming the rank or office itself. As well, the fact that there were ritual uses of clothing in display (*sordes*, the *sumere sagum, toga virilis* and the rituals surrounding the *paludamentum*) also denote the strength of clothing's symbolism in Roman antiquity.

Dress was important to the Romans because "in several significant ways, the Roman world was a *visual* culture." (Petersen 2009, 182: Elsner 1998, 11). Cicero wrote:

> It has been sagaciously discerned either by Simonides or someone else, that the most complete pictures are formed in our minds of the things that have been conveyed to them and imprinted on them by the senses (*a sensu tradita atque impressa*), but that the keenest of all our senses is the sense of sight (*accerimum autem ex omnibus nostris sensibus esse sensum videndi*), and that consequently perceptions received by the ears or by reflection can be most easily retained in the mind if they are also conveyed to our minds by the mediation of the eyes (*commendatione oculorum animis traderentur*).
>
> (Cic. *de Orat.* 2.357)

The Romans recognized that in conveying ideas visual imagery could be more effective than the spoken word, in everything from art to the triumph to monuments. "Less vividly is the mind stirred by what finds entrance through the ears than by what is brought before the trusty eyes (*oculis subiecta fidelibus*), and what the spectator can see for himself (*quael ipse sibi tradit spectator*)," wrote Horace (*Ars* 180–2). We can say with some certainty that the visual system and social symbols in ancient Rome were dynamic elements of Roman life, and that dress was a large part of that system. "Much was at stake in articulating one's role in Roman society, marked as it was by external appearances and, by extension, by the legibility of those appearances" (Petersen 2009, 185–6). There was no established *legal* hierarchy of clothing in ancient Rome, but there was a system of sartorial signs which was unofficial, understood, and acknowledged.

Clothing also had the disturbing ability to renegotiate the body in society. The system of social mobility (within particular boundaries) and the availability of signs of status to all financially well-off men encouraged the usurpation of sartorial signs and the resultant confusion of the social body. In the late second century, Tertullian complained of this sartorial inversion:

> You may see freedmen in the attire of knights, slaves loaded with floggings in that of nobility, captives in that of freeborn, bumpkins in that of city dwellers, buffoons in that of men of the forum, citizens in that of soldiers. The corpse-bearer, the pimp, and the trainer of gladiators: they dress like you.
>
> (*Pall.* 4.8.4).[1]

Ideas, ideology, and power were conveyed through appearance, but these examples of sartorial dissonance show that dress was an unreliable identifier of self. Self-presentation was complex; garments could lie or speak the truth. A keen reader of sartorial signs, however, could perhaps identify more subtle ways to distinguish true rank and status (through the smell of garments, the sharpness and number of folds, cleanliness, how worn a garment was) despite the usurpation of symbols of rank by upstarts. Rank and status were slippery concepts, often intertwined in complex ways.

Despite the fact that male clothing in Roman society was supposed to delineate the social rank and status of each of its members clearly ('the boy,' 'the *eques*'; etc.), the challenge for the dress historian is that often an ancient garment and the rank or status it visualized does not stay in its allotted social slot as belonging to one group or another, but instead migrates between and amongst social categories. In other words, clothing could be polyvalent: a green silk tunic, for example, denoting wealth or effeminacy, or the many different types of cloaks which were to be found on the backs of men of all ranks in Rome. Too, the Romans borrowed garments from other societies, those that partook of the luxurious foreign (the *synthesis*) or the rough-and-ready practical (the *cucullus*).[2]

One of the fascinating things about Roman clothing is that there was little historical change in garments over time. The toga, although it underwent alterations in drape, remained essentially the same garment for five hundred years; not until late antiquity did the normal dress of males see a real transformation: to tunic, trousers, and cloak. Even in the Augustan era, a time of enormous political change, we see the emergence of *sinus* and *umbo* but no abandonment of the toga. This is because the progress of 'fashion' does not follow the path of political change in a simple and satisfying way, but rather the path of *mentalité* (which may or may not itself follow or precede the path of political change, or indeed have anything to do with it). I would argue that there was no *essential* alteration in Roman conceptions of masculinity from the time of P. Scipio Africanus (second century BCE, cited by Aulus Gellius cited in Chapter 5) to the late second century CE and beyond. The four centuries of the central period, despite political modifications, underwent no real shift in the *habitus* or sartorial behavior that pertained to the performance of masculinity. (On the other hand, there is the possibility that our patchy literary and artistic evidence in this area does not allow such detailed evaluations.) For other pre-industrial societies, "clothing signifies in an ongoing process that is organized by time, rhythms and spaces and involves different languages and models of discourse" (Paulicelli 2014, 10) but this was not so for the Romans, whose garments had their own stable and self-perpetuating symbolic life.

One of the frustrations of studying ancient clothing lies in the fact that we have few or no archival sources from Roman antiquity of the sort which give clothing histories in other periods their richness of detail: letters, diaries, receipts, or lists of clothing, for example. What I suspect we have from our Latin literary sources is often discourse upon clothing, and discourse tends to be normative, prescriptive, and idealizing. Thus for instance the Roman habit of referring to the broad stripes on a senator's tunic as the *latus clavus* (that is, in the singular), because ideally the upper-class man wore a toga, in which case only one stripe was visible. It is difficult to know for certain however with what end or for what reason a garment receives mention in any particular source: is the author reflecting the world view? Attacking it? Or presenting his world as it *ought* to be?

And what did the Romans think of their clothes? Is it possible to arrive at a social psychology of Roman clothing? Roman togas and cloaks were uncut lengths of cloth, woven to size on the loom, intended to be draped around the body (Hollander 1978, 5). Since few studies have been done on the psychology of ancient dress, "the personal significance which these fabrics had for those who owned and wore them is difficult to ascertain" (Staples 1979, ii). And in the absence of ancient evidence, of course any such study must remain largely conjectural. Still, one hypothesis runs as follows:

> The sensuous pleasure taken by the hairless human body in the sliding touch of fabric is conjured by any image of draped flesh. Since the feel of drapery involves the action of loose cloth working against the body's motion, it is quite different from the feel of tailored clothes, which provide a constant and immobile tactile reference for the whole surface of the body at once. During the antique draped centuries, the sensation of cloth in motion against the skin must have had a steady, underlying importance.
>
> (Hollander 1978, 184)

Conclusion

Although how the Romans felt in their clothing must necessarily remain the subject of speculation, most individuals surely "cautiously negotiated their way through the more or less explicit 'rules' that governed dress" (Ugolini 2009, 208 of nineteenth-century and early twentieth-century fashion). Ultimately, I hope this study has challenged some long-held generalizations about the production and reproduction of normative Roman male identity. As throughout much of Western history, in Roman antiquity there was a "difficult and unstable relationship between manliness and clothing" (Breward 1999, 155).

Notes

1 *libertinos in equestribus, subuerbustos in liberalibus, dediticios in ingenuis, rupices in urbanis, scurras in forensibus, paganos in militaribus: uespillo, leno, lanista tecum uestiuntur.*
2 [Xen.] asserts that the Athenians drew clothing items from many cultures, Greek and barbarian (*Ath Pol.* 2.8).

Bibliography

Abrahams, E. 1908. *Greek Dress.* London: Murray.
Adams, J. E. 1995. *Dandies and Desert Saints: Styles of Victorian Manhood.* Ithaca: Cornell University Press.
Adams, J. N. 1982. *The Latin Sexual Vocabulary.* Baltimore: Johns Hopkins.
Adkin, N. 2000. "Did the Romans Keep Their Underwear On in Bed?" *CW* 93: 619–620.
Aldrete, G. S., S. Bartell, and A. Aldrete. 2013. *Reconstructing Ancient Linen Body Armor: Unraveling the Linothrax Mystery.* Baltimore: The Johns Hopkins University Press.
Alfaro Giner, C. 2001. "Recent Discoveries of Gold Textiles from Augustan Age Gadir (Cádiz)". In *The Roman Textile Industry and its Influence: A Birthday Tribute to John Peter Wild,* edited by P. W. Rogers, L. Bender-Jørgensen, and A. Rast-Eicher, 77–83. Oxford: Oxbow Books.
Alfaro Giner, C.. 2005. "Gold Textiles from a Roman Burial at Munigua (Mulva, Seville)." In *Northern Archaeological Textiles: NESAT VII,* edited by F. Pritchard and J. P. Wild, 1–4. Oxford: Oxbow Books.
Alfaro Giner, C., and L. Karali, eds. 2008. *Purpureae Vestes II: Vestidos, textiles y tintes: estudios sobre la producción de bienes de consumo en la Antigüedad.* University of València.
Alfaro Giner, C., and M. J. Martinez. 2013. "Purpur und Macht an den Küsten des Mittelmeerraumes." In Tellenbach *et al.* 2013, 55–57.
Alfaro Giner, C., J.P. Wild, and B. Costa, eds. 2004. *Purpureae Vestes: Actas del I Symposium Internacional sobre Textiles y Tintes del Mediterráneo en época romana.* University of València.
Alfaro Giner, C., J.-P. Brun, Ph. Borgard, and R. Peirobon Benoit, eds. 2011. *Purpureae Vestes III: Textiles y tintes en la ciudad Antigua.* Archeology de l'Artisanat Antique, 4. Valencia: University of València. Alföldi, A. 1935. "Insignien und Tracht der römischen Kaiser." *RM* 50: 1–58.
Alföldy, G. 1985. *The Social History of Rome.* Translated by D. Braund and F. Pollock. London and New York: Routledge.
Amiotti, G. 1981. "Religione e politica nell'iniziazione romana. L'assunzione della toga virile." *Contributi dell'Istituto di Storia Antica* 7: 131–140.
André, J. 1949. *Étude sur les termes de couleur dans la langue latine,* Paris: Librairie C. Klincksieck.
André, J. ed. 1981. *Anonyme Latin: Traité de Physiognomonie.* Paris: Les Belles Lettres.

Bibliography

Angelicoussis, E. 1984. "The Panel Reliefs of Marcus Aurelius." *Römische Mitteilungen* 91: 141–205.
Austin, R. G., ed. 1966. *M. Tullius Ciceronis Pro M. Caelio Oratio.* 3rd ed. Oxford: Clarendon Press.
Bablitz, L. 2007. *Actors and Audience in the Roman Courtroom.* London and New York: Routledge.
Baines, P. 1989. *Linen: Hand Spinning and Weaving.* London: Batsford.
Balsdon, J. P. V. D. 1979. *Romans and Aliens.* London: Duckworth.
Baratte, F. 2004. "Le vêtement dans l'antiquité tardive: rupture ou continuité?" *Antiquité Tardive* 12: *Tissus et vêtements dans l'antiquité tardive*: 121–136.
Barber, E. J. W. 1991. *Prehistoric Textiles: The Development of Cloth in the Neolithic and Bronze Ages with Special Reference to the Aegean.* Princeton, NJ: Princeton University Press.
Barbey d'Aurevilly, J. [1845] 1977. *Du dandysme et de G. Brummel.* Paris: Editions d'Aujourd'hui.
Barié, P. and W. Schindler. 1999. *M. Valerius Martialis: Epigramme.* Zurich: Artemis & Winkler.
Barney, S. A., W. J. Lewis, J. A. Beach, and O. Berghof, eds. 2010. *The Etymologies of Isidore of Seville.* Cambridge, UK: Cambridge University Press.
Baroin, C., and E. Valette-Cagnac. 2007. "S'habiller et se déshabiller en Grèce et à Rome (III). Quand les Romains s'habillaient à la grecque ou les divers usages du pallium.". *Revue Historique* 643: 517–551.
Bartman, E. 2001. "Hair and the Artifice of Roman Female Adornment." *AJA* 105: 1–25.
Bartman, E. 2002. "Eros's Flame: Images of 'Sexy Boys' in Roman Ideal Sculpture." In *The Ancient Art of Emulation: Studies in Artistic Originality and Tradition from the Present to Classical Antiquity*, edited by E. Gazda, 249–271. Ann Arbor: Univ. of Michigan Press for the American Academy in Rome.
Barton, C. 1993. *The Sorrows of the Ancient Romans: the Gladiator and the Monster.* Princeton, N.J.: Princeton University Press.
Barton, C. 2001. *Roman Honor: The Fire in the Bones.* Berkeley: University of California Press.
Barton, C. 2002. "Being in the Eyes: Shame and Sight in Ancient Rome." In Fredrick 2002, 216–235.
Batcheller, J. 1995. "A Roman Textile Bracelet from Dorchester, Dorset." *Archaeological Textiles Newsletter* 20: 5–8.
Batten, A. 2014. "The Paradoxical Pearl: Signifying the Pearl East and West." In Upson-Saia et al. 2014, 233–250.
Baudelaire, C. [1863] 1971. *Le Peintre de la Vie Moderne.* Paris: Union Générale d'Éditions.
Bell, Q. 1976. *On Human Finery.* 2nd ed. New York: Schocken Books.
Bedini, A., D. Ferro, and I. A. Rapinessi. 2004. "Testimonianze di filati e ornamenti in oro nell'abigliamento di età romana." In Alfaro Giner et al. 2004, 77–88.
Bender-Jørgensen, L. 2004. "Team Work on Roman Textiles: the Mons Claudianus Textile Project." In Alfaro Giner*et al.* 2011, 69–75.
Bender-Jørgensen, L. 2011. "Clavi and Non-Clavi: Definitions of Various Bands on Roman Textiles." In Alfaro Giner et al. 2011, 75–81.
Benazeth, D. 1989. "Un rare exemple de tissu copte à fil d'or." In *Tissage, Corderie, Vannerie: IX Rencontres Internationales d'Archéologie et d'Histoire, Antibes, Octobre 1988.* Juan-les-Pins: éditions APDCA: 219–228.

Benoist, S. 2012. "Le prince nu. Discours en images, discours en mots. Représentation, celebration, dénonciation." In Gherchanoc and Huet 2012, 261–277.
Beran, Z. 1973. "The Realm of Sensory Perception and its Significance in Petronius' *Satyricon*." *Ziva Antiqua* 23: 227–251.
Berger, J. 1972. *Ways of Seeing*. London: Penguin.
Bergmann, B. 2010. *Der Kranz des Kaisers: Genese und Bedeutung einer römishcen Insignie*. Berlin: Walter de Gruyter.
Bergmann, B. and C. Kondoleon, eds. 1999. *The Art of Ancient Spectacle*. New Haven: Yale University Press.
Bessone, L. 1998. "La porpora a Roma." In Longo 1998, 149–202.
Bevis, E. 2014. "Looking Between Loom and Laundry: Vision and Communication in Ostian Fulling Workshops." In Harlow and Nosch 2014, 306–322.
Bieber, M. 1959. "Roman Men in Greek *Himation* (*Romani pallati*): A Contribution to the History of Copying." *PAPhS* 103: 347–417.
Birk, S. 2011. "Man or Woman? Cross-Dressing and Individuality on Third Century Roman Sarcophagi." In *Life, Death and Representation: Some New Work on Roman Sarcophagi*, edited by J. Elsner and J. Huskinson, 229–260. Berlin: Walter de Gruyter.
Birk, S. 2013. *Depicting the Dead: Self-Representation and Commemoration on Roman Sarcophagi with Portraits*. Aarhus: Aarhus University Press.
Birley, R. 2009. *Vindolanda: a Roman Frontier Fort on Hadrian's Wall*. Chalford: Amberley.
Blanck, H. 1997. "Die *instita* der Matronenstola." In *Festschrift T. Lorenz*, edited by T. Rauscher and H.-P. Mansel, 23–26. Vienna: Phoebus.
Blonski, M. 2014. *Se nettoyer à Rome (IIe siècle av. J.-C.–IIe siècle ap. J.-C.): Practiques et enjeux*. Paris: Les Belles Lettres.
Blonski, M. 2008. "Les sordes dans la vie politique romaine: la saleté comme tenue de travail?" In *S'habiller, se déshabiller dans les mondes anciens*, edited by F. Gherchanoc and V. Huet. *Mètis* 6: 41–56.
Blundell, S. 2002. "Clutching at Clothes." In Llewellyn-Jones, ed. 2002b, 143–169.
Bodel, J. 1989a. "Trimalchio and the Candelabrum." *CP* 84: 224–231.
Bodel, J. 1989b. "Trimalchio's coming of age." *Phoenix* 43: 72–74.
Bodel, J. 1999. "Death on Display: Looking at Roman Funerals." In Bergmann and Kondoleon 1999, 259–281.
Bodiou, L., F. Gherchanoc, V. Huet and V. Mehl, eds. 2011. *Parures et artifices: le corps exposé dans l'Antiquité*. Paris: L'Harmattan.
Bogensperger, I. 2014. "The Multiple Functions and Lives of a Textile: the Reuse of a Garment." In Harlow and Nosch 2014, 335–344.
Bonanno, A. 1988. "Imperial and Private Portraiture: a Case of Non-Dependence." In *Ritratto Ufficiale e Ritratto Privato. Atti della II Conferenza Internazionale sul Ritratto Romano*, edited by N. Binacasa and G. Rizza, 157–164. Rome: Consiglio Nazionale delle Ricerche.
Bonfante, L. 2003. *Etruscan Dress*, 2nd ed., Baltimore: Johns Hopkins University Press.
Bonfante-Warren, L. 1964. "A Latin Triumph on a Praeneste Cista." *AJA* 68. 1: 35–42.
Bonfante-Warren, L. 1970. "Roman Triumphs and Etruscan Kings: the Changing Face of the Triumph." *JRS* 60: 49–66.
Bonfante-Warren, L. 1973. "Roman Costumes: a Glossary and Some Etruscan Derivations." *ANRW* 1. 4: 584–614.

Boon, G. C. 1991. "Tonsor Humanus: Razor and Toilet-Knife in Antiquity." *Britannia* 22: 21–32.
Borgard, P. and M.-P. Puybaret. 2004. "Le travail de la laine au début de l'Empire: l'apport du modèle pompeien. Quels artisans? Quel équipements? Quelles techniques?" In Alfaro Giner et al. 2004, 47–59.
Boscagli, M. 1996. *Eye on the Flesh: Fashions of Masculinity in the Early Twentieth Century.* Boulder, CL: Westview Press.
Boswell, J. 1981. *Christianity, Social Tolerance, and Homosexuality: Gay People in Western Europe from the Beginning of the Christian Era to the Fourteenth Century.* Chicago, Il.: University of Chicago Press.
Bourdieu, P. 1984. *Distinction: A Social Critique of the Judgement of Taste.* Translated by R. Nice. Cambridge, Mass.: Harvard University Press.
Bourdieu, P. 1991. "The Economy of Linguistic Exchanges." In *Language and Symbolic Power*, edited by J. B. Thompson. Translated by G. Raymond and M. Adamson, 37–89. Cambridge, Mass: Harvard University Press.
Bowman, A. K., and J. D. Thomas. 1983. *The Vindolanda Writing Tablets: Tabulae Vindolandenses*, vol. I. London: Society for the Promotion of Roman Studies.
Bradley, K. R. 1994. *Slavery and Society at Rome.* Cambridge, UK: Cambridge University Press.
Bradley, M. 2002. "It All Comes Out in the Wash: Looking Harder at the Roman Fullonica." *JRA* 15: 20–44.
Bradley, M. 2009. *Colour and Meaning in Ancient Rome.* Cambridge, UK: Cambridge University Press.
Bramble, J. C. 1974. *Persius and the Programmatic Satire: A Study in Form and Imagery.* Cambridge, UK: Cambridge University Press.
Brandis, C. 1897. "Ein Schreiben des Triumvirn Marcus Antonius an den Landtag Asiens." *Hermes* 32: 509–522.
Bray, A. 1982. *Homosexuality in Renaissance England.* London: Gay Men's Press.
Bremmer J. 1992. "Walking, Standing and Sitting in Ancient Greek Culture." In Bremmer and Roodenburg, 15–35.
Bremmer, J. and H. Roodenburg, eds. 1992. *A Cultural History of Gesture.* Ithaca, New York: Cornell University Press.
Brennan, T. C. 2008. "Tertullian's *De Pallio* and Roman Dress in North Africa." In *Roman Dress and the Fabrics of Roman Culture*, edited by J. Edmondson and A. Keith, 257–270. Toronto: University of Toronto Press.
Breward, C. 1999. *The Hidden Consumer: Masculinities, Fashion, and City Life 1860–1914.* Manchester, UK: Manchester University Press.
Breward, C. 2002. "Style and Subversion: Postwar Poses and the Neo-Edwardian Suit in Mid Twentieth-century Britain." *Gender and History* 14. 3: 560–583.
Breward, C. 2004. *Fashioning London: Clothing and the Modern Metropolis.* Oxford and New York: Berg.
Breward, C. 2011. Introduction. In Ross (ed.) 2011, 9–13.
Brewster, E. 1918. "The Synthesis of the Romans." *TAPA* 49: 131–143.
Bridgeman, J. 1987. "Purple Dye in Late Antiquity and Byzantium." In *The Royal Purple and the Biblical Blue: Argaman and Tekhelet*, edited by E. Spanier, 159–165. Jerusalem: Keter.
Brown, C. 1983. "From Rags to Riches: Anacreon's Artemon." *Phoenix* 37. 1: 1–15.
Brunt, P. A. 1969. "The Equites in the Late Republic." In *The Crisis of the Roman Republic*, edited by R. Seager, 83–115. Cambridge: Cambridge University Press.

Brunt, P. A. 1983. "Princeps and equites." *JRS* 73: 42–75.
Buechner, K. 1982. *Fragmenta Poetarum Latinorum Epicorum et Lyricorum*. Leipzig: Teubner.
Bulard, M. 1926. *La religion domestique dans la colonie italienne de Délos d'après les peintures murales et les autels historiés*. Paris: E. de Boccard.
Butler, J. 1990. *Gender Trouble: Feminism and the Subversion of Identity*. New York: Routledge.
Butler, J. 1993. "Imitation and Gender Insubordination." In *The Lesbian and Gay Studies Reader*, edited by H. Abelove, M. A. Barale, and D. M. Halperin, 307–320. London and New York: Routledge.
Butrica, J. L. 2002. "Clodius the Pulcher in Catullus and Cicero." *CP*: 507–516.
Butrica, J. L. 2005. "Some Myths and Anomalies in the Study of Roman Sexuality." *Journal of Homosexuality* 49: 209–269.
Callu, J-P. 2004. "L'habit et l'ordre social: le témoignage de l'*Histoire Auguste*." In *Antiquité Tardive* 12: *Tissus et vêtements dans l'antiquité tardive*: 187–194.
Caputo, G. 1959. *Il Teatro di Sabratha e l'Architettura Teatrale Africana*. Rome: L'Erma di Bretschneider.
Cardon, D., and M. Feugère, eds. 2000. *Archéologie des textiles, des origines au Ve siècle. Actes du colloque international de Lattes, oct. 1999*. Monographies Instrumentum,14. Montagnac:.Editions Monique Mergoil.
Cardon, D., W. Nowik, H. Granger-Taylor, N. Marcinowska, K. Kusyk, and M. Trojanowicz 2011. "Who Could Wear True Purple in Roman Egypt? Technical and Social Considerations on Some New Identifications of Purple from Marine Mollusks in Archaeological Textiles." In Alfaro Giner et al. 2011, 197–214.
Carlyle, T. [1831]. 2004. "The Dandiacal Body." In *The Rise of Fashion: A Reader*, edited by D. L. Purdy, 165–173. Minnestoa: University of Minnesota Press.
Carrié, J.-M. 2004. "Vitalité de l'industrie textile à la fin de l'Antiquité: considerations économiques et technologiques." In *Antiquité Tardive* 12: *Tissus et vêtements dans l'antiquité tardive*: 13–44.
Carrigan, T., B. Connell, and J. Lee. 1985. "Towards a New Sociology of Masculinity." *Theory and Society* 14. 5: 551–603.
Carter, M. 2009. "Thomas Carlyle and *Sartor Resartus*." In McNeil and Karaminas 2009a: 72–83.
Casinos Mora, F. J. 2013a. "Kleidung und Gesetz in Rom." In Tellenbach et al. 2013: 53–54.
Casinos Mora, F. J. 2013b. "Repression of Luxury in Rome: the Specific Case of Garments. " In *Luxury and Dress: Political Power and Appearance in the Roman Empire and its Provinces*, edited by C. Alfaro Giner, J. Ortiz García, and M. J. Martínez García, 99–114. València: Universitat de València.
Casson, L. 1983. "Greek and Roman Clothing: Some Technical Terms." *Glotta* 61. 4: 193–207.
Cèbe, J. P. 1987. *Varron: Satires Ménippées*, vol. 8. Collection de L'École française de Rome9. Rome: L'École française de Rome.
Chancellor, E. B. 1927. *Life in Regency and Early Victorian Times: An Account of the Days of Brummell and D'Orsay 1800–1850*. London: B. T. Batsford.
Chastagnol, A. 1975. "*Latus clavus et adlectio*: l'accès des hommes nouveaux au sénat romain sous le HautEmpire." *RHDFE* 53: 375–394.
Chastagnol, A. 1976. "Le laticlave de Vespasien." *Historia* 25: 253–256.
Chaudhuri, S. 2006. *Feminist Film Theorists*. London and New York: Routledge.

Chauncey, G. 1994. *Gay New York: Gender, Urban Culture, and the Makings of the Gay Male World, 1890–1940*. New York: Basic Books.
Chausson, F., and H. Inglebert, eds. 2003. *Costume et société dans l'Antiquité et le haut Moyen Âge*, Paris: Picard.
Chioffi, L. 2004. "Attalica e alter auratae vestes a Roma." In Alfaro Giner et al. 2004: 89–95.
Christ, A. 1997. "The Masculine Ideal of 'The Race that Wears the Toga'." *Art Journal* 56. 2: 24–30.
Citroni, M. 1975. *M. Valerii Martialis Epigrammaton Liber Primus*. Florence: La Nuova Italia.
Clark, A. ed. [1907]. 1956. *Orationum Ciceronis Quinque Enarratio*. Oxford: Oxford University Press.
Clark, A. ed. 1909. *Oratio pro C. Rabirio Postumo*. Oxford: Clarendon Press.
Clark, A. 1918. *The Descent of Manuscripts*. Oxford: Clarendon Press.
Clark, G. 1993. *Women in Late Antiquity: Pagan and Christian Life-Styles*. Oxford and New York: Oxford University Press.
Clark, P. 1998. "Women, Slaves and the Hierarchies of Domestic Violence: the Family of St. Augustine." In Joshel and Murnaghan 1998, 109–129.
Clarke, J. 1998. *Looking at Lovemaking: Constructions of Sexuality in Roman Art 100 B.C.–A.D. 250*, Berkeley, CA: University of California Press.
Clarke, J. 2005. "Representations of the *Cinaedus* in Roman Art: Evidence of a 'Gay' Subculture?" *Journal of Homosexuality* 49: 271–298.
Clarke, J. R. 2001. "Colours in Conflict: Catullus' Use of Colour Imagery in C. 63." *CQ* 51. 1: 163–177.
Clarke, J. R. 2003. *Imagery of Colour and Shining in Catullus, Propertius, and Horace*. Lang Classical Studies13. New York: Peter Lang Publishing.
Cleland, L., M. Harlow, and L. Llewellyn-Jones, eds. 2005. *The Clothed Body in the Ancient World*. Oxford: Oxbow Books.
Cleland, L., G. Davies, and L. Llewellyn-Jones. 2007. *Greek and Roman Dress from A–Z*. London and New York: Routledge. Cohen, B. 2001. "Ethnic Identity in Democratic Athens and the Visual Vocabulary of Male Costume." In *Ancient Perceptions of Greek Ethnicity*, edited by Irad Malkin, 235–274. Washington, DC: Center for Hellenic Studies.
Cole, S. 2000. *Don We Now Our Gay Apparel: Gay Men's Dress in the Twentieth Century*. Oxford and New York: Berg.
Colin, J. 1955. "Luxe oriental et parfums masculins dans la Rome Alexandrine (d'après Cicéron et Lucrèce)." *Revue Belge de Philologie et d'Histoire* 33: 5–19.
Connell, R. W. 1995. *Masculinities*. Cambridge, UK: Cambridge University Press.
Connolly, J. 1998. "Mastering Corruption: Constructions of Identity in Roman Oratory." In Joshel and Murnaghan 1998, 130–151.
Constantinidis, D., and L. Karali. 2011. "A Proposed Survey of East Mediterranean Murex Heaps from the Bronze Age to Roman Times: a GIS Analysis of Possible Trade Networks." In Alfaro Giner et al. 2011, 151–155.
Corbeill, A. 1996. *Controlling Laughter: Political Humor in the Late Roman Republic*. Princeton, NJ: Princeton University Press.
Corbeill, A. 2002. "Political Movement: Walking and Ideology in Republican Rome." In *The Roman Gaze: Vision, Power, and the Body*, edited by D. Fredrick, 182–215. Baltimore: Johns Hopkins University Press.

Cornwall, A., and N. Lindisfarne. 1994. "Dislocating Masculinity: Gender, Power, and Anthropology." In *Dislocating Masculinity: Comparative Ethnographies*, edited by A. Cornwall and N. Lindisfarne, 11–47. London and New York: Routledge.
Courtney, E. 1980. *A Commentary on the Satires of Juvenal*, London: Athlone Press.
Cowie, E. 1993. "From *Fantasia*." In *Contemporary Film Theory*, edited by A. Easthope, 147–161. New York: Longman.
Croom, A.. 2002. *Roman Clothing and Fashion*. Stroud, Gloucestershire and Charleston, SC: Tempus.
Croom, A. 2011. *Running the Roman Home*. Stroud, Gloucestershire: The History Press.
Cumont, F. 1982. *L'Egypte des Astrologues*. Brussels: Fondation égyptologique Reine Elisabeth.
Currie, H. M. 1989. "Petronius and Ovid." In *Studies in Latin Literature and Roman History V*, Collection Latomus 206, edited by C. Deroux, 317–335. Brussels.
D'Ambra, E. 2000. "Nudity and Adornment in Female Portrait Sculpture of the Second century A.D." In *I Claudia II: Women in Roman Art and Society*, edited by D. E. E. Kleiner and S. B. Matheson, 101–114. Austin, TX: University of Texas Press.
D'Ambra, E. and G. P. R. Métraux, eds. 2006. *The Art of Citizens, Soldiers and Freedmen in the Roman World*. BAR International Series 1526. Oxford.
D'Arms, J. 1990. "The Roman *Convivium* and the Idea of Equality." In *Sympotica: a Symposium on the Symposion*, edited by O. Murray, 308–320. Oxford: Oxford University Press.
Dalby, A. 2000. *Empire of Pleasures: Luxury and Indulgence in the Roman World*. London and New York: Routledge.
Dalla, D. 1987*Ubi Venus mutatur: Omosessualita e diritto nel mondo Romano*. Milan: A. Giuffrè.
Dana, F. M. 1919. The Ritual Significance of Yellow Among the Romans. Ph.D diss. Philadelphia, PA:, University of Pennsylvania.
Daniel-Hughes, C. 2011. *The Salvation of the Flesh in Tertullian of Carthage: Dressing for the Resurrection*. New York: Palgrave MacMillan.
Dauster, M. 2003. "Roman Republican Sumptuary Legislation." *Studies in Latin Literature and Roman History* 11:65–93.
Davidson, J. 1997. *Courtesans and Fishcakes: The Consuming Passions of Classical Athens*. New York: Harper Collins.
Davidson, J. 2007. *The Greeks and Greek Love*:London: Weidenfeld & Nicolson.
Davies, G. 2005. "What Made the Roman Toga *Virilis*?" In Cleland *et al.* 2005, 121–130.
Day, F. E. 1956. "Aristotle: Ta bombukia." *Studi Orientalistici in onore di Giorgio Levi della Vida*, vol. I. Rome: Instituto per l'oriente.
De Ruyt, C. 2001. "Les foulons, artisans des textiles et blanchisseurs." In *Ostia: Port et Porte de la Rome Antique*, edited by J.-P. Descoeudres, 186–191. Genève: Musée Rath.
Delbrueck, R. 1932. *Antike Porphyrwerke*. Leipzig: Walter de Gruyter.
Delbourg-Delphis, M. 1985. *Masculin singulier*. Paris: Hachette.
Della Corte, M. 1965. *Casa ed Abitanti di Pompei*. Rome: Faustino Fiorentino.
Dellamora, R. 1996. "Homosexual Scandal and Compulsory Heterosexuality in the 1890s." In *Reading Fin de Siècle Fictions*, edited by L. Pykett, 80–102. London and New York: Longman.

Delmaire, R. 2004. "Le vêtement dans les sources juridiques du bas-empire." In *Antiquité Tardive* 12: *Tissus et vêtements dans l'antiquité tardive*: 195–202.
Dench, E. 1998. "Austerity, Excess, Success, and Failure in Hellenistic and Early Imperial Italy." In *Parchments of Gender: Deciphering the Bodies of Antiquity*, edited by M. Wyke, 121–146. Oxford: Oxford University Press.
Deniaux, E. 2003. "La *toga candida* et les élections à Rome sous la République." In Chausson and Inglebert 2003, 49–56.
Deonna, W. and M. Renard. 1961. *Croyance et superstitions de table dans la Rome antique.* Latomus46.
Déry, C. 1993. "The Lex Sumptuaria." *Liverpool Classical Monthly* 18: 156–157.
Dewar, M. J. 2008. "Spinning the Trabea: Consular Robes and Propaganda in the Panegyrics of Claudian." In Edmondson and Keith 2008, 217–237.
Dionisotti, A.C. 1982. "From Ausonius' Schooldays? A School-Book and its Relatives." *JRS* 72: 83–125.
Dixon, J. 2014. "Dressing the Adulteress." In Harlow and Nosch 2014, 298–305.
Dixon, S. ed. 2001a. *Childhood, Class and Kin in the Roman World.* London and New York: Routledge.
Dixon, S. 2001b. "Familia Veturia: Towards a Lower-Class Economic Prosopography." In Dixon 2000a, 115–127.
Dixon, S. 2001c. *Reading Roman Women: Sources, Genre, and Real Life.* London: Duckworth.
Doerfler, M. 2014. "Coming Apart at the Seams: Cross-Dressing, Masculinity, and the Social Body in Late Antiquity." In Upson-Saia et al. 2014, 37–51.
Dohrn, T. 1968. *Der Arringatore.* Berlin: Gebr. Mann.
Dolansky, F. 2008. "Togam Virilem Sumere: Coming of Age in the Roman World." In Edmondson and Keith 2008, 47–70.
Dover, K. 1978. *Greek Homosexuality.* Cambridge, Mass.: Harvard University Press.
Driel-Murray, C.van 1987. "Roman Footwear: a Mirror of Fashion and Society." *Recent Research in Archaeological Footwear*, The Association of Archaeological Illustrators and Surveyors, Technical Paper8: 32–42.
Driel-Murray, C.van 2001. "Vindolanda and the Dating of Roman Footwear." *Britannia* 32: 185–197.
Duberman, M., M. Vicinus, and G.Chauncey, Jr., eds. 1989. *Hidden From History: Reclaiming the Gay and Lesbian Past.* London: Penguin.
Dubourdieu, A. 1986. "Cinctus Gabinus." *Latomus* 45: 3–20.
Dyck, A. R. 2001. "Dressing to Kill: Attire as a Proof and Means of Characterization in Cicero's Speeches." *Arethusa* 34: 119–130.
Dynes, W.R., and S. Donaldson, eds. 1992. *Homosexuality in the Ancient World.* New York and London: Garland Publishing.
Edgeworth, R. 1978. "What color is 'ferrugineus?'" *Glotta* 56: 297–305.
Edgeworth, R. 1979. "Does 'Purpureus' Mean 'Bright?'" *Glotta* 57: 281–291.
Edmonds, J. 2000. *Tyrian or Imperial Purple Dye.* Historic Dye Series no. 7. Little Chalfont, Buckinghamshire.
Edmondson, J. 2008. "Public Dress and Social Control in Late Republican and Early Imperial Rome." In Edmondson and Keith 2008, 21–46.
Edmondson, J., and A. Keith, eds. 2008. *Roman Dress and the Fabrics of Roman Culture.* Toronto: University of Toronto Press.
Edwards, C. 1993. *The Politics of Immorality in Ancient Rome.* Cambridge, UK: Cambridge University Press.

Edwards, C. 1997. "Unspeakable Professions: Public Performance and Prostitution in Ancient Rome." In Hallett and Skinner 1997, 66–98.
Ehrman, R. K. 1993. "The 'Cornicula' ascribed to Plautus." *Rheinisches Museum für Philologie* 136: 268–281.
Ellis, R. 1889. *A Commentary on Catullus*. 2nd ed. Oxford: Oxford University Press.
Elsner, J. 1995. *Art and the Roman Viewer: The Transformation of Art from the Pagan World to Christianity*. Cambridge, UK: Cambridge University Press.
Elsner, J. 1998. *Imperial Rome and Christian Triumph: The Art of the Roman Empire A.D. 100–450*. Oxford: Oxford University Press.
Emberley, J. V. 1997. *The Cultural Politics of Fur*. Montreal: McGill-Queens University Press.
Epstein, A. G. 1994. "Gods in the Hood." *Proceedings of the Harvard Celtic Colloquium* 14: 90–105.
Fagan, G. G. 1999. *Bathing in Public in the Roman World*. Ann Arbor: University of Michigan Press.
Fantham, E. 2008. "Covering the Head at Rome: Ritual and Gender." In Edmondson and Keith 2008, 158–171.
Faure, P. 2011. "Parures, corps et identites militaires dans l'armée romaine imperial." In Bodiou et al. 2011, 141–154.
Fittschen, K. 1970. "Der Arringatore: ein römischer Bürger?" *Römische Mitteilungen* 77: 177–184.
Fless, F. 1995. *Opferdiener und Kultmusiker auf stadtrömischen historischen Reliefs: Untersuchungen zur Ikonographie, Funktion, und Benennung*. Mainz: Bücher.
Flohr, M. 2003. "Fullones and Roman Society: a Reconsideration." *JRA* 6: 447–450.
Flohr, M. 2013a. "The Textile Economy of Pompeii." *JRA* 26: 53–87.
Flohr, M. 2013b. *The World of the Fullo: Work, Economy, and Society in Roman Italy*. Oxford: Oxford University Press.
Fögen, T. 2009. "Sermo Corporis: Ancient Reflections on Gestus, Vultus, and Vox." In Fögen and Lee 2009, 15–43.
Fögen, T. and M. Lee, eds. 2009. *Bodies and Boundaries in Graeco-Roman Antiquity*. Berlin: Walter de Gruyter.
Forbes, R. J. 1964. *Studies in Ancient Technology*, vol. IV. 2nd ed. Leiden: Brill.
Forbes, W. T. M. 1930. "The Silkworm of Aristotle." *CP* 25: 22–26.
Foucault, M. 1985. *The History of Sexuality*, vol. 2: *The Uses of Pleasure*, translated by R. Hurley. New York: Pantheon Books.
Foulkes, N. 2003. *Scandalous Society: Passion and Celebrity in the Nineteenth Century*. London: Abacus.
Fox, M. 1998. "The constrained man." In Foxhall and Salmon 1998b: 6–22.
Foxhall, L. 1998. "Introduction." In Foxhall and Salmon 1998a, 1–9.
Foxhall, L., and J. Salmon, eds. 1998a. *When Men Were Men: Masculinity, Power and Identity in Roman Antiquity*. Routledge: London and New York.
Foxhall, L., and J. Salmon. eds. 1998b. *Thinking Men: Masculinity and its Self-Representation in the Classical Tradition*. Routledge: London and New York.
Frank, T. 1940. *Economic Survey of Ancient Rome* vol. V: *Rome and Italy of the Empire*. Baltimore: the Johns Hopkins University Press.
Fraschetti, A. 1996. "Jeunesses romaines." In *Histoire des jeunes en Occident de l'antiquité à l'époque moderne*, edited by G. Levi and J. C. Schmitt, 63–100. Seuil: Paris.
Fredrick, D. 1995. "Beyond the Atrium to Ariadne: Erotic Painting and Visual Pleasure in the Roman House." *Classical Antiquity* 14. 2: 266–288.

Fredrick, D. ed. 2002. *The Roman Gaze: Vision, Power, and the Body*. Baltimore: Johns Hopkins University Press.
Freyburger-Galland, M.-L. 1993. "Le rôle politique des vêtements dans l'*Histoire romaine* de Dion Cassius." *Latomus* 52: 117–128.
Fuentes, N. 1987. "The Roman Military Tunic." In *Roman Military Equipment:the Accoutrements of War. Proceedings of the Third Roman Military Equipment Research Seminar*, edited by M. Dawson, BAR International Series, 336, 41–75..Oxford
Gabelmann, H. 1977. "Der Ritterliche Trabea." *JDAI* 92: 322–374.
Gabelmann, H. 1985. "Römische Kinder in Toga Praetexta." *JDAI* 100: 517–541.
Gage, J. 1993. *Colour and Culture: Practice and Meaning from Antiquity to Abstraction*. London: Thames & Hudson.
Galinier, M. 2012. "Domi forisque: les vêtements romains de la Vertu." In Gherchanoc and Huet 2012, 189–208. Gallia, A. B. 2014. "The Vestal Habit." *CP* 109: 222–240.
Gardner, J. 1998. "Sexing a Man: Imperfect Men in Roman Law." In Foxhall and Salmon 1998a, 136–152.
Garelick, R. K. 1998. *Rising Star: Dandyism, Gender, and Performance in the Fin de Siècle*. Princeton, NJ: Princeton University Press.
Geddes, A. G. 1987. "Rags and Riches: the Costume of Athenian Men in the Fifth Century." *CQ* 37. 2: 307–331.
Geertz, C. 1973. *The Interpretation of Cultures: Selected Essays*. New York: Basic Books.
Geffcken, K. A. 1973. *Comedy in the Pro Caelio*. Mnemosyne suppl. 30. Leiden: Brill.
Gelder, K. 2007. *Subcultures: Cultural Histories and Social Practices*. London and New York: Routledge.
George, M. 2001. "A Roman Funerary Monument with a Mother and Daughter." In Dixon 2001a, 178–189.
George, M. 2002. "Slave Disguise in Ancient Rome." *Slavery & Abolition* 23: 41–54.
George, M. 2003. "Images of Black Slaves in the Roman Empire." *Syllecta Classica* 14: 161–185.
George, M. 2006. "Social Identity and the Dignity of Work in Freedmen's Reliefs." In D'Ambra and Métraux 2006, 19–29.
George, M. 2008. "The 'Dark Side' of the Toga." In Edmondson and Keith 2008, 94–112.
Gercke, W. B. 1968. Untersuchungen zum römischen Kinderportrait. Diss. Hamburg.
Gherchanoc, F. ed. 2015. *L'histoire du corps dans l'Antiquité; bilan historiographique*. Dialogues d'histoire ancienne, suppl. 14. Besançon: Presses Universitaires de Franche Comté. Gherchanoc, F. and V. Huet . 2007. "S'habiller et se déshabiller en Grèce et à Rome (I): pratiques politiques et culturelles du vêtements: essai historiographique." *Revue Historique*, no. 641: 3–30.
Gherchanoc, F. and V. Huet. eds. 2008a. *S'habiller, se déshabiller dans les mondes anciens*. Mètis6. Paris: Editions de L'EHESS.
Gherchanoc, F. and V. Huet, eds. 2012. *Vêtements antiques: s'habiller, se déshabiller dans mondes anciens*. Paris: Editions Errance.
Giacometti, G. 1998. "Il colore della porpora e la meccanica quantistica." In Longo 1998a, 29–40.
Gibson, R. ed. 2003. *Ovid Ars Amatoria Book 3*, Cambridge, UK: Cambridge University Press.
Gilmore, D. 1990. *Manhood in the Making: Cultural Concepts of Masculinity*. New Haven and London: Yale University Press.
Gillis, C. and M.-L. B. Nosch, eds. 2007. *Ancient Textiles: Production, Craft, Society*. Oxford: Oxbow Books.

Gleason, M. W. 1990. "The Semiotics of Gender: Physiognomy and Self-Fashioning in the Second Century C.E." In *Before Sexuality: the Construction of Erotic Experience in the Ancient Greek World*, edited by David M. Halperin, J. Winkler, and F. Zeitlin, 389–416. Princeton, NJ: Princeton University Press.
Gleason, M. W. 1995. *Making Men: Sophists and Self-Presentation in Ancient Rome.* Princeton, NJ: Princeton University Press. Gleason, M. 1999. "Elite Male Identity in the Roman Empire." In *Life, Death, and Entertainment in the Roman Empire*, edited by D. S. Potter and D. Mattingly, 67–84. Ann Arbor: University of Michigan Press.
Gleason, M. W. 1999. "Elite Male Identity in the Roman Empire. In *Life, Death, and Entertainment in the Roman Empire*, edited by D. S. Potter and D. Mattingly, 67–84. Ann Arbor: University of Michigan Press.
Gleba, M. 2000. "Textile Production at Poggio Civitate (Murlo) in the 7th C. BC." In Cardon and Feugère 2000, 75–80.
Gleba, M. 2004. "Linen Production in Pre-Roman and Roman Italy." In Alfaro Giner et al. 2004, 29–38.
Gleba, M. 2008a. "Auratae Vestes: Gold Textiles in the Ancient Mediterranean." In Alfaro Giner and Karalli 2008, 61–77.
Gleba, M . 2008b. *Textile Production in Pre-Roman Italy.* Ancient Textile Series4. Oxford: Oxbow Books. Gledhill, C. ed. 1987. *Home is Where the Heart Is: Studies in Melodrama and Women's Film.* London: BFI.
Goethert, F. W. 1939. "Studien zur Kopienforschung, I: Die stilund trachtgeschichtliche Entwicklung der Togastatue den beiden ersten Jahrhunderten der römischen Kaiserzeit." *RM* 54: 176–219.
Goette, H. R. 1986. "Die Bulla." *BJb* 186: 133–164.
Goette, H. R. 1988. "*Mulleus – Embas – Calceus.*" *JdL* no. 103: 401–464.
Goette, H. R. 1989. "Beobachtungen zu römischen Kinderportraits." *AA* 453–471.
Goette, H. R. 1990. *Studien zu römischen Togadarstellungen.* Mainz: von Zabern.
Goette, H. R. 2013. "Die römische 'Staatstracht' -toga, *tunica* und *calcei.*" In Tellenbach et al. 2013, 39–52. Goffman, E. 1959. *The Presentation of Self in Everyday Life.* Garden City, N.Y.: Doubleday.
Gold, B. 1998. "Vested Interests in Plautus' *Casina*: Cross-Dressing in Roman Comedy." *Helios* 25: 17–29.
Goldman, N. 1994a. "Reconstructing Roman Clothing." In Sebesta and Bonfante 1994, 213–237.
Goldman, N. 1994b. "Roman Footwear." In Sebesta and Bonfante 1994, 101–129.
Goldman, R. B. 2013. *Color-Terms in Social and Cultural Context in Ancient Rome.* New Jersey: Gorgias.
Gomez, J. A. M. 2013. "Zur Kleidung römischer Priester im öffentlichen Kult." In Tellenbach et al. 2013, 64–65.
González, J. 1984. "Tabula siarensis, fortunales siarenses et municipia civium Romanorum." *ZPE* 55: 55–100
Goody, J. 1982. *Cooking, Cuisine, and Class: A Study in Comparative Sociology.* Cambridge, UK: Cambridge University Press.
Goold, G. P. 1965. "Amatoria Critica." *Harvard Studies in CP* 69: 1–107.
Gowers, E. 1993. *The Loaded Table: Representations of Food in Roman Literature.* Oxford: Oxford University Press.
Graf, F. 1992. "Gestures and Conventions: the Gestures of Roman Actors and Orators." In Bremmer and Roodenburg 1992, 36–58.
Grainger, R. 1998. *The Social Symbolism of Grief and Mourning.* London: Jessica Kingsley.

Granger-Taylor, H. 1982. "Weaving Clothes to Shape in the Ancient World: the Tunic and Toga of the Arringatore." *Textile History* 13. 1: 3–25.
Granger-Taylor, H. 1987. "The Emperor's Clothes: the Fold-Lines." *Bulletin of the Cleveland Museum of Art* 74. 3: 114–123.
Granger-Taylor, H. 2000. "The Textiles from Khirbet Qazone (Jordan)." In Cardon and Feugère 2000, 149–162.
Granger-Taylor, H. 2006. "Textiles from Khirbet Qazone and the Cave of Letters, Two Burial Sites near the Dead Sea: Similarities and Differences in Find Spots and Textile Types." *Riggisberger Berichte* 13: 113–133.
Granger-Taylor, H. 2007. "'Weaving Clothes to Shape in the Ancient World' 25 Years On: Corrections and Further Details with Particular Reference to the Cloaks from Lahun." *Archaeological Textiles Newsletter* 45: 26–35.
Granger-Taylor, H. 2008. "A Fragmentary Roman Cloak Probably of the 1st C CE and Off-Cuts from Other Semi-Circular Cloaks." *Archaeological Textiles Newsletter* 46: 6–16.
Grant, M. 2004. "Colourful Characters: a Note on the Use of Colour in Petronius." *Hermes* 132: 244–247.
Graver, M. 1998. "The Manhandling of Maecenas: Senecan Abstractions of Masculinity." *AJPh* 119: 607–632.
Greene, E. M.forthcoming. "Metal Fittings on the Vindolanda Shoes: Podiatry and Footwear in the Roman World." In *Shoes, Slippers and Sandals: Feet and Footwear in Classical Antiquity*, edited by S. Pickup and S. Waite. Farnham, UK: Ashgate.
Gregori, G. L. 1994. "Purpurarii." In *Epigrafia della produzione e della distribuzione*. Actes de la VIIe rencontre franco–italienne sur l'épigraphie du monde romaine (Colloque de Rome, 1992), 739–743. Rome: Università di Roma-La Sapienza.
Griffin, J. 1985. *Latin Poets and Roman Life*. London: Duckworth.
Grondona, M. 1980. *La religione e la superstizione nella Cena Trimalchionis di Petronio*. Brussels.
Gunderson, E. 1998. "Discovering the Body in Roman Oratory." In Wyke 1998, 169–190.
Gunderson, E. 2000. *Staging Masculinity: the Rhetoric of Performance in the Roman World*. Ann Arbor: University of Michigan Press.
Gunderson, E. 2003. *Declamation, Paternity and Roman Identity: Authority and the Rhetorical Self*. Cambridge: Cambridge University Press.
Guralnick, E. 2008. "Fabric Patterns as Symbols of Status in the Near East and Early Greece." In *Reading a Dynamic Canvas: Adornment in the Ancient Mediterranean World*, edited by C. Colburn and M. Heyn, 84–114. Newcastle, UK: Cambridge Scholars Publishing.
Hafner, G. 1969. "Etruskische togati." *Antike Plastik* 9: 23–45.
Hall, J. 2014. *Cicero's Use of Judicial Theater*. Ann Arbor: Univ. of Michigan Press.
Hallett, C. 2005. *The Roman Nude: Heroic Portrait Statuary 200 B.C.–A.D. 300*. Oxford: Oxford University Press.
Hallett, J., and M. Skinner, eds. 1997. *Roman Sexualities*. Princeton: Princeton University Press.
Halleux, R. 1981: *Les alchimistes grecs*. Paris: Belles Lettres
Halperin, D. 1990. *One Hundred Years of Homosexuality and Other Essays on Greek Love*. London and New York: Routledge.
Harlow, M. 2004. "Clothes Maketh the Man: Power Dressing and Elite Masculinity in the Later Roman World." In *Gender in the Early Medieval World: East and West,*

300–900, edited by L. Brubaker and J. M. H. Smith, 44–69. Cambridge: Cambridge University Press.
Harlow, M. 2005. "Dress in the Historia Augusta: the Role of Dress in Historical Narrative." In Cleland *et al.* 2005, 143–153.
Harlow, M. 2012. "Dressing to Please Themselves: Clothing Choices for Roman Women." In *Dress and Identity*, edited by M. Harlow, 37–46. Archeopress: Oxford.
Harlow, M. 2013. "Dressed Women on the Streets of the Ancient City: What to Wear?" In *Women and the Roman City in the Latin West*, edited by E. Hemelrijk and G. Woolf, 225–242. Leiden: Brill.
Harlow, H., and M. L. Nosch, eds. 2014. *Greek and Roman Textiles and Dress: An Interdisciplinary Anthology*. Oxford: Oxbow Books. Harte, N. B. 1976. "State Control of Dress and Social Change in Pre-Industrial England." In *Trade, Government, and Economy in Pre-Industrial England*, edited by D. C. Coleman and A. H. John, 132–165. London: Weidenfeld & Nicolson.
Harte, N. B. and K. G. Ponting, eds. 1983. *Cloth and Clothing in Medieval Europe: Essays in Memory of E. M. Carus-Wilson*. London: Pasold Research Fund and Heineman.
Haley, E. 1986. "Suetonius 'Claudius' 24,1 and the Sons of Freedmen." *Historia: Zeitschrift für Alte Geschichte* Bd. 35.1:115–121.
Harvey, J. 1995. *Men in Black*. Chicago: University of Chicago Press.
Hawley, R. 2007. "Lords of the Rings: Ring-wearing, Status, and Identity in the Age of Pliny the Elder." In *Vita Vigilia Est: Essays in Honour of Barbara Levick*, edited by E. Bispahm, G. Rowe, with E. Matthews, 103–111. London: Institute of Classical Studies.
Hayward, M. 2009. *Rich Apparel: Clothing and the Law in Henry VIII's England*. Farnham, UK: Ashgate.
Haywood, R. M. 1938. "Roman Africa." In *Economic Survey of Ancient Rome* vol. IV: *Roman Africa, Roman Syria, Roman Greece, Roman Asia*, edited by T. Frank. Baltimore: Johns Hopkins University Press.
Helbig, W. 1904. "Toga und Trabea." *Hermes* 39. 2: 161–181.
Henriksen, C. 2012. *A Commentary on Martial, Epigrams Book 9*. Oxford: Oxford University Press.
Henzen, W. 1874. *Acta Fratrum Arvalium quae supersunt*. Berolini: G. Reimeri. Herdt, G. 1994. *Third Sex, Third Gender: Beyond Sexual Dimorphism in Culture and History*. New York: Zone Books.
Hersch, K. 2010. *The Roman Wedding: Ritual and Meaning in Antiquity*. Cambridge: Cambridge University Press.
Herter, H. 1959. "Effeminatus." *RAC* 4: 620–650.
Herzfeld, M. 1985. *The Poetics of Manhood: Contest and Identity in a Cretan Mountain Village*. Princeton, NJ: Princeton University Press.
Heskel, J. 1994. "Cicero as Evidence for Attitudes to Dress in the Late Republic." In Sebesta and Bonfante 1994, 133–145.
Hildebrandt, B. 2013. "Seidenkleidung in der römischen Kaiserzeit." In Tellenbach et al. 2013, 58–61.
Hill, D. K. 1972. "An Unknown Roman Togatus." *Antike Kunst* 15: 27–32.
Hinton, J. 1972. *Dying*, 2nd ed. Harmondsworth: Penguin Books.
Hird, M. J. 2000. "Gender's Nature: Intersexuality, Transsexualism and the 'Sex'/ 'Gender' Binary." *Feminist Theory* 1. 3: 347–364.
Hofenk-De Graaff, J. 1983. "The Chemistry of Red Dyestuffs in Medieval and Early Modern Europe." In Harte and Ponting 1983, 71–79.

Hollander, A. 1994. *Sex and Suits*. New York: Knopf.
Hollander, A. 1978. *Seeing Through Clothes*. New York: Viking Press.
Hollander, A. 2002. *Fabric of Vision: Dress and Drapery in Painting*. London: National Gallery Company.
Holleran, C. 2012. *Shopping in Ancient Rome: The Retail Trade in the Late Republic and the Principate*. Oxford: Oxford University Press.
Hollis, A. S. ed. 1977. *Ovid Ars Amatoria Book I. With Introduction and Commentary*. Oxford: Clarendon Press.
Holmes, L. 1992. "Myrrh and Unguents in the Coma Berenices." *CP* 87. 1: 47–50.
Hölscher, T. [1987]. 2004. *The Language of Images in Roman Art*, translated by A. Snodgrass and A. Künzl-Snodgrass. Cambridge: Cambridge University Press.
Holtheide, B. 1980. "Matrona stolata – femina stolata." *ZPE* 38: 127–134.
Hopman, M. 2003. "Satire in Green: Marked Clothing and the Technique of Indignatio at Juvenal 5.141–145." *AJP* 124: 557–574.
Horn, A. 2009. *Juke-Box Britain: Americanisation and Youth Culture, 1945–60*. Manchester and New York: Manchester University Press.
Howell, P. 1980. *A Commentary on Book One of the Epigrams of Martial*. London: The Athlone Press.
Howgego, C. 1995. *Ancient History From Coins*. London and New York: Routledge.
Huet, V. 2008. "Jeux de vêtements chez Suétone dans les Vies des Julio-Claudiens." In Gherchanoc and Huet 2008, 127–158.
Huet, V. 2012. "Le voile du sacrifiant à Rome sur les reliefs romains: une norme?" In Gherchanoc and Huet 2012, 47–62.
Hughes, L. 2007. "Dyeing in Ancient Italy? Evidence for the *Purpurarii*." In Gillis and Nosch 2007, 87–92.
Humphrey, J., J. O. Oleson, and A. N. Sherwood, eds. 1998. *Greek and Roman Technology: A Sourcebook*. London and New York: Routledge.
Hunink, V. 2005. *Tertullian De Pallio: a Commentary*. Amsterdam: J. C. Gieben.
Hunink, V. 2001. *Apuleius of Madauros Florida*. Edited with a commentary. Amsterdam: J. C. Gieben.
Jahn, O. 1843. *Persii, Iuvenalis, Sulpiciae Saturae*. Leipzig.
Jenkins, I., and D. Williams. 1985. "Sprang Hair-Nets: Their Manufacture and Use in Ancient Greece." *AJA* 39: 411–418.
Johns, C. 1982. *Sex or Symbol: Erotic Images of Greece and Rome*. New York: Routledge.
Johnson, M. 2016. *Ovid on Cosmetics: Medicamina Faciei Femineae and Related Texts*. London: Bloomsbury.
Jones, A. H. M. 1955. "The elections under Augustus." *JRS* 45: 9–21.
Jones, A. R., and P. Stallybrass. 2000. *Renaissance Clothing and the Materials of Memory*. Cambridge: Cambridge University Press.
Joshel, S. 1992. *Work, Identity, and Legal Status at Rome: a Study of the Occupational Inscriptions*. Norman: University of Oklahoma Press.
Joshel, S., and S. Murnaghan, eds. 1998. *Women and Slaves in Greco-Roman Culture: Differential Equations*. London and New York: Routledge. Juan-Tresseras, J. 2000. "El uso de plantas para el lavado y teñido de tejidos en época romana. Análisis de residuos de la fullonica y la tinctoria de Barcino." *Complutum* 11: 245–252.
Kampen, N. 1981. *Image and Status: Roman Working Women in Ostia*, Berlin: Mann.
Kampen, N. 2009. *Family Fictions in Roman Art*. Cambridge: Cambridge University Press.

Kanold, I., and R. Haubrichs. 2008. "Tyrian Purple Dyeing: an Experimental Approach with Fresh Murex Trunculus." In Alfaro Giner and Karali 2008, 253–255.
Karaminas, V. 2009. "Introduction" In McNeil and Karaminas 2009b, 147–151.
Kaster, R. 2005. *Emotion, Restraint, and Community in Ancient Rome.* Oxford: Oxford University Press.
Kaufman, D. B. 1932. "Roman Barbers." *The Classical Weekly.* (Mar. 21), 145–148.
Kellum, B. 1999. "The Spectacle of the Street." In Bergmann and Kondoleon 1999, 283–299.
Kelly, I. 2005. *Beau Brummel: The Ultimate Dandy.* London: Hodder & Stoughton.
Kennedy, D. 1992. *The Arts of Love: Five Studies in the Discourse of Roman Love Elegy.* Cambridge, UK: Cambridge University Press.
Kenney, E. J. ed. 1965. *Ars Amatoria and Other Love Poems.* Oxford, UK: Oxford Classical Texts.
Kenyon, F. 1893. "A Rescript of Marcus Antonius." *Classical Review* 7: 476–478.
Kilian-Dirlmeier, I. 1988. "Jewellery in Mycenaean and Minoan 'Warrior Graves'." In *Problems in Greek Prehistory,* edited by Elizabeth B. French and K. A. Wardle, 161–165. Bristol: Bristol Classical Press.
Kleiner, D. E. E. 1987. *Roman Imperial Funerary Altars With Portraits.* Rome: G. Bretschneider.
Kleiner, F. 1991. "The Roman Toga." [review of Goette 1990]. *JRS* 4: 219–221.
Kleiner, D. E. E. 1992. *Roman Sculpture.* New Haven and London: Yale Univ. Press.
Kleiner, D. E. E., and F. Kleiner. 1980–1. "Early Roman Togate Statuary." *Bolletino della commissione archeologica communale di Roma* 87: 125–133.
Kockel, V. 1993. *Porträtreliefs Stadtrömischen Grabbauten: ein Beitrag zur Geschichte und zum Verständnis des spätrepublikanisch-frühkaiserzeitlichen Privatporträts,* Mainz am Rhein: P. von Zabern.
Kolb, F. 1973. "Römische mäntel: paenula, lacerna, mandye." *RM* 80: 69–167.
Koloski-Ostrow, A. 1997. "Violent Stages in Two Pompeian Houses: Imperial Taste, Aristocratic Response, and Messages of Male Control." In *Naked Truths: Women, Sexuality, and Gender in Classical Art and Archaeology,* edited by A. Koloski-Ostrow and C. L. Lyons, 243–266. London and New York: Routledge.
Konstan, D.1993. "Sexuality and Power in Juvenal's Second *Satire.*" *LCM* 18. 1: 12–14.
Konstan, D. 2002. "Enacting Eros." In *The Sleep of Reason: Erotic Experience and Sexual Ethics in Ancient Greece and Rome,* edited by M. Nussbaum and J. Sihvola, 354–373. Chicago: University of Chicago Press. Kosofsky-Sedgwick, E. 1985. *Between Men: English Literature and Male Homosocial Desire.* New York: Columbia University Press.
Kraus, C. S. 2005. "Hair, Hegemony, and Historiography: Caesar's Earliest Critics." *Proceedings of the British Academy* 129: 97–115.
Kuchta, D. 1996. *"The Making of the Self-Made Man: Class, Clothing, and English Masculinity, 1688–1832."* In *The Sex of Things: Gender and Consumption in Historical Perspective,* edited by V. de Grazia and E. Furlough, 54–78. Berkeley: University of California Press.
Kuchta, D. 2002. *The Three-Piece Suit and Modern Masculinity: England 1550–1850.* Berkeley: The University of California Press.
Kuefler, M. *2001. The Manly Eunuch: Masculinity, Gender Ambiguity, and Christian Ideology in Late Antiquity.* Chicago and London: University of Chicago Press.
Kurke, L. 1992. "The Politics of Habrosyne in Archaic Greece." *CA* 11: 91–120.

Bibliography

Labate, M. 1984. *L'arte di farsi amare: modelli culturali e progetto didascalico nell'elegia ovidiana*. Biblioteca di MD2. Pisa: Giardini.
Laes, C. 2003. "Desperately Different? *Delicia*-Children in the Roman Household." In *Early Christian Families in Context: An Interdisciplinary Dialogue*, edited by D. L. Balch and C. Osiek, 298–326. Michigan: W. B. Eerdmans Pub. Co.
Laes, C. 2010. "Delicia-Children Revisited: the Evidence of Statius' Silvae." In *Children, Memory, and Family Identity in Roman Culture* edited by V. Dasen and T. Späth, 245–272. Oxford and New York: Oxford University Press.
La Follette, L. 1994. "The Costume of the Roman Bride." In Sebesta and Bonfante 1994, 54–64.
Leach, E. 2001. "Gendering Clodius." *CW* 94: 335–359.
Leach, E. 2006. "Freedmen and Immortality in the Tomb of the Haterii." In D'Ambra and Métraux 2006, 1–17.
Leary, T. J. 1990. "The 'Aprons' of St Paul – Acts 19:12." *Journal of Theological Studies* 41. 2: 527–529.
Leary, T. J. 1996. *Martial Book XIV: The Apophoreta*, London: Duckworth.
Lee, M. 2005. "Constru(ct)ing Gender in the Feminine Greek *Peplos*." In Cleland*et al.*2005, 55–64.
Lee, M. 2015. *Body, Dress, and Identity in Ancient Greece*. Cambridge, UK: Cambridge University Press.
Leeman, A. D. 2001. "Julius Caesar, the Orator of Paradox". In *The Orator in Action and Theory in Greece and Rome*, edited by C. B. Wooten, 97–110. Leiden: Brill.
Lenski, N. 2013. "Working Models: Functional Art and Roman Conceptions of Slavery." In *Roman Slavery and Roman Material Culture*, edited by M. George, 129–157. Toronto: University of Toronto Press.
Levick, B. 1991. "A Note on the Latus Clavus." *Athenaeum* 79: 239–244.
Lilja, S. 1983. *Homosexuality in Republican and Augustan Rome*. Helsinki: Finnish Society of Sciences and Letters.
Linderski, J. 2001. "Silver and Gold of Valor: the Award of *Armillae* and *Torques*." *Latomus* 60. 1: 3–15.
Linderski, J. 2002. "The Pontiff and the Tribune: the Death of Tiberius Gracchus." *Athenaeum* 90. 2: 339–366.
Lindheim, S. 1998. "Hercules Cross-Dressed, Hercules Undressed: Unmasking the Construction of the Propertian Amator in Elegy 4.9." *AJPh* 119: 43–66.
Lintott, A. 1999. *Violence in Republican Rome*. 2nd ed. Oxford: Oxford University Press.
Liu, J. 2009. *Collegia Centonariorum: the Guilds of Textile Dealers in the Roman West*. Leiden: Brill.
Llewellyn-Jones, L. 2002a. "Introduction." In Llewellyn-Jones 2002b, vii–xv.
Llewellyn-Jones, L., ed. 2002b. *Women's Dress in the Ancient Greek World*, Swansea, Wales: Classical Press of Wales.
Llewellyn-Jones, L. 2003. *Aphrodite's Tortoise: the Veiled Woman of Ancient Greece*, Swansea, Wales: Classical Press of Wales.
Longo, O., ed. 1998a. *La Porpora: realtà e immaginario di un colore simbolico*. Venice: Instituto Veneto di Scienze, Lettere ed Arti.
Longo, O. 1998b. "La zoologia delle porpore nell'antichità Greco-Romana." In Longo 1998a, 79–90.
Lovén, L. Larsson. 1998. "Male and Female Professions in the Textile Production of Roman Italy." In *Textiles in European Archaeology: Report from the 6th NESAT*

Symposium, 7–11th May 1996 in Borås. GOTARC Series A, vol. 1, edited by L. Bender-Jørgensen and C. Rinaldo, 73–78. Göteborg: Göteborg University Department of Archaeology.

Lovén, L. Larsson. 2013. "Römische Frauen, Kleidung und öffentliche Identitäten." In Tellenbach*et al*.2013, 98–103.

Lowe, B. 2004. "The Industrial Exploitation of Murex: Purple Dye Production in the Western Mediterranean." In *Colour in the Ancient Mediterranean World*, edited by L. Cleland and K. Stears, 46–8. Oxford: Oxford University Press.

MacMahon, A. 2003. *The Taberna Structures of Roman Britain*. Oxford: Oxford University Press.

MacMullen, R. 1982. "Roman Attitudes to Greek Love." *Historia* 31:484–502.

Macheboeuf, C. 2004. "Pourpre et matières textiles: des ateliers aux *tabernae*." In Alfaro Giner*et al*.2004, 137–143.

Macheboeuf, C. 2008. "Remarques sur l'ars aria." In Alfaro Giner and Karali 2008, 247–250.

Maiuri, A. 1953. *The Great Centuries of Painting: Roman Painting*. Lausanne: Skira.

Maiuri, A. 1965. *Ercolano: Nuovi Scavi*. Rome: Istituto poligrafico dello Stato, Libreria della Stato.

Manfredini, A. 1985. "Qui commutant cum feminis vestem." *RIDA* 32: 257–271.

Mannering, U. 2000a. "Roman Garments from Mons Claudianus." In Cardon and Feugère 2000, 283–290.

Mannering, U. 2000b. "The Roman Tradition of Weaving and Sewing: a Guide to Function?" *Archaeological Textiles Newsletter* 30: 10–16.

Marshall, A. J. 1984. "Symbols and Showmanship in Roman Public Life." *Phoenix* 38: 120–141.

Marshall, A. R. 2008. "Law and Luxury in Augustan Rome." *Journal of Ancient Civilization* 23: 97–117.

Marshall, F. H. 1907. *Catalogue of the Finger Rings, Greek, Etruscan, and Roman, in the Departments of Antiquities, British Museum*. London: Trustees of the British Museum.

Martorelli, R. 2004. "Influenze religiose sulla scelta dell'abito nel primi secoli cristiani." In *Antiquité Tardive* 12: *Tissus et vêtements dans l'antiquité tardive*: 231–248.

Masterson, M., N. Rabinowitz, and J. Robson, eds. 2014. *Sex in Antiquity: Exploring Gender and Sexuality in the Ancient World*. London and New York: Routledge.

McDaniel, W. B. 1925. "Roman Dinner Garments." *CP* 20: 268–270.

McDonnell, M. 2006. *Roman Manliness: Virtus and the Roman Republic*. Cambridge: Cambridge University Press.

McDowell, C. 1997. *The Man of Fashion: Peacock Males and Perfect Gentlemen*. London: Thames and Hudson.

McGinn, T. A. J. 1998. *Prostitution, Sexuality, and the Law in Ancient Rome*. Oxford: Oxford University Press.

McGinn, T. A. J. 2014. "Prostitution: Controversies and New Approaches." In *A Companion to Greek and Roman Sexualities*, edited by T. K. Hubbard, 83–101. Chichester, UK: Wiley-Blackwell.

McNeil, P. 1999. "'That Doubtful Gender:' Macaroni Dress and Male Sexualities." *Fashion Theory* 3. 4: 411–448.

McNeil, P. 2000. "Macaroni Masculinities." *Fashion Theory* 4. 4: 373–403.

McNeil, P., and V. Karaminas. 2009a. "Introduction: the Field of Men's Fashion." In McNeil and Karaminas 2009b, 1–11.

McNeil, P., and V. Karaminas, eds. 2009b. *The Men's Fashion Reader*. Oxford and New York: Berg.

Métraux, G. P. R. 2008. "Prudery and Chic in Late Antique Clothing." In Edmondson and Keith 2008, 271–293.

Meyer, H. 1993. "Ein Denkmal des Consensus Civium." *Bollettino Comunale di Archeologia*, 95: 45–67.

Milanezi, S. 2005. "On Rhakos in Aristophanic Theatre." In Cleland *et al.* 2005, 75–86.

Miller, J. 1969. *The Spice Trade of the Roman Empire 29 B.C. to A.D. 641*. Oxford: Clarendon Press.

Millar, F. 1977. *The Emperor in the Roman World*. Ithaca, N.Y.: Cornell University Press.

Miller, M. C. 1992. "The Parasol: an Oriental Status Symbol in Late Archaic and Classical Athens." *JHS* 112: 91–105.

Miller, M. C. 1997. *Athens and Persia in the Fifth Century BC: A Study in Cultural Receptivity*. Cambridge, UK: Cambridge University Press. Mills, H. 1984. "Greek Clothing Regulations: Sacred and Profane." *ZPE* 55: 255–265.

Moeller, W. O. 1976. *The Wool Trade of Ancient Pompeii*. Leiden: Brill.

Moers, E. 1960. *The Dandy: Brummell to Beerbohm*. London: Secker & Warburg.

Mohler, S. 1940. "Slave Education in the Roman Empire." *TAPA* 71: 262–280.

Moliner-Arbo, A. 2003. "'Imperium in virtute esse non decore:' le discours sur le costume dans l'Histoire Auguste." In Chausson and Inglebert 2003, 67–84.

Monteix, N. 2010. *Les lieux de métier: boutiques et ateliers d'Herculanum*. Collection du Centre Jean Bérard34. Rome: École Française.

Morgan, T. 1999. "Victorian Effeminacies." In *Victorian Sexual Dissidence*, edited by R. Dellamora, 109–126. Chicago: University of Chicago Press.

Morley, N. 1996. *The Metropolis and Hinterland: The City of Rome and the Italian Economy 200 BC–AD 200*. Cambridge, UK: Cambridge University Press.

Mottahedeh, P. E. 1984. "The Princeton Bronze Portrait of a Woman with Reticulum." In *Festschrift für Leo Mildenberg: Numismatik, Kunstgeschichte, Archäologie*, edited by A. Houghton, S. Hurter, P. E. Mottahedeh, and J. A. Scott, 203–208. Wetteren, Belgium: Editions NR.

Muggleton, D. 2000. *Inside Subculture: The Postmodern Meaning of Style*. Oxford and New York: Berg.

Mulvey, L. 1975. "Visual Pleasure and Narrative Cinema." *Screen* 16. 3: 6–18.

Mulvey, L. [1981] 1989a. "Afterthoughts on 'Visual Pleasure and Narrative Cinema' Inspired by King Vidor's Duel in the Sun (1946)." In Mulvey 1989c, 29–37.

Mulvey, L. [1977] 1989b. "Notes on Sirk and Melodrama." In Mulvey 1989c, 39–44.

Mulvey, L. 1989c. *Visual and Other Pleasures*. Basingstoke: Macmillan.

Munro, J. 1983. "The Medieval Scarlet and the Economics of Sartorial Splendour." In Harte and Ponting 1983, 13–70.

Murgatroyd, P. 1977. "Tibullus and the Puer Delicatus." *Acta Classica: Proceedings of the Classical Society of South Africa* 20: 105–119.

Murgatroyd, P. 1980. *Tibullus I: A Commentary on the First Book of the Elegies of Albius Tibullus*. Pietermaritzburg:University of Natal Press.

Musurillo, H. 1954. *Acts of the Pagan Martyrs*. Oxford: Oxford University Press.

Napoli, J. 2004. "Ars purpuraire et législation a l'époque Romaine." In Alfaro Gineret *al.* 2004, 123–136.

Nappo, S. Cirro. 1989. "Fregio dipinto dal 'praedium' di Giulia Felice con rappresentazione del foro di Pompei." *RSP* 3: 79–96.

Néraudau, J.-P. 1979. *La jeunesse dans la littérature et les institutions de la Rome républicaine.* Paris: Belles Lettres, Collection d'études anciennes.

Nilson, K. A., C. B. Persson, S. Sande, and J. Zahle. 2008. "The Foundation and the Core of the Podium and of the Tribunal." In *The Temple of Castor and Pollux,* iii. *The Augustan Temple,* edited by K. A. Nilson, C. B. Persson, S. Sande, and J. Zahle, 21–73. Rome: L'Erma Di Bretschneider.

Noé, E. 1974. "La produzione tessile nella Gallia cisalpina in età Romana." *Rendiconti dell'Istituto lombardo-accademia di scienze e lettere* 108: 918–932.

Nosch, M.-L., and H. Koefoed, eds. 2012. *Wearing the Cloak: Dressing the Soldier in Roman Times.* Oxford: Oxbow Books.

Novokhatko, A. 2009. *The Invectives of Sallust and Cicero: Critical Edition with Introduction, Translation, and Commentary.* New York and Berlin: Walter de Gruyter.

Obermayer, H. P. 1998. *Martial und der Diskurs über männliche 'Homosexualität' in der Literatur der fruhen Kaiserzeit.* Tübingen: Gunter Narr.

Olson, K. 2002. "*Matrona* and Whore: the Clothing of Roman Women." *Fashion Theory* 6. 4: 387–420.

Olson, K. 2003. "Roman Underwear Revisited." *CW* 96. 2: 201–210.

Olson, K. 2004–5. "*Insignia lugentium*: Female Mourning Garments in Roman Antiquity." *American Journal of Ancient History* 3–4: 89–130.

Olson, K. 2008. *Dress and the Roman Woman: Self-Presentation and Society.* London and New York: Routledge.

Olson, K. 2014a. "Masculinity, Appearance, and Sexuality: Dandies in Roman Antiquity." *The Journal of the History of Sexuality* 23. 2: 182–205.

Olson, K. 2014b. "Toga and Pallium: Status, Sexuality, Identity." In Masterson *et al.* 2014, 422–448. O'Sullivan, T. 2011. *Walking in Roman Culture.* Cambridge, UK: Cambridge University Press.

Overing, J. 1986. "Men Control Women? The 'Catch 22' in the Analysis of Gender." *International Journal of Moral and Social Studies* 1. 2: 135–156.

Palmer, R. E. A. 1998. "Bullae insignia ingenuitatis." *American Journal of Ancient History* 14: 1–69.

Palombi, D. 1990. "Gli horrea della via Sacra: dagli appunti di G. Boni ad un ipotesi su Nerone." *DialA* 8: 53–72.

Panagiotakopulu, E., P. C. Buckland, P. Day, C. Doumas, A. Sarpaki, and P. Skidmore. 1997. "A Lepidopterous Cocoon from Thera and Evidence of Silk in the Aegean Bronze Age." *Antiquity* 71. 272: 420–429.

Parani, M. 2008. "Defining Personal Space: Dress and Accessories in Late Antiquity." In *Objects in Context, Objects in Use: Material Spatiality in Late Antiquity,* edited by L. Lavan, E. Swift, and T. Putzeys, 497–529. Leiden: Brill.

Parker, G. 2002. "'Ex Oriente Luxuria': Indian Commodities and Roman Experience." *Journal of the Economic and Social History of the Orient* 45. 1: 40–95.

Parker, G. 2008. *The Making of Roman India.* Cambridge: Cambridge University Press.

Parker, H. 1997. "The Teratogenic Grid." In Hallett and Skinner 1997, 47–65.

Paulicelli, E. 2014. *Writing Fashion in Early Modern Italy: From Sprezzatura to Satire.* Farnham, UK: Ashgate.

Pausch, M. 2008. *Die römische Tunika.* Augsberg: Wißner.

Perrot, P. 1994. *Fashioning the Bourgeoisie: A History of Clothing in the Nineteenth Century,* translated by R. Bienvenu. Princeton, N.J.: Princeton University Press.

Petersen, L. H. 2006. *The Freedman in Roman Art and Art History.* Cambridge: Cambridge University Press.
Petersen, L. H. 2009. "'Clothes Make the Man:' Dressing the Roman Freedman Body." In Fögen and Lee 2009, 181–214.
Pleket, H. 1988. "Greek Epigraphy and Comparative Ancient History: Two Case Studies." *Epigraphica Anatolica* 12: 25–37.
Pocock, L. G. 1967. *A Commentary on Cicero In Vatinium, with an Historical Introduction and Appendices.* Amsterdam: A. M. Hakkert.
Pomeroy, A. J. 1992. "Trimalchio as Deliciae." *Phoenix* 46: 45–53.
Pollini, J. 1999. "The Warren Cup: Homoerotic Love and Symposial Rhetoric in Silver." *The Art Bulletin* 81: 21–52.
Pollini, J. 2003. "Slave-Boys for Sexual and Religious Service: Images of Pleasure and Devotion." In *Flavian Rome: Culture, Image, Text*, edited by A. J. Boyle and W. J. Dominik, 149–166. Leiden and Boston: Brill.
Pollini, J. 2012. *From Republic to Empire: Rhetoric, Religion, and Power in the Visual Culture of Ancient Rome.* Norman: University of Oklahoma Press.
Puybaret, M.-P., P. Borgard, and R. Zérubia. 2008. "Teindre comme à Pompéi: approche expérimentale." In Alfaro Giner and Karali 2008, 143–147.
Quinn, K. (ed.)1970. *Catullus: The Poems. Edited with Introduction, Revised Text and Commentary.* London: Macmillan. New York: St Martin's Press.
Raschke, M. G. 1978. "New Studies in Roman Commerce with the East." *ANRW* 2. 9: 604–1361.
Rawson, B. 2003. *Children and Childhood in Roman Italy.* Oxford: Oxford University Press.
Rebbechi, F. 1999. "Per l'iconografia della 'transvectio equitum:' altre considerazioni e nuovi documenti." In *L'ordre équestre. Histoire d'une aristocratie (Ier siècle av. J.-C.–IIIe siècle ap. J.-C)*, Actes du colloque de Bruxelles-Leuven (octobre 1995), edited by M.-T. Raepsaet-Charlier and S. Demougin, Collection de l'École française de Rome257: 191–214.
Rehak, P. 2001. "Aeneas or Numa? Rethinking the Meaning of the Ara Pacis Augustae." *The Art Bulletin* 83. 2: 190–208.
Reinhold, M. 1970. *History of Purple as a Status Symbol in Antiquity.* Coll. Latomus116. Brussels.
Reinhold, M.1971. "The Usurpation of Status and Status Symbols in the Roman Empire." *Historia* 20: 275–302.
Ribbeck, O. 1865. *Der echte und der unechte Juvenal: eine kritische Untersuchung.* Berlin: I. Guttentag.
Rich, B. R. 1990. "In the Name of Feminist Film Criticism." In *Issues in Feminist Film Criticism*, edited by P. Erens, 268–287. Bloomington: Indiana University Press.
Richardson, E. H., and L.Richardson, Jr. 1966. "Ad Cohibendum Bracchium Toga: an Archaeological Examination of Cicero, Pro Caelio 5.11." *Yale Classical Studies* 19: 251–268.
Richardson, T. W. 1986. "Further on the Young Trimalchio." *Phoenix* 40: 201.
Richlin, A. 1992. *The Garden of Priapus.* 2nd ed. Oxford: Oxford University Press.
Richlin, A. 1993. "Not Before Homosexuality: The Materiality of the *Cinaedus* and the Roman Law against Love between Men." *Journal of the History of Sexuality* 3: 523–573.
Richlin, A. 1995. "Making up a Woman: the Face of Roman Gender." In *Off With Her Head: the Denial of Women's Identity in Myth, Religion, and Culture*, edited by

W. Doniger and H. Eilberg-Schwartz, 185–213. Berkeley, CA: University of California Press.
Richlin, A. 1997. "Gender and Rhetoric: Producing Manhood in the Schools." In *Roman Eloquence: Rhetoric in Society and Literature*, edited by W. J. Dominik, 90–110. London and New York: Routledge.
Roche, D. 1994. *The Culture of Clothing: Dress and Fashion in the Ancien Régime*, translated by J. Birrell. Cambridge and New York: Cambridge University Press.
Roisman, J. 2005. *The Rhetoric of Manhood: Masculinity in the Attic Orators*. Berkeley: University of California Press.
Roller, L. 1999. *In Search of God the Mother: the Cult of Anatolian Cybele*. Berkeley: University of California Press.
Rose, G. 2001. *Visual Methodologies: An Introduction to the Interpretation of Visual Materials*, London: Sage.
Ross, G. A., ed. 2011. *The Day of the Peacock. Style for Men 1963–1973*. London: V&A Publishing.
Rossbach, O. 1896. *L. Annaei Flori Epitomae, libri II, et P. Annii Flori fragmentum de Vergilio oratore an poeta*. Leipzig: Teubner.
Rothfus, M. A. 2010. "The Gens Togata: Changing Styles and Changing Identities." *AJP* 131: 425–452.
Rowe, C. 1972. "Conceptions of Colour and Colour Symbolism in the Ancient World." *Eranos* 41: 327–364.
Rowe, G. 2002. *Princes and Political Culture: The New Tiberian Senatorial Decrees*. Ann Arbor: University of Michigan Press.
Rubin, G. 1975. "The Traffic in Women: Notes on the 'Political Economy' of Sex." In *Toward an Anthropology of Women*, edited by R. Reiter, 157–210. New York: Monthly Review Press.
Ryberg, I. S. 1967. *Panel Reliefs of Marcus Aurelius*. AIA Monographs, 14. New York.
Saiko, M. 2005. *Cura dabit faciem: Kosmetik in Altertum-literarische, kulturhistorische, und medizinische Aspekte*, Bochumer Altertumswissenschaftliches Colloquium6. Trier.
Saller, R. 1982. *Personal Patronage Under the Early Empire*. Cambridge: Cambridge University Press.
Salles, C. 2003. "Le costume satirique dans la poésie satirique latine." In Chausson and Inglebert, 57–66.
Salzman-Mitchell, P. 2005. *A Web of Fantasies: Gaze, Image, and Gender in Ovid's Metamorphoses*. Columbus: The Ohio State University Press.
Sampaolo, V. 1999. "IX.7.7: Officina coactiliaria di Verecundus." *Pompei: pitture e mosaici*, vol. 9: 774–778. Rome.
Sapsford, T. 2015. "The Wages of Effeminacy? Kinaidoi in Greek documents from Egypt." *EuGeStA* 5: 103–123.
Sartre, J.-P. 1947. *The Age of Reason*. Trans. E. Sutton. London: H. Hamilton.
Scheidel, W. 2003. "Germs for Rome." In *Rome the Cosmopolis*, edited by C. Edwards and G. Woolf, 158–176. Cambridge, UK: Cambridge University Press.
Schmeling, G. 2011. *A Commentary on the Satyrica of Petronius*. With the collaboration of A. Setaioli. Oxford: Oxford University Press.
Scholte, A. 1873. *Observationes Criticae in Saturas D. Junii Iuvenalis*. Utrecht.
Scholz, B. 1992. *Untersuchungen zur Tracht der römischen Matrona*. Köln: Böhlau.
Schoonhoven, H. 1980. *Elegiae in Maecenatem. Proglomena, Text, and Commentary*. Grönigen: Bouma's Boekhuis.

Scobie, A. 1986. "Slums, Sanitation, and Mortality in the Roman World." *Klio* 68: 399–433.
Sebesta, J. L. 1994a. "Symbolism in the Costume of Roman Women." In Sebesta and Bonfante 1994, 46–53.
Sebesta, J. L. 1994b. "*Tunica Ralla, Tunica Spissa*: the Colors and Textiles of Roman Costume." In Sebesta and Bonfante 1994, 65–76.
Sebesta, J. L. 1997. "Women's Costume and Feminine Civic Morality in Augustan Rome." *Gender and History* 9. 3: 529–541.
Sebesta, J. L. 2005. "The *Toga Praetexta* of Roman Children and Praetextate Garments." In Clelande*t al.*2005 , 113–120.
Sebesta, J. L., and L. Bonfante, eds. 1994. *The World of Roman Costume*. Madison, Wis.: University of Wisconsin Press.
Sherwin-White, A. N. 1966. *The Letters of Pliny: A Historical and Social Commentary*. Oxford: Clarendon Press.
Shively, D. H. 1964–5. "Sumptuary Regulation and Status in Early Tokugawa Japan." *Harvard Journal of Asiatic Studies* 25: 123–164.
Siedschlag, E. 1977. *Zur Form von Martials Epigrammen*. Berlin: Mielke.
Silverman, K. 1992. *Male Subjectivity at the Margins*. London and New York: Routledge.
Silverman, K. 1986. "Fragments of a Fashionable Discourse." In *Studies in Entertainment: Critical Approaches to Mass Culture*, edited by T. Modleski, 139–154. Bloomington: Indiana University Press.
Simpson, M. 1994. "Here Come the Mirror Men: Why the Future is Metrosexual." http://www.marksimpson.com/here-come-the-mirror-men/ (June 20, 2016).
Simpson, M. 1996. *It's a Queer World: Deviant Adventures in Pop Culture*. London and New York: Routledge.
Simpson, M. 2002. "Meet the Metrosexual." http://www.salon.com/2002/07/22/metrosexual/ (June 20, 2016).Sinfield, A. 1994. *The Wilde Century: Effeminacy, Oscar Wilde, and the Queer Movement*. New York: Columbia University Press.
Skinner, M. 1979. "Parasites and Strange Bedfellows: a Study in Catullus' Political Imagery." *Ramus* 8: 137–152.
Skinner, M. 1982. "Pretty Lesbius." *TAPA* 112: 197–208.
Skinner, M. 2005. *Sexuality in Greek and Roman Culture*. Malden, MA.: Blackwell.
Smallwood, E. M. 1967. *Documents Illustrating the Principates of Gaius, Claudius, and Nero*. Cambridge, UK: Cambridge University Press.
Smith, M. S. (ed.) 1975. *Petronii Arbitri Cena Trimalchionis*. Oxford: Clarendon Press.
Smith, R. R. R. 2002. "The Use of Images: Visual History and Ancient History." In *Classics in Progress: Essays on Ancient Greece and Rome*, edited by T. P. Wiseman, 59–102. Oxford: Oxford University Press.
Snow, E. 1989. "Theorising the Male Gaze: Some Problems." *Representations* 25. 1: 30–41.
Southern, P. 2006. *The Roman Army: A Social and Institutional History*. Santa Barbara, CA: ABC-CLIO.
Speidel, M. P. 1994. *Die Denkmäler der Kaiserreiter*. Köln: Rheinland-Verlag.
Speidel, M. P. 1997. "Late-Roman Military Decorations II: Gold-Embroidered Capes and Tunics." *Antiquité Tardive* 5: 213–237.
Speidel, M. P. 2012. "Dressed for the Occasion: Clothes and Context in the Roman Army." In *Wearing the Cloak: Dressing the Soldier in Roman Times*, edited by M.-L. Nosch and H. Koefoed, 1–12. Oxford: Oxbow Books.

Spier, J. 1992. *Ancient Gems and Finger Rings: Catalogue of the Collections*. Malibu: The J. Paul Getty Museum.
Sponsler, C. 1992. "Narrating the Social Order: Medieval Clothing Laws." *Clio* 21: 265–283.
Spooner, C. 2004. *Fashioning Gothic Bodies*. Manchester: Manchester University Press.
Stafford, E. J. 2005. "Viewing and Obscuring the Female Breast: Glimpses of the Ancient Bra." In Cleland, *et al.* 2005, 96–110.
Staples, L. N. 1979. *Cloth and Class: the Prestige of Fabric*. New Haven: Yale University Art Gallery.
Steele, V. 1985. "The Social and Political Significance of Macaroni Fashion." *Costume* 19: 89–101.
Stewart, S. 2007. *Cosmetics and Perfumes in the Roman World*. Stroud: Tempus.
Stilp, F. 2001. *Mariage et Suovetaurilia: Etude sur le Soi-disant 'Autel Ahenobarbus.'* RdA Supplementi26. Rome: Giorgio Bretschneider.
Stone, S. 1994. "The Toga: from National to Ceremonial Costume." In Sebesta and Bonfante 1994, 13–45.
Stout, A. M. 1994. "Jewelry as a Symbol of Status in the Roman Empire." In Sebesta and Bonfante 1994, 77–100.
Strocchia, S. T. 1992. *Death and Ritual in Renaissance Florence*. Baltimore and London: Johns Hopkins University Press.
Sumi, G. 2005. *Ceremony and Power: Performing Politics in Rome between Republic and Empire*. Ann Arbor: University of Michigan Press.
Sumner, G. 2002. *Roman Military Clothing I: 100 BC–AD 200*. Oxford: Osprey Publishing.
Sumner, G. 2009. *Roman Military Dress*. Stroud: The History Press.
Syme, R. 1961. "Who was Vedius Pollio?" *JRS* 51: 23–30.
Tarbell, F. B. 1906. "The Forms of the Chlamys." *Classical Philology* 1: 293–299.
Taylor, G. W. 1983. "Detection and Identification of Dyes on Pre-Hadrianic Textiles from Vindolanda." *Textile History* 2: 115–124.
Taylor, L. 1983. *Mourning Dress: A Costume and Social History*. London: Allen and Unwin.
Taylor, R. 1997. "Two Pathic Subcultures in Ancient Rome." *Journal of the History of Sexuality* 7. 3: 319–371.
Tellenbach, M., R. Schulz, and A. Wieczorek, eds. 2013. *Der Macht der Toga: DressCode im Römischen Welt*. Regensburg: Schnell and Steiner.
Thompson, D. 1947. *A Glossary of Greek Fishes*. Oxford: Oxford University Press.
Thompson, L. A. 1989. *Romans and Blacks*. London and Oklahoma: Routledge and Oklahoma University Press.
Threadgold, T. 1990. "Introduction." In *Feminine Masculine, and Representation*, edited by T. Threadgold and A. Cranny-Francis, 1–35. London: Allen and Unwin.
Torelli, M. 1982. *Typology and Structure of Roman Historical Reliefs*. Ann Arbor: University of Michigan Press.
Tosh, J. 1999. *A Man's Place: Masculinity and the Middle-Class Home in Victorian England*. New Haven and London: Yale University Press.
Tracy, V. 1976. "Roman Dandies and Transvestites." *EMC* 20: 60–63.
Treggiari, S. 1991. *Roman Marriage: Iusti Coniuges From the Time of Cicero to the Time of Ulpian*. Oxford: Oxford University Press.

Treggiari, S. 2002. *Roman Social History*. London and New York: Routledge.
Treherne, P. 1995. "The Warrior's Beauty: the Masculine Body and Self-Identity in Pre-Modern Europe." *Journal of European Archaeology* 3. 1: 105–144.
Trumbach, R. 1991. "The Birth of the Queen: Sodomy and the Emergence of Gender Equality in Modern Culture, 1660–1750." In Duberman*et al.*, 129–140.
Tuori, K. 2009. "Dig. 34.2.33: Return of the Cross-Dressing Senator." *Arctos* 43: 191–200.
Turcan, M., ed. 2007. *Tertullian Le Manteau (De Pallio)*. Paris: Les éditions du Cerf.
Ugolini, L. 2009. "Autobiographies and Menswear Consumption in Britain, c. 1880–1939." *Textile History* 40. 2: 202–211.
Upson-Saia, K. 2011. *Early Christian Dress: Gender, Virtue, and Authority*. London and New York: Routledge.
Upson-Saia, K., C. Daniel-Hughes, and A. Batten, eds. *2014. Dressing Judeans and Christians in Antiquity*. Farnham, UK: Ashgate.
Vainshtein, O. 2009. "Dandyism, Visual Games, and the Strategies of Representation." In McNeil and Karaminas 2009b, 84–107.
Vanggaard, J. 1988. *The Flamen: A Study in the History and Sociology of Roman Religion*. Copenhagen: Museum Tusculanum Press.
Van Wees, H. 2005. "Clothes, Class and Gender in Homer." In *Body Language in the Greek and Roman Worlds*, edited by F. Cairns, 1–36. Swansea: The Classical Press of Wales.
Veblen, T. 1899. [1934] *The Theory of the Leisure Class: an Economic Study of Institutions*. New York: The Modern Library.
Veyne, P. 1960. "Iconographie de la transvectio equitum." *Revue des études ancienne* 62: 100–113.
Veyne, P. 1985. "Homosexuality in Ancient Rome." In *Western Sexuality: Practice and Precept in Past and Present Times*, edited by P. Ariès and A. Béjin, and translated by A. Forster, 26–35. Oxford: Basil Blackwell.
Vicaire, M., and R. Le Tourneau. 1937. "La fabrication du fil d'or à Fès." *Hespéris* 24: 67–88.
Vigarello, G. 1988. *Concepts of Cleanliness: Changing Attitudes in France Since the Middle Ages*. Trans. J. Birrell. Cambridge: Cambridge University Press.
von Hase, F. W. 2013. "Zur Kleidung im frühen Etrurien." In Tellenbach*et al.* 2013, 72–79.
Vout, C. 1996. "The Myth of the Toga: Understanding the History of Roman Dress." *Greece and Rome* 43. 2: 204–220.
Wace, A. J. B. 1948. "Weaving or Embroidery?" *AJA* 48: 51–55.
Wallace-Hadrill, A. 1996. "Engendering the Roman House." In *I, Claudia: Women in Ancient Rome*, edited by D. E. E. Kleiner and S. B. Matheson, 104–115. Austin: University of Texas Press.
Wallace-Hadrill, A. 2008. *Rome's Cultural Revolution*. Cambridge, UK: Cambridge University Press.
Walsh, P. 1970. *The Roman Novel. The Satyricon of Petronius and the Metamorphoses of Apuleius*. Cambridge, UK: Cambridge University Press.
Walters, J. 1993. "'No More Than a Boy': the Shifting Construction of Masculinity from Ancient Greece to the Middle Ages." *Gender & History* 5. 1: 20–33.
Walters, J. 1998. "Juvenal, Satire 2: Putting Male Sexual Deviants on Show." In Foxhall and Salmon 1998b, 148–154.
Warden, P. G. 1983. "Bullae, Roman Custom, and Italic Tradition." *OpRom* 14: 69–75.

Watson, A., trans. 1985. *The Digest of Justinian.* Latin text edited by Th. Mommsen with P. Kreuger. Philadelphia: University of Pennsylvania Press.
Waywell, G. B. 1978. *The Free Standing Sculptures of the Mausoleum at Halicarnassus.* London: British Museum Publications.
Weeks, J. 1989. "Inverts, Perverts, and Mary-Annes: Male Prostitution and the Regulation of Male Homosexuality in England in the Nineteenth and Early Twentieth Centuries." In Duberman, *et al.* 1989, 195–211.
Wessely, K. 1921. *Catalogus Papyrorum Raineri.* Series Graeca. Pars I. Textus Graeci papyrorum. *Studien zur Paläographie und Papyruskunde* 20.
Wiedemann, T. 1989. *Adults and Children in the Roman Empire.* London and New York: Routledge.
Wild, J. P., 1964. "The Textile Term *Scutulatus.*" *CQ* 14. 2: 263–266.
Wild, J. P. 1976. "Textiles." In *Roman Crafts,* edited by D. Strong and D. Brown, 167–177. London: Duckworth.
Wild, J. P. 1977. *The Textiles from Vindolanda 1973–1975.* VindolandaIII. Haltwhistle, Northumberland: Vindolanda Trust.
Wild, J. P. 1979. "Roman Textiles from Vindolanda, Hexham, England." *The Textile Museum Journal* 18: 19–24.
Wild, J. P. 1992a. "*Colorator.*" *Glotta* 70: 96–99.
Wild, J. P. 1992b. "Vindolanda 1985–1989: First Thoughts on New Finds." In *Archaeological Textiles in Northern Europe: Report from the 4th NESAT Symposium, 1–5 May 1990 in Copenhagen,* edited by L. Bender-Jørgensen and E. Munksgaard, 66–74. Copenhagen: Konservatorskolen.
Wild, J. P. 1993. "Vindolanda 1985–1988: the Textiles." In *Vindolanda III: Preliminary Reports on the Leather, Textiles, Environmental Evidence and Dendrochronology,* edited by R. E. Birley, 76–90. Bardon Mill, Northumberland.
Wild, J. P. 1994. "Tunic no. 4219: an Archaeological and Historical Perspective." *Riggisberger Berichte* 2: 9–36.
Wild, J. P. 2008. "Textile Production." In *The Oxford Handbook of Technology and Engineering in the Classical World,* edited by J. P. Oleson, 465–482. Oxford: Oxford University Press.
Wild, J. P. 2011. "Vindolanda and its Textiles: Gavvo and his *Tosseae.*" In Alfaro Giner *et al.* 2011, 69–73.
Wild, J. P. 2013. "Textilien und das römische Konzept von Luxus." In Tellenbach *et al.* 2013, 62–63.
Wild, J. P., F. C. Wild, and A. J. Clapham. 2008. "Roman Cotton Revisited." In Alfaro Giner and Karali 2008, 143–147.
Williams, C. A., ed. 2004. *Martial Epigrams Book Two.* Oxford: Oxford University Press.
Williams, C. 2010. *Roman Homosexuality: Ideologies of Masculinity in Classical Antiquity.* 2nd ed. Oxford and New York: Oxford University Press.
Williams, C. 2013. "The Meanings of Softness: Some Remarks on the Semantics of *Mollitia.*" *EuGeStA* 3: 240–263. Williams, C. A. 2014. "The Language of Gender: Lexical Semantics and the Latin Vocabulary of Unmanly Men." In Masterson *et al.* 2014, 461–481.
Wilson, A. 2003. "The Archaeology of the Roman *Fullonica.*" *JRA* 16: 442–446.
Wilson, L. M. 1924. *The Roman Toga.* Baltimore: Johns Hopkins University Press.
Wilson, L. M. 1938. *The Clothing of the Ancient Romans.* Baltimore: Johns Hopkins University Press.

Winkler, J. J. 1990. *The Constraints of Desire: The Anthropology of Sex and Gender in Ancient Greece*. London and New York: Routledge.

Wiseman, T. P. 1970. "The Definition of 'Eques Romanus' in the Late Republic." *Historia* 19: 67–83.

Wiseman, T. P. 1979. *Clio's Cosmetics: Three Studies in Greco-Roman Literature*, Leicester: Leicester University Press.

Wolters, X. 1935. *Notes on Antique Folklore on the Basis of Pliny's Natural History L. XXVIII.22–29*. Amsterdam: H. J. Paris.

Wray, D. 2001. *Catullus and the Poetics of Roman Manhood*. Cambridge: Cambridge University Press.

Wrede, H. 1988. "Zur Trabea." *JDAI 103*: 381–400.

Wyke, M. 1994. "Woman in the Mirror: the Rhetoric of Adornment in the Roman World." In *Women in Ancient Societies: An Illusion of the Night*, edited by L. Archer, S. Fischler, and M. Wyke, 134–151. London and New York: Routledge.

Wyke, M., ed. 1998. *Parchments of Gender: Deciphering the Bodies of Antiquity*, Oxford: Oxford University Press.

Yadin, Y. 1963. *The Finds from the Bar Kokhba Period in the Cave of Letters*. Jerusalem: Israel Exploration Society.

Young, G. K. 2001. *Rome's Eastern Trade: International Commerce and Imperial Policy, 31 BC–AD 305*. London and New York: Routledge.

Zanda, E. 2011. *Fighting Hydra-Like Luxury: Sumptuary Legislation in the Roman Republic*. London: Bristol Classical Press.

Zanker, P. 1988. *The Power of Images in the Age of Augustus*. Trans. A. Shapiro. Ann Arbor: Univ. of Michigan Press.

Index

abolla 69, 111, 118, 146
ad cohibendum bracchium 43–4, 54
Alexander Severus (emperor) 73, 108
alicula 71
Antonius, M. (Mark Antony) 79, 116–17, 103 n26, 126, 149
Ara Pacis 16, 31, 35
Arringatore statue 20, 23, *24*, *29*, 45, 123
Augustus (emperor) 17, 19, 23, 31, *32*, 35–6, 50, 53, 80, 81, *84*, 97, 110, 111, 119, 126

balteus 9, 33, 34, 35, 39, 41
bardocucullus 7–8, 69, 92
beards 94, 96, 97, 98, 99, 100, 136, 144, 147, 149, 152
black 91, 94, 95, 97, 100, 109, 117, 121, 147; see also *pullus*
blue 93, 113, 114, 141
boots 86, 116, 117
borders 29, 44–8; construction of 46; location on toga 45
boys' clothing and ornament 17, 27–9, 43–4, 45, 46–7, 54, 62–5, 70–1, 95, 123
brooches 69, 70, 72, 73, 77, 115, 121
bulla 27, 48, 62–5, *63*, *65*; as apotropaic 64–5; contents of 64; materials of 63

Caligula (emperor) 32, 48, 86, 116, 126, 142
callainus 113
capite velato 31, 43
capitium see *thorax*
cenatoria see *synthesis*
cerasinus 114
chlamys 69–71, 73, 77, 115, 119
cinaedus 10, 135–6, 145; appearance of 136, 141, 145, 147, 148, 153–4
cinctus Gabinus 43, 54, 115

Claudius (emperor) 19, 49, 51, 53, 72, 97, 98, 120
cleanliness 5, 53, 94, 124–5, 168; see also *lautus*
cloaks and capes 15, 68–79, 91, 94, 95, 96, 107, 109, 115, 122, 142, 146, 147, 149, 168; of poor men 92–3; terminology for 68; water-resistant 71, 73, 93; see also *abolla, alicula, bardocucullus, cucullus, chlamys, endromis, lacerna, laena, pallium, paenula, paludamentum, sagum*
clotheshorse 122–3
clothes-press 122, 123–4
cobblers 82
color 1, 93, 106, 108–14, 118, 119, 124–5, 141, 149; terminology of 109
Commodus (emperor) 73, 108
comptulus 152, 154
cosmetics 138, 147, 148
costume, definition of 4
courtrooms 53, 72, 97–8
cross-dressing 119, 141, 150, 156–7 n23
cucullus 7–8, 69, 71, 93, 112, 113, 114, 168
cultus 4, 5

dalmatic 56 n23
dandies 10, 111, 114, 123, 135, 146, 151–4
dark clothing see black
delicati/deliciae 136, 139, 147
depilation 122, 136, 137, 139, 144, 146, 147, 148, 153
Didymoi 4, 110, 128 n20
dirt 91, 92, 93, 96, 97, 99, 101, 114, 117, 124, 137, 138
Domitian (emperor) 53, 70
dress, chronological change in 3, 168–9
duplex 69, 72, 77

effeminacy 2, 10, 16, 75, 81, 106, 108, 111, 116, 121, 123, 127, 135–6, 138–54; pre-modern 149–51, 153–4
Elegabalus (emperor) 108
endromis 71
equestrian dress 19, 20, 45, 53, 67, 72, 84, 85, 100, 115–16, 141, 146, 154; *see also* tunics: *angustus clavus*; shoes: equestrian
ethics of clothing 137, 143
Etruscan clothing 9, 29, 30, 49, 62, 63, 82, 115
exoletus 143
expense of cloth and clothing 8–9, 52–3, 63, 92; *see also* retail trade

face-patches 138–9
fascia see *feminalia*
fashion 82, 146, 169; definition of 4
felt 90 n61
feminalia 81
folds in clothing 123–4, 168
footwear *see* shoes
freedmen 32, 35, 48, 54, 63, 64, 66–7, 80, 106, 114, 146, 168
fringe 71, 73, 142
fulling 53, 71, 91, 92, 123, 124–5
fuscus 141, 146

galbinus 114, 141
Gallic dress 7, 8, 51, 69, 72, 77, 78, 86, 117, 142
gausapa 73, 79, 92, 107, 122
gaze 151
gender 5–6, 135, 139, 145, 151
gesture 138
gold 62, 63, 77; on clothing 49, 108, 111, 115; hairnet 139; rings 65–7, 105; sellers of 8; on slaves 122; on *socci* 116
Greek dress 1, 7, 27–9, 29–31, 44, 51, 65, 69–71, 74–7, 87, 116–17, 118, 123, 142
green 81, 110, 112–13, 114, 141, 168; see also *galbinus*

habitus 4
Hadrian (emperor) 34, *36*, *37*, 76
hair 94, 96, 97, 99, 100, 108, 121, 136, 137, 138, 146, 147, 148, 152; body 139, 140, 146; curly 139, 145, 147; long 139
hats 71, 80, 142
heteroeroticism 135, 147–52, 153
himation 27, 29, 30, 49, 73, 74–7; see also *pallium*

history of fashion 1–2
homoeroticism 135–6, 141, 145, 148, 149, 153, 154
hoods 69, 71, 73, 80; see also *bardocucullus*, *cucullus*
hysignum 112

insignia 97, 99–101

jewellery 7, 8, 121, 140, 142, 153; *see also* rings
Julius Caesar, C. 63–4, 80, 86, 125, 139, 142, 143, 144

lacerna 9, 71–2, 92, 93, 111, 112, 113, 114, 115, 117, 122, 149
laena 72, 93, 111, 118
late antique clothing 2, 4, 8, 16, 73, 79, 81, 115, 116, 124, 142, 144, 168
lautus 5, 110
leather 64, 73, 82, 84, 93, 138
legacies of clothing 18
leggings see *feminalia*
legislation on clothing 53, 108
linen 9, 44, 107, 108, 125
lower-class appearance 5, 15, 48, 53, 64, 68, 71, 72, 73, 76, 78, 81, 82, 91–4, 100–1, 102, 108, 110, 113–14, 124; colors 114
luna 67, 68, 85, 110, 153
luxury in dress 5, 8, 69, 105, 106, 108, 109–12, 117–19, 141, 145, 153

Macaronis 151
Maecenas, C. 20, 74, 139, 141, 143, 147, 149
mantles 68, 69, 71, 74–6
Marcus Aurelius (emperor) 35, *38*, *39*, 77, 79, 123
masculinity, Roman 6, 10, 75, 94–5, 109, 126, 127, 135–6, 137, 138, 140–1, 144, 145, 148, 149–50, 152, 154, 169, 170
masculinity studies 5–6, 149
metonymy 26, 65, 71, 73, 79, 80, 86–7, 102, 139
military dress 2, 4, 8, 16, 43, 66, 69, 70, 71, 73, 77–9, 81, 85, 112, 115, 118
mollitia see effeminacy
Mons Claudianus 4, 15, 21, 22
mourning dress 4, 64, 65, 91, 94–6, 100–1, 102, 121

Nero (emperor) 48, 49, *64*, 86, 111, 115, 118, 119, 126
nightwear 92

orators 4, 52, 75, 106, 140; toga of 41–3, 141, 144, 145

paenula/penula 18, 69, 73, 107, 114, 121, 122, 149
pallium 7, 15, 29–31, 44, 69, 70, 71, 72, 73, 74–7, 96, 98, 112, 117, 118, 119, 124, 147
paludamentum 77, 79, 167
pattern 141–2
pearls 8, 116
perfumes 8, 92, 99, 136, 139–40, 141, 144, 146, 147, 148, 153
pilleum 71, 80
Pompeii 4, 14–15, 20, 45
poverty *see* lower-class appearance
prasinus 114
prostitutes 33, 43, 52
pullus 93, 94, 95, 96, 100, 147
purple 7, 8, 49–50, 77, 96, 107, 109–11, 112, 113, 115, 116, 122, 141, 142, 145, 146, 147, 149; as apotropaic 44–5; borders 44–8, 49; color of in antiquity 44, 111–12; counterfeit 110; legislation on 125–6; on slaves 122; smell of 85, 110, 124, 168; *socci* 116; stripes 18–20, 141; Tyrian 45, 67, 71, 93, 109–11, 112, 118, 146, 153

rank 6, 7, 19–20, 26, 49, 65–8, 68–9, 81, 86, 87, 105, 106, 109, 111, 117, 167, 168
red *see* scarlet
retail trade 8–9, 14–15, 20, 82, 117
rings 8; effeminate 140, 147, 148; of equestrians 66–7, 105; of freedmen 66–7; with gems 114, 119–21, 127, 153; of iron 65, 66; *ius anuli aurei* 6, 7, 66, 87, 125, 167; of senators 65–6, 99, 100, 105; of slaves 66, 122; status in 119–21
ritual 43, 44, 45–6, 48, 73, 77, 78–9, 94–6, 100, 102, 113, 115, 116, 167
Roman dress: definition of 4; general 1–2; golden mean in 137–8; imported 7, 168; as inner reflection of self 10; male 2, 119, 167–70; prescription in 19, 68–9, 85, 87, 169; social psychology of 169–70

Roman Egypt 4, 9, 12 n30, 13–14, 21, 68, 142, 155 n2; *see also* Mons Claudianus, Didymoi
russus 114
rustic clothing 53, 85, 92, 110, 118, 137, 138, 146

sagulum 77
sagum 69, 77–9, 118, 121, 167
sartorial code 136–8
saturnalia 53–4, 80, 117, 118
scarlet 77, 85, 109, 111–12, 113, 115, 116, 117, 141, 142, 146; on slaves 122
scutulatus 141–2
secondhand clothing 9, 18, 68, 110
senatorial directives on clothing 78, 99
senators' dress 19, 20, 31, 65–8, 72, 82–6, 97, 119, 126; *see also* tunics: *latus clavus*; shoes: senatorial
sexuality 54, 65, 71, 135–6, 138, 141, 151
shoes 6; *calceus* 72, 82–6, 93, 144; *caliga* 78, 117; clogs 93; *cothurnus* 85, 112, 117; equestrian 84, 85; *gallicae* 117; with gems 117; hobnails 82, 117; loose 93, 136, 137; of lower-class men 93; *luna* 67, 68, 85; metonymy 86–7; patrician *mulleus* 67, 84–5, 117, 153; *phaecasia* 116–17; sale of 9; sandals 7, 74, 86, 87, 93, 116, 117, 127, 147; senatorial 67–8, 72, 82–6, 117; status in 116–17; terminology for 82; white 114, 117; see also *socci*
silk 8, 44, 107–8, 127, 140–1, 142, 145, 168
sinus 29, 30, 31, 32, 42, 43, 55, 74, 147
slave clothing 5, 9, 16, 18, 20, 28–9, 48, 54, 63, 72, 73, 76, 78, 80, 81, 92, 102, 106, 117, 121–2, 124, 137, 142, 143, 147; branding-marks 139; in cosmetics 138; hair of 139; rich dress of 7, 112, 114, 121–2, 168; shoes 93
sleeves *see* tunics
soccus 74, 82, 116, 140
socks 86
sordes 91, 93, 96, 97–101, 102
sources 2–4, 25–9, 169
squalor 97, 101
status 4, 6, 7, 26, 49, 67, 72, 81, 87, 91, 94, 105–34, 153–4, 168
stripes *see* tunic
sulphur 113, 124
sumptuary legislation 105, 106, 125–6
synthesis 117–19, 142, 168

200   *Index*

tailoring and sewing 15, 22, 40, 93
tebenna 29
textiles: archaeological finds of 4, 15, 18, 21–2, 108, 116; production 4
thorax 81, 141
thrift 31, 92, 93, 105, 106, 125, 126, 137
Tiberius (emperor) 19, 52, 65, 70, 108, 126, 140
tibiale see *feminalia*
toga 1, 9–10, 23–55, 71, 74, 75, 76, 78, 86, 94, 110, 111, 117, 125, 126, 142, 153, 168; Antonine 35–9, 52; on the Ara Pacis 31; artistic evidence for 25–9; in the Augustan age 31–3; Augustan togas 31–3, 34, 35–9, 41, 55, 107, 147, 168–9; badly-fitting 137; *balteus* 9, 33, 34, 35, 39; banded toga (*toga contabulata*) 39–41; boys' 46–8; *candida* 113; changes in drape 25–6, 29–44, 55, 168; of citizens 51–2, 53, 54; of clients 52, 53, 92; color of 113, 114; construction 23, 32–3; in the courts 97, 98; disheveled 43; draping of 24–5, 31, 33–4; 35–9, 39–40, 41, 42, 53, 101; effeminate 144; Etruscan 9, 29; *exigua* 31–2; fabric of 23, 33, 37, 107–8; fashions in togas 31, 37, 41, 43; fastening of 24; as ideogram 26; as ideological symbol 26; inconvenience of 53, 54–5; of the late first-second century CE 33–5; of lower-class men 92, 93; newly laundered 23; omission of 52–4; orator's toga 41–3; *pallium*-drape 29–31, 44; '*palmata*' 50; *perversa* 101–2; *picta* 49–51, 92, 115; *praetexta* 29, 44–9, 62, 68, 71, 79, 95, 99, 100, 111, 122; of prostitutes 33; *pulla* 95–6, 101; *purpurea* 49, 51, 125; putting it on 24–5; Republican togas 29–31; senators' 72; shape of 23; symbolism of 51–2, 78, 79; transparent 108, 141, 149; as 'typical' dress 29; *virilis/libera/pura* 48–9, 65, 108; weights for 25; width of 23; without a tunic 16, 81, 91; woollen 23; see also *ad cohibendum bracchium*; *cinctus Gabinus*; *capite velato*, *sinus*, *umbo*
toga *virilis* ceremony 17, 19, 48, 65, 167
togula 91, 92
trabea 115–16

trossulus 152–3, 154
trousers 77, 81
tunic 7, 9–10, 13–23, 71, 74, 107, 117, 168; and age 17–18; *angustus clavus* 7, 19, 20, 67; archaeological remains of 21–2; cincture 16, 19, 136, 142–4, 147, 148; color 147; construction 13–15; cost of 8; of equestrians 20, 67; the *exomis* 91; late antique tunics 16, 73, 81; *latus clavus* 6, 7, 14, 19, 99, 125, 144, 167, 169; of lower-class men 20–2, 91–2; number of stripes 18–19; *palmata* 49–51, 115; *pulla* 94, 147; *recta* 17–18; of senators 19, 67, 99, 107; of slaves 18; sleeves 15–16, 142, 144–5; stripes on 18–23, 141; ubiquity of 20; undertunic (*tunica intima*) 81, 93, 125, 137; unstriped 22–3; *vestes clavatae* 18–23; wealthy 9; white 117; width of stripes 19, 20, 22
tunicula 91
twining 45

umbo 29, 31, 32, 55, 74
underwear 16, 80–1, 93, 121, 125, 137
urbanity in dress 146, 149, 153, 154
usurpation 7, 67–8, 105, 168

veiling see *capite velato*
venetus 114
Vespasian (emperor) 19, *34*
vestis domestica 22–3
vestis forensia 22–3
Vicomagistri relief 26
visuality 6–7, 51–2, 91, 99, 102, 167–8
Vitellius 23, 79, 97

washing *see* fulling
wealth 7, 10, 32, 55, 63, 72, 75, 92, 101, 105, 106, 110, 112, 113, 114, 116, 117–19, 120, 123, 124–5, 125–6, 137, 146, 153, 154, 168
white 77, 81, 91, 94, 96, 97, 98, 107, 113–14, 117, 118, 121, 153; *socci* 116
wool 23, 86, 93, 95, 100, 107, 121, 123; as apotropaic 44

yellow 107, 113, 141, 142, 148
youthful clothing 145–6, 149

Printed in the United States
by Baker & Taylor Publisher Services